# Writing is Dialogue: Teaching Students to Think (and Write) Like Writers

# Writing is Dialogue: Teaching Students to Think (and Write) Like Writers

Jeff House

Christopher-Gordon Publishers, Inc.
Norwood, Massachusetts

# Credits

Christopher-Gordon Publishers, Inc.
*Bridging Theory and Practice*

1502 Providence Highway, Suite 12
Norwood, MA  02062
800-934-8322
781-762-5577
www.Christopher-Gordon.com

Printed in the United States of America

10 9 8 7 6 5 4 3 2 1                                        09 08 07 06

ISBN: 1-929024-92-4

Library of Congress Catalogue Number: 2005907503

# Dedication

*To my family, who put up with a lot, most of it by choice:*

*My sister, who helped me write my first Sunday School speeches, pointing out the power of anecdotes and figurative language.*

*My mother, the word maven, who does crossword puzzles in ink, beats all comers in Boggle, and still owns the family's original Scrabble dictionary.*

*My father, like me, a reporter on his high school newspaper, whose skills at analysis prevented me from winning an argument with him until I was twenty-two, and by then it didn't matter.*

*And to Spunky, who listened, supported, gave more than anyone should, and never, ever, stopped believing.*

# Contents

# Acknowledgments

I think there are about a half dozen original ideas in this text; the rest came out of discussions and interminably long meetings with colleagues from all the schools I have taught at, so many of whom make me proud to do what I do.

In lecturing around the country, I have faced the challenge of "instructing" some immensely talented teachers who have helped me hone and develop all the ideas that inform both this text and the courses I teach.

My colleagues at the San Jose Area Writing Project, in particular Jonathan Lovell and Charleen Delfino, for championing my lectures and the book.

College Board gave me my first opportunities to meet and work with teachers all over the Western states, and I am particularly grateful to George Henry, Sharron Heinrich, and my "big sis" Betsy James, all of whom supported me and made the occasional rough patches easy to bear.

Sue Canavan of Christopher-Gordon Publishers, Inc., was enthusiastic about this book from the first—some six years ago—and in addition to her support and humor, she has hooked me up with the company's best, including my editor, Jennifer Bengston. She also farmed out early versions of the text to a number of reviewers, including Leila Christenbury, Marianne Kent-Stoll, George E. Newell, Duane Roen, Helen Poole Shillito, Charleen Silva Delfino, and Bonnie Sunstein, whose feedback focused and sharpened my work.

As this project approached completion, my colleagues at Georgiana Bruce Kirby Preparatory School have born my ego and challenges, encouraging me with their own time, ideas, and humor. In their receptivity to all I have pursued, they have made me feel welcomed and appreciated as our young school continues its journey. I am particularly grateful to my colleague Joe Poirot, for his enthusiastic support and willingness to carve out new curriculums with me. And to Marianne Kent-Stoll, who believes in me still and remembers what it was like to swim uphill against the tide.

Finally, my students, the hundreds whose faces still tumble through my brain despite our differing paths. I doubt most of them believed me when I told them how much easier they made my day when the mornings got rough. I thank them for teaching me, for proving how powerful and enriching language is, and for sharing this lifelong dialogue of learning.

My colleague Joe Poirot created a shorthand acronym to teach his students the basic writing components: FADS (facts, anecdotes, detail, speech).

# Sheep Talk:
# How I Learned
# to Teach Inductively

*Nothing is more chilling than the dawn of a new conception.*
—Suzanne K. Langer

*Broadly conceived your whole life is a writing process consisting of every moment of every experience, awake or asleep in actuality or imagination; every thought and feeling explored or repressed; every person and phenomenon known or observed; every bit of information learned and used or filed away; everything you've read. Indeed, the artists of any kind— painter, writer, dancer, musician, athlete, chef—if asked how long it takes to learn the craft or to perfect a particular aspect of it could truly answer, "All my life." From this perspective the writing process is continuous, without beginning, without end.*

—Lynn Z. Bloom, *Fact and Artifact: Writing Nonfiction*

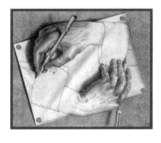 If my mother is to be believed, I never had a first word. I had a first sentence. Its utterance was an occasion for relief, as I had passed the stage by which most infants begin talking. My parents discussed taking me to a specialist to see why I refused to speak. But the anticipated moment came on a Sunday afternoon while I rode in the backseat of the family car. The suburbs behind us, we moseyed through farm lands when, spotting a wooly creature, I pulled myself up to the window and declared, "Hi, lamb."

Apparently, I was holding off speaking until I got it right.

*Writing is Dialogue: Teaching Students to Think (and Write) like Writers*

I hope the story's true, because it explains the way I learn. I didn't know how to swim until I was twelve, and then I took to water like a turtle. I didn't become a good student until I went back to college. And it took over two decades of teaching to develop the methods explained in this book.

In twenty-five years of teaching, you can get enough things wrong so that you start to ask "why" questions. Like, why were activities I enjoyed doing so much on my own—reading and writing—so boring for many students? Why could I get them to crank out perfect five-paragraph essays that nevertheless had all the scintillation of lead? Why did they turn in interesting creative pieces and, then, compose numbingly bad analytic papers? Why did they pass grammar drills and subsequently hand in work rife with comma splices, fragments, and run-ons? Why, no matter what range of topics I suggested for writing, did their papers share the same dull, academic voice?

The closer we get to the truth, the harder it is to define; so, I can't reduce the lessons I've learned to a phrase or two. However, I've come to believe the following about how students learn:

- Students learn best when they become active learners, not passive ones; when they apply, and not merely regurgitate, their knowledge.

- Students learn best when they understand a skill they are required to use.

- Students learn best when they acquire a skill and then apply it in varied ways.

- Students learn best when they understand the relation between specific and abstract language.

- Students learn best when they find skills reinforced and developed throughout a curriculum, not when those skills are merely repeated year to year.

- Students learn best when they see how unit objectives lead to course objectives which lead to program objectives that clarify what they've learned and where the class is heading.

- Students learn best when they move beyond memorizing rules to understanding the concepts behind the rules.

- Students learn best when they see the connection between classroom writing and the larger goals of oral and written expression.

- Students learn best when they read for tone, theme, and style, not only plot.

- Students learn best when they apply the thinking processes required in the classroom to their own lives, when they see the connection between classroom study and the world they must negotiate.

- Students learn best when they are given the freedom and responsibility to choose their own writing topics as well as decide how best to represent their thinking in written and oral form.

- Students learn best when they encounter open-ended assignments, realizing there are no right answers, only well-defended ones.

- Students learn best when they connect writing to self-expression.

These observations are the foundation for the writing, models, methods, and lessons discussed in *Writing is Dialogue: Teaching Students to Write (and Think) Like Writers*. Because writing is a highly intuitive process, it lends itself to guidelines better than formulae. The point of a writing program is to write, not allow drills and exercises to dominate instruction so that ideas sink beneath the muck of methodology. Teachers know the possibilities for exploration that writing offers. However, like many, I wonder at the emphasis on mechanics over expression, and the use of writing techniques that teachers, in our own writing, never utilize. If such methods are foreign to our love of composition, why are they appropriate for our students?

## Where I Come From

I received my teaching credential six months after California voters passed Prop. 13, the Howard Jarvis initiative that rolled back property taxes and displaced firemen, policemen, and teachers onto the unemployment roles. Staggered by the revenue loss, public schools offered nothing but one-year teaching contracts, so I moved my belongings to four different homes as I fulfilled four different teaching assignments before landing on terra firma my fifth year. Forced to adapt quickly and frequently, I developed a bag of teaching tricks, but I was particularly skilled in one area: I could get kids to crank out five-paragraph essays.

My first school had recently adopted what came to be called The Sparks Method, also called Power Writing, because it assigned numerical values to differing sentences: a thesis was a first power sentence, a point sentence was a second power, an example was a third power, and a commentary was a fourth power. A model of reductionism, Power Writing was easy to teach and easy to grade. Some students balked at the shoehorning of ideas into one of four sentence types, but they inevitably jettisoned their frustrations and adopted the simplified structure. It took little to master, and, within a month of each opening school year, all my classes perfunctorily churned out pristine, five-paragraph essays.

I was good at this. I taught the Powers Method at seminars and to my colleagues. Kids who'd never scored well on essays became fans, and history teachers stopped me in the hall to thank me for teaching kids how to finally answer test questions. A few colleagues and parents balked at the strictures, but I had no need to alter my teaching.

But I did.

Six years into the program, I stopped teaching Power Writing. The essays were as competent as they'd been when I'd first taught the method, but they bored me (and I know they bored the kids). The sole advantage of Power Writing was its ability to teach the structuring of a five-paragraph essay, but those essays lacked voice, style, and sophistication. More disturbing, Power Writing offered no approach to composition other than five-paragraph papers. Four classes of thirty students apiece meant twice a quarter I read the same ideas—in nearly identical tones and voices—120 times. I wanted to kill something.

But my fifth class was yearbook, and drawing off my journalism background, I made the publication into a writing course. Encouraged to explore their talents, the kids turned interviews and research into feature stories and personal essays, sports analyses, and news reports. Within three years, the book began winning national awards and continued to do so for the next seven years. Several students went on to writing or journalism careers. I loved the class: the writing was vivid, creative, trenchant, and fun. So I accepted my lot: I did my writing duty in four of my classes and explored methodologies in my fifth. It didn't occur to me to adapt the writing ideas of the yearbook course to my other classes. First, our traditional program emphasized five-paragraph literary analysis; the only deviations from the coursework were the occasional "creative" pieces (which, ironically, students and teachers both wanted more of). Second, echoing my colleagues, I declared that most kids couldn't learn complicated structures and styles—just look at how they struggled to write interesting five-paragraph essays.

But two events altered the course of my instruction. In the early 1990s, I came across Nancy Atwell's *In the Middle*, her argument for student-based learning. In opposition to how my colleagues and I taught, Atwell insisted entire periods should be given to students to write, the teacher floating about to provide on-the-spot feedback and instruction. Lectures weren't abandoned; they were replaced by mini-lessons on topics and techniques relevant to what students were currently working on, short (five- to ten-minute) presentations that didn't interrupt the flow of the working period. But even more compelling, Atwell moved students to the center of the writing experience, encouraging them to create topics, subject matter, style, structure, and voice appropriate to their compositions. Dispelling the laments my colleagues and I uttered, she insisted students could write, could push themselves, and—most heretically— often knew better what they needed. When presented with a work in progress, Atwell refused to read it, instead asking her students what they felt the paper needed. Invariably, she was right: the writer had a sense of what to work on. In Atwell's world, the teacher was less a lecturer than a facilitator, someone whose expertise enabled her to guide students and not dictate to them.

The second insight came the year I began teaching timed writings. The first time I handed out a timed writing to my AP class, the students hunched over their desks, made notes for five or ten minutes, and began to write. Nothing unusual. But that same week I conducted a timed writing with my non-AP kids; two minutes after I'd handed out the poem, the class was writing. Many halted during the period, frustrated, and several didn't finish before the period ended. The next day I asked, "Why did you start writing so quickly?"

"We didn't have a lot of time," they insisted. "What else were we supposed to do?"

"Read the poem again," I responded, "and again and again, all the while making notes and thinking about your findings." Their eyes widened.

"We'd run out of time," they insisted.

"But I watched you," I said. "A lot of you stuttered and stopped, many turning in incomplete analyses; you were so concerned about getting started that you didn't bother to find where you were going before you began."

I explained about looking for specifics in a poem—images, figures of speech, sound devices, structure—and using those as a starting point to investigate the poem's deeper meanings. "You struggle because the first thing you try to do," I pointed out, "is write the thesis—the crux of your paper—before you've found the evidence that would lead you to it. Trust me," I pleaded, "you can only compose a thesis AFTER your evidence has led you to it. The thesis might be in the first part of your paper, but it's the conclusion of your thinking."

And as I labored over what I wanted to say, the revelation floated to the surface. I wanted them to think inductively, to gather their evidence and work it into higher levels of thought until they arrived at an argument. So I began teaching my classes to think and write inductively. It was a revelation for all of us. Students asked, "Why didn't anyone teach us this before?"

"I've just figured it out myself," I responded, but taking my cue from Atwell, I applied the inductive method to a range of writing types and set aside time in class for what I now called Writing Workshops.

Shortly after publishing a description of the inductive method in *English Journal* ("Writing the Essay Backwards"), I began lecturing for the College Board, passing on the inductive method to teachers at Saturday sessions. Workshop participants echoed my kids: Why didn't anyone teach us this before? I explained how inductive approaches to writing were universal, whether students wrote literary analyses, poetry, feature articles, reviews, opinion pieces, memoirs, historical or scientific observations—the inductive method was the unified field theory of writing. I'm not vying for canonization. I've not found the Grail, ascended Mt.

Sinai, or cured the common cold. My students are normal, meaning some of them forego their homework, some turn in papers late or incomplete, and others still ignore my charm and charisma and skip directions. But I know this like I know pigs love mud: because of these inductive approaches, the quality of student work I see is vastly more interesting and compelling. More students actually want to write in my courses, and less frequently am I driven to drink by boring, vapid writing that is perfectly structured but intellectually and emotionally soulless.

At last: this is power writing.

## Why I Want to Hate My Sister but Can't

My sister was the salutatorian at the Sacramento high school we both attended before she went on to college and graduated cum laude. Obviously, I couldn't compete, so I didn't. A "C" student, I entered sophomore year English expecting to like the reading and hate the writing. Mrs. Jane Veglia was the teacher: young, compassionate, and looking for ways to hook her students. It was 1967 and journaling was a new technique. We would free write for ten minutes at the beginning of each class, Mrs. Veglia announced, on anything we wanted.

"Anything?" I wanted to know.

"Anything," she assured me. So I took her at her word and produced a week's worth of suspiciously creative writing. The following Monday, I opened my graded journal to find Mrs. Veglia's comments: "Nice metaphors." I had no idea what metaphors were, but apparently I could write them, and apparently I could write them well. So I looked up the definition, honed the technique, and began a year that ended with a self-published book of poetry and stories, as well as a new identity. I was a poet, I assured anyone who asked, and I had a talent for writing. And when the school started a journalism program the next year, Mrs. Veglia pulled the newspaper instructor aside and advised her to invite me onto the staff. Three years later I joined my college paper, graduating with a BA in journalism before starting my career as a police reporter for the *Las Vegas Review-Journal*.

That was three decades ago.

"I never really thought of myself as a writer," Kelsey wrote me last summer, "but because of your encouragement and your teaching I'm on the newspaper staff and a poem of mine is about to get published in your book." The accompanying CD-ROM is filled with the work of students who didn't think of themselves as writers, and it's one of the joys of seeing this project completed to give so many of them an audience. Their enthusiasm and creativity saved me from long nights of boredom, and the suitcase of photocopied examples they provided for my lectures made my points better than my talking could. I trust you'll enjoy their writing as I have.

This book is divided into three sections. The first part argues that too many programs turn writing into a formulaic activity. Chapter 1, "Making the Angels Dance," lays the argument out by contrasting the formulaic approach—a kind of deductive philosophy—with the open inquiry of induction. Deductive teaching tells students in advance what they must produce, no matter the assignment. In such curricula, emphasis is placed on dictating the number of paragraphs in a work, the number of sentences in a paragraph, placement of specific guides—thesis, topic sentence, and transitional phrases—and the importance of avoiding a hardcore list of grammar errors. In such a program, students quickly learn that voice, content, and thought are less important than form and presentation. Worse, they know that the paper they compose will look very like the paper their peers turn in. Students taught under such predetermined conditions rarely ask how to create empathic pieces, how to phrase effectively, how to modulate tone, how to write for someone other than the teacher. By contrast, inductive programs emphasize guidelines, not formulas. Students become active—not passive—participants in their writing when they know that the aim is less to produce a "correct" piece than an effective one.

The errors of a deductive philosophy are reinforced by a writing curriculum that predominantly focuses on textual analysis. As I argue in Chapter 2, "Beyond the Omelete," students become better writers the more they expand their compositional palette. If the goal is to teach literary analysis, emphasizing such writing will only produce such writers. But I would argue that—detached from a wider range of writing techniques—students in such programs will write even less effective analyses than students exposed to a variety of techniques. Ideas make sense only within a context, and students exposed to a multiplicity of styles, formats, voices, and techniques are better prepared to write. An expanded writing curriculum complements the free inquiry philosophy of inductive instruction, encouraging students to find their own voices, manipulating writing techniques to produce a range of work.

Unit II gets into the specifics of the inductive method. Chapter 3, "The Matrix of Meaning," explains how induction can be taught. Chapter 4, "Rummaging the Cupboard," details what students must first do as they approach their material inductively. This first stage—which I refer to as "gathering"—involves accumulating the building blocks of writing: anecdotes, quotations, specific details, and facts. These specifics, in one combination or other, are the ground upon which the work's structure is built and from which its focus emerges. Because writing is recursive, we move back and forth between these specifics and our focus, creating a dialogue between the concrete and the abstract, the specific and the general. The second stage of induction involves the structuring of our specifics, the focus of Chapter 5, "The First Shall Be Last." In contrast to deductive approaches—which tell students in advance what structure their paper will take—an inductive approach argues that structure emerges from specifics, organically evolving from the material. Chapter 5 presents a variety of structural formats, drawn from across the writing curriculum, but even these must be thought of as guides and not the only acceptable models on the market. Ultimately, if we encourage students to think inductively and to explore their own voices, they will arrive at structures appropriate to their work.

The "Rhetoric and Poetics" discussion of Chapter 6 details specific ways to teach style and voice, discussing some hopefully refreshing— and occasionally alternative—ways to approach diction, syntax, tone, and punctuation. Much of *Writing is Dialogue* approaches the teaching of writing conceptually, shifting the emphasis from mechanics to expression, from rules to intent. I do not find, for example, much result from teaching grammar drills and the memorization of rules. Instead, I discuss punctuation as a stylistic technique: markings that aid the writer in creating a voice the reader can hear. Learning punctuation, like diction and syntax, is important only insofar as its instruction is integrated into the writing experience directly, not separated out into drills and worksheets.

Finally, Chapter 7, "Piece by Piece," argues again for an expanded writing program, specifically in the instruction of analysis. Just as too much curricula focuses on the five-paragraph essay, too much instruction centers on textual analysis, which ignores additional (and quite often more accessible) approaches: mythological, sociological, psychological, and deconstructive. Students are more empowered as they consider a range of structures, styles, and writing techniques. Thus, they find more success when given a number of ways to approach a text critically.

The book's final section addresses the "What now?" issue. My hope is that teachers will see the importance of sequenced units based around skills. Comparing the hodgepodge of many department curricula to a stew, "Stew Versus Souffle" insists that students—and teachers—benefit when skills are developed and expanded upon. In light of the large variety of structures, analytic approaches, and instructional activities I cover here, I'm not arguing that they all be taught in a single course. Though teachers can certainly adapt individual ideas from *Writing is Dialogue* into their present classes, those classes are strengthened when colleagues reinforce their work and establish a continuum of skill development. Drawing from the studies of child psychologist Jean Piaget and others, I argue in Chapter 8 that sequenced programs should parallel the emotional and mental development of students. Classes should work to expand students' worldview from the personal to the communal as they age.

I've supplemented the text with a CD-ROM containing downloadable handouts (all passages in boxes), which are some of the writing assignments that generated much of the work discussed in the book, and dozens of student samples drawn from across the continuum of writing projects.

And believing I should practice what I preach, I've composed *Writing is Dialogue: Teaching Students to Think (and Write) Like Writers* with my own techniques in mind, which means it's larded with anecdotes, quotes, specific details, and facts. Each chapter begins with a statement of focus and a list of sections; each section contains specific examples and arguments.

## Coda

My intent is to make writing a pleasure for students and teachers, to convince departments that skill-based instruction is the most effective way to develop methodologies, and to turn the classroom into a community of explorers who find writing essential to developing thought. Big goals. But I enjoy writing and reading good work. I've leapt onto chairs to read a passage from a student work-in-progress, pounded a desk on occasion, wielded pens of varied colors to make comments, and unashamedly choked up when reading a particularly strong piece. I believe words matter, that they bring the abstractions of thought into the material world. And I believe that realization burbled somewhere in my brain half a century ago when I stood in the backseat of my family's car and spoke to the sheep.

The King of Hearts advised Alice:
*"Begin at the beginning, and go on until you come to the end: then stop."*

# Unit 1:
# Laying the Foundation

*"I write to make peace with the things I cannot control. I write to create fabric in a world that often appears black and white. I write to discover. I write to uncover. I write to meet my ghosts. I write to begin a dialogue."*

—Terry Tempest Williams, from *"Why I Write"*

# Chapter 1

# Writing is Dialogue:
# Making the Angels Dance

Focus: <u>Writing is not a one-dimensional, linear act. Rather, it is a series of dialogues between ourselves, others, our environments, and our expectations</u>.

**Sections:**
- The Inductive Act
- Writing is Dialogue
- Making the Angels Dance

*One of the best ways to think of the task before you when you are asked to write about art is to approach it as a kind of dialogue between you and the work. It is your business, when you write about art, to record this dialogue.*

—Henry Sayres, *Writing About Art*

*A rule says, "You must do it this way."*
*A principle says, "This works, and has."*

—William James

Thomas Aquinas, the Medieval theologian, is rumored to have wondered how many angels could dance on the head of a pin. However, the tale is likely apocryphal because his writings record no such discussion. Aquinas did, however, debate the number of angels that could share the same place. One, he wrote.

Who, then, misquoted Aquinas and created a question both abstruse and absurd? It's a satirical jab worthy of Rabelais, the French satirist who lampooned the foibles of the Church, but Alexander Pope and his contemporaries appear more likely to have started the jest. Latecomers to the Renaissance, Pope and company were rationalists, raised on Francis Bacon and idolizing Isaac Newton. The stuffy school of Aquinas, John Duns Scotus, and the rest of the Scholastics earned their ire, not their praise.

Because the Scholastics wrote in the twelfth century before the scientific method arose concurrently with the Renaissance, they did not take open inquiry as their mantra. Defenders of the Church and smitten with Aristotle, they aimed not to pursue truth wherever it led them, but determined in advance what it had to be. The answers were foreordained, so it was merely a matter of assembling a logical argument that would end with the determined answers.

By contrast, the scientific method was inductive. The truth was not to be defended so much as revealed. The conclusion was not foregone. It resulted instead from an open investigation. Scholastics knew what the answer was in advance; they only had to figure out how to get there. But the Renaissance scientists didn't know where their journey would end until their horse carts arrived there. Truth was not a goal; it was a result.

Which, like riders in horse carts, brings us to the point.

So let me be melodramatic: the writing programs of America are bedeviled with Scholastics, bound by formulas that chain students like Prometheus, discouraging investigation, prizing instead predetermined structures, topics, and therefore—most lamentably—thought. William Blake's mind-forged manacles are all the rage in the classroom where drills, exercises, and worksheets take time away from the very activity they proclaim to serve: writing. Our kids don't write; they produce like assembly line workers.

## The Inductive Act

*Abstract and concrete are polar forms of verbal expression, and the movement between them describes something essential about the activity of all thought. In good writing they are controlled to engage the mind of the reader by involving it progressively with the development of the writer's idea.*

—Marie Ponsot and Rosemary Deen,
*Beat Not the Poor Desk*

Inductive thinking is an exploration, a rummaging of the cabinet in search of something to cure what ails us. It gathers particulars and then, sensing a pattern, begins to assemble them into a coherent whole. As poet Charles Simic writes, "Somewhere in the city of New York there are four or five still-unknown objects that belong together. Once together they'll make a work of art." Induction is the gathering, then grouping, of those objects until they make a work that did not exist before.

This is the notion Montaigne exemplified as he mused over a disparate range of writings. Another child of the Renaissance, Montaigne cut his teeth on Classical writers, emulating their styles and amassing quartos of quotations. But having gathered the observations of others over the years, Montaigne began to draw his own conclusions, finally writing them up in a compositional style he had no precedent for. He called them what they were, *l'essai:* "I attempt." So the first essays were explorations into the undefined, forages for fact and thought.

I wish we could restore Montaigne's curiosity to the classroom. Instead, the word "essay" disenchants and unnerves students as they greet writing assignments with dread and boredom. Montaigne's inductive explorations find no place in school and are replaced by straitjacketing topics that are limited nearly always to literary interpretation and hopelessly devoid of passion or interest. No wonder a former colleague of mine once observed, "Grading essays is the worst part of my job."

How sad. In the era of objective testing—whose spirit guides the creation and grading of its educational corollary, the five-paragraph essay—the rambling observations of Bacon, Joseph Addison, Charles Lamb, John Stuart Mill, E. B. White, and James Thurber seem as distant as Alpha Centauri. But such work lives in our newspapers and magazines, in the writing of Pico Iyer, Calvin Trillin, Robert Hughes, Garrison Keillor, and Joel Stein. Philip Lopate publishes annual collections of moving, compelling, and provocative essays, as does the publishing house of Houghton-Mifflin, which provides the year's best work in essays, science, sports writing, and travelogues. The essay is alive and well everywhere in America except its classrooms.

But let's not (as a few instructors do) blame the students. Taught that their voices are valued only insofar as they echo academese, that the only notable writing is a literary analysis, and that the prerequisite to composition is a series of drills and worksheets, most students tolerate classroom composition. When a teacher ventures to say that writing is exploration, that it is an expression of the self or the development of a thought, students sit, befuddled, at their desks: what's this guy talking about?

# *Writing is Dialogue*

*Abstract and concrete work together to make identity—
a unity in variety and variety in unity. They limit and
complete each other. The concrete limits the speculativeness of
the abstract and develops its schemes; the abstract structures
the exuberance of the concrete and develops its implications.
The abstract reduces the concrete but also frees it from a
general or predetermined form. The concrete enlivens the
abstract and stabilizes it. Together they make up the identity of*

*an idea and express it as description and definition—perhaps
even a truth embodied or an accurate sweetness.*

—Marie Ponsot and Rosemary Deen, *Beat Not the Poor Desk*

Writing is dialogue, a process that moves inductively from specifics to abstraction. Effective composition—whether it be prose or poem, article or essay, fiction or nonfiction—weds concrete details with the abstraction of thought. You've read the student work that ignores one or the other: the poem packed with platitudes and generalities, but no images or details to place us somewhere in its heart; the list of quotations/facts that lead to no conclusion, the overarching observation that explains what all the specifics suggest. Composition that lacks details is a gathering of abstractions that have no heft. An accretion of concrete details without observation provides no insight. These are nothing more than lists. Writing is the dialogue of the specific and the general, the inductive act of distilling meaning from details.

"The most useful act to readers and writers," argues teacher Leo Rockas, "is the ready apprehension of the concrete in the abstract and the abstract in the concrete." Which is why writing is a recursive activity, shuttling back and forth between insight gleaned from specifics and the search for more specifics to clarify insight. Inductions result from following hunches suggested by specifics. Dialogue occurs when we follow inductions back to their roots and then ascend the ladder of thought yet again. Our thinking both expands and clarifies as we gather more specifics, and our specifics regroup as we find tighter patterns of classification. We dialogue as we first entertain a notion, we dialogue as we seek to shape it, and we dialogue as we revise our writing to sharpen our point.

This is another way of saying that writing is a process, an organic working out of memory, observation, research, and experience. Writing is not a noun, it is a verb; the result of competing and similar states of ideas or experiences that conjure up something greater than they are individually. As these differing voices interact they produce new patterns of thought. Writing is the result of these dialogues, these back-and-forth discursions:

## The dialogue between teacher and student

The more formulaic writing becomes, the less the student composes the work. The more we dictate the terms of the work, the less the student is a part of it. The more we predetermine every step of the process, the less the student learns how to write. The best teaching is a dialogue, yet if teachers take over that conversation, the student voice is buried. I was terrified to teach my first AP class, particularly because the previous teacher habitually met with each student when papers were assigned, a commitment that appeared time-consuming and intimidating. I felt obligated to do the same but couldn't imagine how the meetings should go: what advice would I give? Luckily, my fear worked for me: unable to figure out what to say, I started each interview by asking questions: What did the student like about the book? What didn't he like? What ideas seemed intriguing or disturbing? What parts didn't make sense? As the students answered, I found they hadn't needed my direction. Against all my teacherly instincts, I came to see they'd usually been thinking about the book, and what they needed was someone to bring their thoughts to the surface. This was a key insight: I wasn't to tell them what to write. I was to help them develop what they'd begun seeing on their own. This insight was, in my tenth year of instruction, epiphanic. As I expanded my repertoire of writing tricks, I came to believe that students had an innate sense of their interests and thoughts, which meant the more I dictated their direction, the more I got in the way of their working. This is what Nancy Atwell explains in *In the Middle* when she writes that she will not read a student's work in progress. Instead, she asks the student what he perceives the problem with his paper to be. This is important: Atwell believes the student is the key player in the writing's composition, and by treating the student as if this is the truth, she reinforces that truth for the student.

## The dialogue between our various selves

Writing is one of the most interior of artistic endeavors. The dancer moves through space, the musician shapes his voice, the actor creates physical drama. Even the sculptor and painter display their finished works in their fullness. But the writer creates most frequently in verbal and physical solitude: the conditions of composing demand the speaking of interior voices. All artists debate their creative choices, but most can be present when the audience views their work. However, the writer's audience is distant: they read his work in silence, recreating his voice. If the writer succeeds, his voice is heard in the mind of the reader; if he fails, the rest is silence. "I do what the voices inside my head tell me to do," declares a T-shirt, an irony writers understand. The integrity of our work is proportional to our willingness to ask ourselves questions that are tough, intimate, sometimes embarrassing, and frequently unsettling. But the more honestly we answer, the more likely what we say will have the weight of truth. Those who rely on clichés, on the banal and superficial, evidence their fear of plumbing their own depths. They opt instead to echo the voices of others, something teachers encourage when they dictate how a final work will look or sound. Instead, let the students do what the voices inside their heads tell them to.

## The dialogue between students

Because writing is an interior act, its completion requires an audience. Who we are is defined in part by how we see ourselves as well as how others see us. Writing for ourselves has its satisfactions, but the way others respond to what we think and feel alters us. Teachers who read student work to the class recall moments when a student's peers turned in their seats to examine the classmate they thought they'd known. Frequently, a student changes when others in his class begin to regard him as unexpectedly talented. I know the pitfalls of peer evaluation, but much of that is remedied when students are given specific items to look for rather than when directed to merely correct grammar errors or vaguely to "provide feedback." I conduct writing workshops, whole periods where students write as I float and discuss; when I come across a particularly vibrant passage, I stop the class and read it aloud. When I read finished work to the class, I ask the writer to explain particular passages or techniques. In short, I treat them like writers until they regard each other that way. Then they come to seek and value the feedback of their peers.

## The dialogue between teachers

I spent six years as a department chair, which exposed me to the methodologies of my colleagues. Expected to evaluate them, I more often became their cheerleader and passed on their ideas to the rest of the department. But what surprised me was how little colleagues knew about what went on in each others' classrooms. Even more unsettling was how little they knew about the writing expectations of their peers. Each June, AP teachers gather from around the nation in hotels and conference rooms to read student exams, poring over hundreds of handwritten essays for several days. But the first morning begins with calibrations, the reading of "anchor papers" to determine how readers will apply the 1 to 9 grading scale. It's humbling in these first hours to sit with dozens of other AP teachers, experienced and erudite, and watch the spread of ratings before we begin to understand and apply the grading rubric. These calibrations, which I encouraged my own department to try, stimulate dialogue as teachers explain what they value and what they believe students need to learn. As colleagues clarify what they envision good writing to be, they sharpen their own arguments and develop a common vocabulary. Inevitably, students benefit when teachers—individually and departmentally—are clear on what they expect. Chapter 8 discusses scope and sequence and explains that after we determine what we want within our classrooms, we need to sit down with colleagues and determine what our programs must do for our students.

## The dialogue between lesson plans and graduation goals

The daily paperwork of teaching makes it difficult to do more than plan the week, much less the unit, the year, and graduation outcomes. Inspired by ideas collected from Saturday workshops, instructional manuals, and teacher gatherings, we often sandwich new ideas within established units without regard to their long-term effects. As a result, the hodgepodge of lessons we gather, multiplied by the number of teachers within the department, means that long-term, department goals become less focused than daily ones. Chapter 8 explains the increased effectiveness that results when daily lessons are planned in league with graduation goals, so that teachers understand how what they do on any given day reinforces department goals and student development. But such planning—scope and sequencing—requires a linking between the specifics of the daily lesson and the abstractions of graduation goals. This dialogue between the concrete and the general strengthens a writing program, enables students to see the connections between units, courses, and levels, and allows for a more effective development of skills. Thus, teachers benefit themselves, their colleagues, and, most importantly, their students when they dialogue about long- and short-term planning.

## The dialogue of writing experiences

The monochromatic nature of writing programs splits the writing program into purportedly serious (five-paragraph literary analysis) and the more frivolous writing (so-called creative writing). Such a dichotomy is neither true to the world of composition nor helpful to students. Frustrated by the perceived failure of students to master the literary analysis, teachers often insist they must repeat the experience before students can attempt other writing styles. This is patent nonsense. The belabored repetition of a single writing experience works against the development of writing skills, not for it. We would not call our students readers if they perused only Jane Austen, nor would we call them grammarians if they only learned the uses of the comma. No discipline is enhanced by a narrow focus. Rather, skills are developed when employed in varied circumstances. Chapter 2 argues for the benefits of an expanded writing program—a dialogue within a range of writings that allows students to pursue a particular skill (e.g., structuring, researching, developing voice, or creating a focus) within different contexts. As perspective is the result of different vantage points, skill is the result of varied experiences. The dialogue of voices that a varied writing program develops enhances student ability.

## *Making the Angels Dance*

The notebooks of Leonardo Da Vinci illustrate the peregrinations of a Renaissance mind. Driven by curiosity to know how to paint the human form, Da Vinci literally laid out the muscle beneath the skin. A wondrous potpourri of disengaged limbs and body parts, the notebooks are gatherings of scribbles, illustrations, and ink stains, a graveyard cum playground from which Leonardo induced the structure of the human body. Here was no Scholastic. Da Vinci pinned back the flesh of arms to see what nature wrot, the data of his senses developing the abstractions of his mind. While the Scholastics sought God in the colored light of stained glass, the scientific methodists let flow the blood of flesh. Perhaps, paradoxically, the scientists were more interested in God's work than His existence.

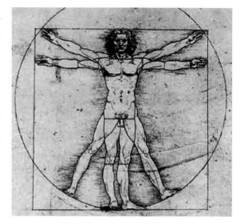

When students ask me how many paragraphs their work should contain, how many sentences within each paragraph, how long a sentence normally is, I hear Aquinas counting angels. I tell them that these are the wrong questions, that these are not important. I do not want my students to wonder how many angels can congregate in a limited space. I want their writing to make those angels dance.

—·—

To understand how induction can aid a writing program, we first need to know what that writing program could look like. Chapter 2, "Beyond the Omelet: A Writing Continuum," argues for a program tapping a variety of writing types, thereby developing a wide range of writing skills.

# Beyond the Omelet:
# A Writing Continuum

---

Focus: Students better understand and utilize writing techniques when the writing they compose is varied. An effective writing program incorporates a range of styles, types, structures, and perspectives.

---

**Sections:**
- Five-Paragraph Problems
- Squelching the Personal
- The Suggestive, the Informative & the Critical: A Writing Continuum
- Social Justice Composition
- Student Samples

*Finally, if the range of possible audience responses is as broad as even this limited picture of discourse possibilities suggests, then our writing programs at the college and secondary levels are far too narrow to be of maximum benefit to our students. The implication for practice is surely to expand the repertoire.*

—George Hillocks, Jr., *Teaching Writing as Reflective Practice*

*If we teach standard patterns as ways of organizing whole texts, we falsify the reality of how writers write. If we teach them as ways of organizing parts of texts, we don't help students learn when to apply them. If we teach students that our little repertoire of patterns represents the larger reality of writing, we teach what is not true.*

—William S. Robinson, "On Teaching Organization: Patterns, Process and the Nature of Writing"

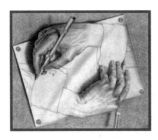The fact that students too often believe writing consists of nothing more than five-paragraph essays and creative writing prompts suggests we have failed to apprise them of varied forms of expression. When students create multiple kinds of writing, they begin to understand the underlying patterns in all writing. Hence, the student exposed solely or predominantly to the five-paragraph essay learns how to produce little more than the five-paragraph essay. More importantly, students focused on one product fail to learn how the skills involved in its creation can be applied to other kinds of writing. The apprentice chef, for instance, who only learns to prepare an omelet, may make great omelets, but never learns the underlying principles of cooking that would enable him to cook anything else. Similarly, the student well versed in the five-paragraph essay may eventually learn to produce five-paragraph essays, but he will not see how its structure applies to writing in general because he has never been taught how writing works—he has only been taught how to replicate a structure.

James Moffett, who first argued for teaching a range of writing in 1968, explains in *Teaching the Universe of Discourse* that

> if the reader images a continuum going from the one extreme of stichomythia to the other extreme of the polished solo publication, he has then an instrument of pedagogical value. For the gradations of the continuum are steps in a natural evolution from dialogue to written composition. (85)

Noting that writing moves from the intensely personal and implicit to the analytic and objective discussion of the masses, Moffett's continuum parallels the studies of child psychologists Jean Piaget and Erik Erikson. Our psyches evolve, according to Piaget, from the personal to the communal; adulthood is signaled by surpassing the subjectivity of personal experience and developing the ability to empathize with the group:

> One can say that all needs tend first of all to incorporate things and people into the subject's own activity, i.e., to "assimilate" the external world into the structures that have already been constructed….The successive modes of incorporation evolve from those of perception and movement to those of the higher mental operations…and the progressive organization of mental development appears to be simply an ever more precise adaptation to reality. (21)

Piaget calls this evolutionary process "adaptation," the increasing addition of more complex systems of thought to previous, more simple ones so that the individual continues to function despite the bombardment of, often, contradictory ideas. Thus, in early stages, children know little beyond their own experiences, but as they adapt, they supplement personal memories with the memories and experiences of others. Ultimately, children distill these collective memories and experiences into an elaborate system of thought, the framework by which they organize their own experiences, a framework that will be revised as they age.

So, the maturing individual increasingly utilizes a range of perspectives—in both time and point of view—to order his universe. To describe water as hot, we must experience it as cold. Moffett's continuum is ordered around perspective; witness his anthology of fiction *Points of View*, a sequencing of literary formats from the personal to the communal: stream of consciousness, diary, journal, memoir, letter, article, etc. This progression of thought moves from the interior monologue to mass communication:

- Reflection: Intrapersonal communication between two parts of one nervous system.

- Conversation: Interpersonal communication between two people in vocal range.

- Correspondence: Interpersonal communication between remote individuals or small groups with some personal knowledge of each other.

- Publications: Impersonal communications to a large anonymous group extended over space and/or time.

Of this sequence Moffett explains that "Each kind of discourse is more selective, composed, and public than those before." (1968, 56)

Writing programs, then, should draw from a wide range of student perspectives and experiences. To do otherwise, to focus on a narrow selection of perspectives, is to disconnect the classroom from the students' culture. We often argue that writing is a highly evolved form of expression, a way to declare who we are in dialogue with others. So, writing programs that ignore this truth only reinforce the belief that the classroom has nothing to do with the outside world.

So, a writing continuum. Encouraging the personal and the communal, a varied writing program offers several benefits:

- Learning a range of writing styles, students are prepared for a wider range of collegiate writing experiences.

- Application of writing techniques in a variety of formats makes clearer how those techniques work.

- A varied writing program improves reading comprehension as students experiment with techniques they encounter in their reading.

- Taught a range of writing styles, students can ultimately choose their own formats, content, and style instead of relying on instructors to choose them.

This chapter argues that in developing a writing continuum, departments can better educate students in crafting expressive, insightful work in a variety of formats.

# *Five-Paragraph Problems*

*The linguist Leon A. Jakobovits suggests that "stale art" is algorithmic—produced by a known algorithm, "defined as a computational device that specifies the order and nature of the steps to be followed in the generation of a sequence." One could say that the major kind of essay too many students have been taught to write in American schools is algorithmic, so mechanical that a computer would readily be programmed to produce it. When a student is hurried or anxious, he simply reverts or regresses to the only program he knows, as if inserting a single card into his brain.*

—Janet Emig, *The Web of Meaning*

*[Students] learn that a "good" paragraph should have a topic sentence (though according to Braddock (1974) few actually do in the textbook sense) or that arguments consist of propositions supported by reasons. But those same students may not be able to generate a "good" paragraph or a developed argument. In fact, Flower and Hayes (1981) report that when writers first focus on the final form of discourse and try to produce its parts, as these texts would have them do, they short-circuit the normal generating processes and become mired in an unmanageable task that blocks writing.*

—George Hillocks, Jr.,
*Teaching Writing as a Reflective Practice*

Despite the earnest efforts of many English teachers, secondary level emphasis on the five-paragraph essay distresses many on the collegiate level. Professor Gregory Shafer argues against the reasons high school teachers cite for teaching the five-paragraph essay:

Implicit in this practice is the early twentieth century theory that students are linguistically deprived, that they can't organize, and that they must learn to write in a decidedly behavioristic way—one that attributes no linguistic ability to the writer. And each year, these same teachers bemoan the clichés, the trite writing, the lack of critical thinking skills. It is an ironic scenario that imposes authoritarian mandates while secretly hoping for the spirit of the subversive. We shouldn't wonder why it never works. (*English Journal* September 2000, 29)

In "The Ill Effects of the Five Paragraph Theme," Kimberley Wesley cites a number of interviews with college instructors who decry the failure of students to understand writing as anything more than a five-paragraph experience:

> In "Articulation and Student Voices," D.R. Randsell and Gregory Clau report findings from a survey of first-year college composition students who recommend that their high school English teachers quit "driving the five-paragraph thing into our brains" and that "there must be more [types of essays] taught." (57)

Wesley cites university professor Thomas Nunnally's comment in "Breaking the Five Paragraph Theme Barrier," and laments what has become a "national phenomenon." Wesley's own observations lead to the following conclusions:

> My primary objection to the five-paragraph theme [FPT] is its tendency to stunt students' critical thinking abilities. Moreover, I have found the essays that best fulfill format requirements turn out to be neatly packaged but intellectually vapid. A 1992 University of Hawaii study of student responses to writing assignments, including the FPT, reports similar findings:
>
> > In structuring their arguments, [student writers] all wanted to exceed formulaic limits, but their teacher would allow no deviation. Clearly, whatever their instructor's intentions, these students were discovering thoughts and feelings through composing. And their discovery experiences proved incompatible with the prescribed essay structure. So the students left the writing experience with considerable frustration. (Marsella et al. 180)
>
> Marsella et al. also conclude that students only challenge their own beliefs when "their contexts allow, even encourage, risk taking" (185). As a teacher assuming a rigid, artificial writing format for my students, I have been limiting their ability to take intellectual risks and discouraging the kind of learning that I believe only writing allows them to do. (59)

Finally, Wesley quotes a 1992 critique of classes of discourse by Richard Larson, who concludes that

> high school English teachers too often ask students to engage in what British educators refer to as a 'dummy run': an activity that has no pur-

pose with identified readers but is designed to display the writer's ability to produce a frozen form. (59)

Wesley argues that abandoning the five-paragraph essay does not mean ignoring "principles of unity, coherence, and development."

> Rather, I suggest that we continue to teach the essay as a rhetorical form with three units—an introduction, a body, and a conclusion. The introductory unit of the essay (which may be more than one paragraph, depending on the scope of the rhetorical problem) serves to grab the reader's attention, establish common ground, and define the problem and perhaps the process undertaken to solve that problem. The thesis (which most likely will occur at the beginning or the end of the introductory unit—there are good models of both) states the writer's focus or position on the problem (without sub-points because—as seen in the above discussion—a rigid number of sub-points can inhibit student thought). The body unit of the essay should be an unspecified number of paragraphs with each paragraph serving one of a variety of purposes: to define terms, to review the literature, to present evidence in favor of the thesis, to analyze that evidence, and to accommodate and/or refute opposing views. Finally, the concluding unit of the essay should serve to reassert the writer's position, to remind the reader of the importance to him/her of the problem at hand, and to pose questions on the issue that could be addressed by other writers. (59)

William S. Robinson lays much of the blame for the dominance of five-paragraph essay instruction in the laps of teachers who do not encourage students to expand their structural repertoire:

> Several writers have noted that in evaluating the work of students, we teachers tend, unfortunately, to value simplistic organizational patterns more highly than we do more subtle ones. [Marie] Foley notes that teachers often penalize more complex organizational schemes simply because they don't recognize them, looking as they do for simplistic over-signaled forms. (3)

Similarly, Richard H. Haswell found that among student essays he studied, the "logically simpler the organization the higher the grade." Especially in impromptu writing, students, he noted, were "doubly" tempted to use simple forms such as the five-paragraph essay:

> Quickly conceived and easily remembered, they allow for high output of words; facile logical compartments can be plumped with examples and detail. And it is the long, fully supported, conspicuously compartmented essay that teachers often react to positively. ("The Organization of Impromptu Essays")

And in another essay:

Spivey found that her academic raters gave their highest scores to symmetrically organized comparison essays, failing to note that such symmetries do not necessarily characterize professional writing. ("On Teaching Organization: Patterns, Process and the Nature of Writing," NCTE)

In contrast to formulaic writing programs, inductive teaching requires we emphasize the skill, not the product, thus enabling students to apply the skill in a variety of situations. Hence, writing programs that are diverse prepare students for collegiate and nonclassroom experiences better. As P. L. Thomas notes in "The Struggle Itself: Teaching Writing as We Know We Should,"

> teachers have to be patient and persistent, allowing students numerous opportunities to write and exposing them to hundreds of models of effective writing. (*English Journal*, September 2000, 43)

Deborah M. Dean echoes the sentiment in "Muddying Boundaries: Mixing Genres with Five Paragraphs." She writes that "understanding various contexts and how to write within them really gives our students more options" (*English Journal*, September 2000, 54). Dean also quotes Lad Tobin, who argues for a multiplicity of writing styles in his "The Case for Double-Voiced Discourse." Tobin writes that "essays should reflect the way we think and experience the world. And the fact is: we often think and experience the world in a multidimensional, multivoiced way"

## *Squelching the Personal*

> *Current traditional rhetoric has been widely influential for a long time because it works so efficiently, but its work does not lie in teaching people how to write.*
>
> —Sharon Crowley, *The Methodical Memory: Invention in Current-Traditional Rhetoric*

> *We do not sit down to write an essay. We sit down to write an essay about a particular subject.*
>
> —George Hillocks, Jr., *Teaching Writing as Reflective Practice*

Unfortunately, not only is the five-paragraph essay the dominant writing experience in high school, it is nearly exclusively applied to literary analysis, so that students get a double whammy: writing is restricted in both structure and content. This dominance of critical writing also means that forays into other kinds of writing (infrequently into the suggestive, rarely into the informative) do not receive the same attention of instruction that teachers often lavish on critical pieces. Thus, teachers grade noncritical writing with fewer expectations. The same attention teachers bring to the structure of a literary analysis is forgotten when explaining the composition of a poem, personal essay, or the sources of a reportorial piece. Students are shocked if we grade a poem with similar strictness expected from literary analysis because we rarely teach them how to write a poem the way we teach an analytic essay. Our inconsistency in this is shown when we, as English teachers, dissect the poetry of Shakespeare, Robert Browning, or Sylvia Plath, referring to the works' structures, use of figurative language, rhythm and pacing, and yet fail to require such rhetorical devices in the fictional work of our students. A poem should receive no less instruction in its structure—and evaluation of its effectiveness—than a literary analysis.

By applying inconsistent standards of evaluation to differing writing experiences, we send mixed signals about what we value (i.e., literary analysis is more important than writing a poem), and contradict our own classroom discussion wherein we extol the beauty and construction of a poem or a story—unless it is written by a student. Students not required to write suggestive works that incorporate the same techniques as the poetry they analyze in class will not fully appreciate what professional writers achieve.

English programs similarly fail students when teaching the personal essay. Though such programs often accord the personal essay more legitimacy than a poem or short story (perhaps because the word "essay" gives it validity), it is taught more frequently only as a narrative. And even here, educators often teach the personal essay as if it were a five-paragraph exercise, imposing the formulaic format of the literary analysis on the personal essay. It is a procrustean requirement.

Personal essays can take on a number of shapes and purposes—reflective, meditative, narrative, and reactive—and their versatility requires a similarly versatile approach to organizing their material. Ironically, as with fictional work, our students are often exposed to excellent personal essays (for example, pieces by Maya Angelou, E.B. White, Russell Baker, and others), but we fail to explain how structure and rhetoric work in such writing, instead focusing on the author's meaning or theme. In the wake of writing projects that emerged in the 1970s, many colleges recognized the difference between rhetoric and literary analysis and began staffing separate departments for the two disciplines. In such programs, students learn the difference between analyzing a piece for its literary meaning and analyzing it for its rhetorical effectiveness. Unfortunately, high schools often fail to delineate the difference between literature and rhetoric, instead proposing a one-size-fits-all approach to reading and writing. Thus, the personal essay is given short shrift, taught only as a piece in need of literary dissection. Students thereby fail to learn how to write personal essays.

This is a particular shortcoming in that college testing and entrance exams rarely require literary analyses, but now they do require personal essays. The revised SAT I, for instance, requires written responses to prompts. Students are called on to provide reflective or persuasive responses, drawing from their recollections, current events, and reading. Here are examples of such prompts:

- Think carefully about the following quotation and the assignment that follows. Then plan and write your essay according to the instructions.

  "Don't take risks; better safe than sorry."

  Do you agree with this statement? Write an essay in which you support your opinion with specific examples from history, contemporary life, readings, or personal observations.

- Think carefully about the following quotation and the assignment that follows. Then plan and write your essay according to the instructions.

  "The American dream is to get something for nothing."

  Do you agree with this statement? Write an essay in which you support your opinion with specific examples from history, contemporary life, readings, or personal observations.

- In a well-organized composition, describe a situation in which an event that you had especially not looked forward to turned out to be the opposite of what you had expected. Include the following in your essay:

    an account of why you had not looked forward to the event

    an account of why the event turned out well

  Be specific.

- "The majority is often wrong"

  Choose a specific example from your reading, personal experience, or current events as the basis for an essay that agrees or disagrees with this statement.

Note that these prompts require the synthesizing of varied experiences (including personal accounts), but none requires a literary analysis.

Finally, personal essays are an integral part of the college application process. Amidst the mind numbing wealth of test scores and GPAs, admissions officers look to the personal essay to find the personality of the applicant. Instead, the majority of students (who too often find the college essay their first exposure to the personal essay) settle for rote, formulaic responses, unaware how important their individual voice is. In "Inside College Admissions," *TIME* writer Jodie Morse attacks the myth that,

   the essay counts only in close calls....Before even glancing at grades or
   test scores, admissions officers at Bowdoin College in Brunswick, Maine,

rate a student's personal statement. That first impression can color the whole discussion. (76)

Interviewing admissions officers from Rice and Cornell, Morse notes the importance of the personal essay in the application process, and the need for a sense of personality on the writer's part: "A little warmth and humor never hurt" (77). Following one set of admissions officers as they read a student's particularly humorous and touching essay, Morse observes the committee's enthusiasm for the piece, which "sent them straight for the ADMIT stamp. Otherwise, the student's B record would not have got him in." (77)

In *Essays that Worked: 50 Essays from Successful Applications to the Nation's Top Colleges*, Boykin Curry and Brian Kasbar relate the tale of an admissions officer's visceral reaction to a clever personal essay: "I chuckled with delight upon reading it, jumped up from my chair, and rushed into the hallway to share it with my colleagues" (36). An officer at Williams College wrote of one essay, "It offers such a direct view into the contradictions and complexities of a highly imaginative and complex person. It is both bold and sensitive, amazingly rich in imagery and unusual in structure. Dylan is a good bet to be a mold-breaker, an innovator" (66–67). The authors add "anyone who doubts the importance of the application essay, imagine having that officer rooting for you in an admissions conference!" (67)

Clearly, as Curry and Kasbar note, admissions officers seek essays with voice and personality, not retread observations, clichés, Hallmark sentiments, or formulas: "But please, God, not another piece on 'what-I-learned-by-working-so-hard-as-yearbook-editor.'" (4)

In short, as important as critical writing and literary analysis are, students who do not receive an equal training in the personal essay—and other kinds of writing—are inadequately prepared for the collegiate experience. Our students become better writers the more they vary their writing. Programs that focus on a select number of products, repeated to the exclusion of other writings, run the risk of emphasizing formula over process. By the senior year, students should be encouraged and able to explore writing for which there is no precedent in their instruction. If they have learned the skills behind the product—and not just the product itself—this will not be a daunting task. If they have had opportunity to apply writing skills in a variety of assignments, the more likely they are to have understood those skills and know how to manipulate them. Like the cook preparing the omelet, it is hard to understand the principles of cooking via a single meal of eggs, cheese, and milk. Better to draw from an array of foods, preparing a gamut of dishes. That is how one becomes a chef.

# *The Suggestive, the Informative &*
# *the Critical: A Writing Continuum*

As writing moves from the implicit to the explicit, it changes purpose, draws from different materials, and selects new formats. We move from the immediate experience to the distant in time and space. Writing that is intensely implicit is dominated by fiction, operating by suggestion rather than direct statement, communicating through figures of speech and allusion rather than scientific criteria. Its perspective is personal, subjective, operating, as Emily Dickinson writes, so that we tell "the truth, but tell it slant." As writing becomes more explicit, it shifts perspective, moving from the personal to incorporate the experiences and views of others, intending to find common ground. Because it seeks less to suggest and more to explicate, its intent is informative in nature, examining an idea from an increasing distance of time and space so that our understanding of it is shared. Finally, writing that is intensely explicit seeks to define with reference to common criteria. Scientific in execution, critical discourse aims to persuade or argue for a shared action. Because the truth it arrives at must be agreed on by many instead of one, it needs to establish a common language for discourse, often relying on logical statement. Analytic in intent, it does not merely express as does suggestive writing, or seek understanding as informative works do; rather, it intends to convert. We can employ the experience of movie going to illustrate the range of the continuum: in the realm of the suggestive, we write the movie; in the realm of the informative, we explain the movie; in the realm of the critical, we evaluate the movie.

| A Writing Continuum | | |
|---|---|---|
| **The Suggestive** | **The Informative** | **The Critical** |
| First-person | | Third-person |
| Implicit | | Explicit |
| Impressionistic | Reportorial | Evaluative |
| Intuitive | Evidential | Declarative |
| Mythic | Historic | Scientific |
| Individualistic | Communal | Cultural |
| Subjective | Perspectival | Persuasive |
| Connotative | Denotative | Analytic |

## The Suggestive

*A spiritual guide should not tell the naked truth. He should use images, allegories, figures, wondrous speech, or other roundabout ways.*

—Paracelsus

*Literature in which everything is explicit is no fun to read: part of the pleasure of engaging with a writer is unraveling some allusions and admitting defeat by others. The purpose of allusive writing is to arouse associations deep in the reader's mind and feelings, not necessarily to communicate plainly.*

—Felipe Fernandez-Armesto, *Civilizations*

Writing that is highly figurative or allusive finds truth by suggestion rather than definition, believing that language and logic do less to pin truth down than to actually muddle our understanding of it. An Eastern proverb states, "That part of the All which can be defined is not the All." The proverb asserts that truth is better understood intuitively than definitively. Such writing implies its meaning, preferring to communicate by indirect rather than direct statement. It operates predominantly in the realm of fiction, where the writer prefers the connotations of language operating in a kind of controlled ambiguity. It is a world frustrating to those who prefer their truth in concrete, measurable units. It is the bane of students who, after examining a poem, ask of the teacher, "Why doesn't the author just say what he means?" (To which I note that if the author had just said what he meant, he'd have written an essay, not a poem.) Such writing draws heavily from myth and has much in common with the world of spirit, attracting readers who find truth transcendent and not one-dimensional. It is, by nature of its subjectivity, intensely personal, exemplified in the stream of consciousness writings of James Joyce and Virginia Woolf, or the private symbols of W.B. Yeats. Even as it veers toward the more explicit, suggestive writing prefers the personal essay to the informative or critical piece, valuing the perspective of the author over the communal truth of the masses. Though such work is often written in recollection, it feels immediate, as expressed in the goals of writers of such diversity as Wordsworth, who in the Preface to *Lyrical Ballads* argued, despite his elaborate sonnets, for "the spontaneous overflow of emotion," and Walt Whitman, whose long lines spun out in juxtapositions of coordinated sections that influenced the 1950s work of such Beats as Allen Ginsberg, Jack Kerouac, and William S. Burroughs.

## The Realm of the Suggestive

As we move from intensely implicit to slightly more explicit writing, we travel from the intensely personal to the shared personal.

*Stream of Consciousness:* The symbolic expression of interior states as in the work of James Joyce, Virginia Woolf, and William Faulkner. Much of the work of the Surrealists would fall into this category.

*Confessional Poetry*: Highly personal symbols as found in the works of Sylvia Plath, Robert Lowell, Ted Hughes, and Allen Ginsberg.

*Psychological Realism:* The projection of interior states onto exterior objects, frequently found in the expressionism of Franz Kafka, Eugene O'Neill, or the drama of Jean Paul Sartre.

*Hyper Realism:* The highly focused use of realistic images to suggest transcendent states as in the work of Gabriel Garcia Marquez (and other practitioners of magical realism), Thomas Pynchon, Joyce Carol Oates, and Don DeLillo.

*Lyric Poetry:* Expression of interior states via more conventional images and language. Found in the classic works of Metaphysical, Carpe Diem, Romantic, and Late Victorian writers.

*Memoir*: A prose recitation of personal events. The autobiographical work of Annie Dillard, Richard Rodriguez, and Maya Angelou falls into this category, as do the personal essays of Charles Lamb, E. B. White, and Annie Lamotte.

## *The Informative*

Writing that wishes to inform often utilizes the personal, but weds it to a multiplicity of perspectives to emphasize comprehension over the mere relating of experience. If suggestive writing draws heavily from memory, informative writing mixes memory with shared perspective to find common ground. Informative work culls a variety of sources—memory, direct observation, interview, and recorded material—to create a sense of depth much like a Renaissance painting that creates perspective by placing elements in contrasting space. Because informative writing draws from a variety of vantage points, it can incorporate first-, second-, or third-person sources. But unlike suggestive writing, whose first-person subjectivity is its own charm and validation, and unlike critical writing, whose third-person objectivity fits its tone of declaration and authenticity, informative writing seeks neither subjectivity nor complete objectivity. We apply the term "media" to much of this work because it acts as a medium between its sources and the reader, intending less to pass itself off as truth (the goal of the critical) than as a conduit by which the reader can make his own truth. Nevertheless, truth is a goal of the informative, but in a distinctly different way from the suggestive, which believes the view of the individual has its own validity. By contrast, the realm of the informative believes truth increases in credibility when varied perspectives establish a common denominator. The value of the informative for writers lies in its requirement that they not only draw from a variety of sources, but that such variety references a range of diverse, and often opposing, viewpoints. Because of this, informative writing draws more on skills of synthesis than the other realms.

---

### The Realm of the Informative

As we continue to move from implicit to more explicit writing, we travel from the personal expressions of the reporter to the communal perspective of mass media.

*Participatory Journalism:* First-person involvement in the event under study often mixed with second- or third-hand sources. Found in the works primarily of Hunter S. Thompson, as well as pieces by Tom Wolfe, Joan Didion, and John McPhee.

*Dramatized Journalism:* Fictionalized interpretations of current or historical events based on research and interviews. *In Cold Blood* by Truman Capote, *The Electric Kool-Aid Acid Test* by Tom Wolfe, *The Executioner's Song* by Norman Mailer, and *The Perfect Storm* by Sebastian Junger are prime examples.

*Feature Writing:* Feature writing often has a first-person feel but is less oriented toward the perspective of the writer and more freely incorporates outside sources. Found predominantly in magazines and feature sections of newspapers.

*Summary News:* In this form of journalism, the first-person perspective has disappeared, the intent of the work being objectivity. Summary news writing eschews the dramatic for the factual. The meat and potatoes of newspapers and broadcast journalism.

*Interview:* With the interview, the first-person angle has disappeared completely as we are absorbed in the view of the source. Studs Terkel's many works showcase interviewing at its best as does the broadcast work of NPR's Terry Gross and Inside the Actor's Studio's James Lipton.

*Biography:* As we move toward the realm of the critical, we encounter such work as the biography, wherein a range of sources and perspectives convey the world or culture of a subject separate from the writer.

## *The Critical*

The realm of the academic, critical writing fully intends to communicate its meaning. Here the emphasis is on analysis, the "what" supplanted by the "how" or "why." Characterized by persuasion, such pieces require the direct over the suggestive, the concrete over the allusive. It is here the scholar uses analysis to unearth the meaning of a text, the speechwriter uses language to enlighten, or the editorial writer seeks to change our point of view. Informative writing is content to enlighten, but critical writing insists that such enlightenment requires action: we must do more than understand a belief; we must share it. This is why critical writing often establishes criteria for evaluation: the validity of what one argues is weakened if its foundational arguments are flawed. We expect the movie critic to do more than applaud or deride a film; before we will plunk down our $10, we need to know what in the film convinced him to declare as he does. Ironically, advertising does not meet critical criteria, despite its intent to persuade; drawing as it does from images and connotations (common techniques of the suggestive), most advertising campaigns fail to establish criteria, preferring to motivate emotively, not rationally. Students most frequently (in the poorest cases, exclusively) encounter critical writing through literary analysis, a discipline whose intent is to unearth meaning that lodges in the interstices of fictional language. As I have already argued, such writing experiences are valuable, but they must be balanced with other experiences so that a student can develop a range of stylistic tricks.

---

### The Realm of the Critical

Writing that is increasingly explicit chooses language, formats, and styles that are more formal and accessible.

*Performance Critique:* Reviews are recapitulations of a performance while critiques evaluate a performance's merits. In doing the latter, the writer has moved beyond a mere collection of information to add another level to the discussion, placing the rehearsal of events within a larger discussion of value. Reviews of a variety of events fill newspapers and magazines; the commentaries of film critic Roger Ebert and art critic Robert Hughes are particularly insightful.

*Editorial:* Like a critique, an editorial weighs the merits of a case, but with the additional intent to persuade the reader to share that evaluation. Letters to the editor and the opinions pages of media publications demonstrate the power of the editorial.

---

cont.

> *Informal Analysis:* This is a first-person treatment of a subject, the author interpreting material gathered from numerous sources. Informal analysis is the tone of choice for popular columnists and writers like science essayist Stephen Jay Gould, media analyst Todd Gitlin, and cultural critic Camille Paglia.
>
> *Academic Analysis:* Third-person in perspective, academic analysis—a more formal approach to the subject matter—prefers a dispassionate approach to discussion as to lend weight and gravitas to the author's nevertheless subjective work.

Students benefit from experience in all three categories of writing and by understanding that research is required in each. Suggestive writing requires brainstorming or clustering, so that students recall anecdotes, conversations, and descriptive details that give their subjective accounts—whether poem, short story, or reflective essay—a richness that communicates the intensity of their experience. Informative writing expands the range of sources, encouraging students to supplement their own experiences and observations with the experiences and observations of others, which can be gathered from both interview and recorded sources (print material, CD-ROMs, online sites, film, and cultural artifacts). Finally, critical writing requires an awareness of the material under discussion—how it operates, what it intends—so that the writer can communicate to others that same awareness and understanding.

Having learned how to adjust perspective as the assignment requires, the student more effectively learns how to address his material. Like the apprentice who learns to make more than omelets—who uses a variety of foods, mixing them in varied combinations—a writer experimenting with varied formats does not make only a single product, but instead understands the process of creation itself. Only then does the omelet maker earn the title of chef, and only then can we declare the student a writer.

## *Social Justice Composition*

> *I came to understand that the key to reaching my students and building community was helping students excavate and reflect on their personal experiences, and connecting them to the world of language, literature, and society.*
>
> —Linda Christensen, *Reading, Writing and Rising Up*

The five girls and three boys who quietly filed into the small room took seats toward the back and, at my request, pulled out notebooks. For the next hour, I told them about mythological journeys, inviting them to see themselves as the heroes of their own narratives. To prepare them for the writing I wanted them to do, I recited a self-deprecating tale of my own half-heroism, the time I braved a cross-country flight, white knuckles gripping my arm rests as a lightning storm buffeted the plane heading toward Bangor, Maine. As the plane "attempted" to land (the pilot's ill-chosen verb), I squeezed back into my seat, immobile. Then the first drop of water hit me. Forced out of my partial paralysis, I examined the plane's ceiling, where drops of water were clearly forming. Shocked into awareness, I knew I had to alert the flight attendant to our imminent disaster. She came in response to my ring, bent over, and smiled. I coughed up my news.

"The plane is leaking," I whispered, not wanting to terrify my co-passengers.

She, who had clearly known flyers like me before, smiled and whispered in a light British tone, "It's condensation, sir," and returned to her seat.

Honestly, my effort to save the plane was heroic, if mildly pathetic.

The story always gets laughs from my students, as it did now, so I encouraged them to brainstorm a list of incidents wherein they had acted heroically. Ten minutes later, they quietly shared. One girl recalled the night she ordered her father out of the house, his drinking and infidelity too much for her mother and siblings. Another girl recalled the time she told her father his physical abuse was unacceptable, and he must leave. Still another student recalled the day she said goodbye to her brother, his employment future bleak, so he had enlisted to fight in Iraq and was now overseas. The family heard from him infrequently.

These were kids in the AVID program, a San Diego-based company that targets economically challenged students in the hope of teaching them skills they'll need to reach college. These students hailed from the Watsonville area near Monterey, a city marked by a heavy employment of migrants, mostly Hispanic. They wanted an education, and they had stories to tell.

Linda Christensen discusses the needs of similar kids in her *Reading, Writing, and Rising Up: Teaching about Social Justice and the Power of the Written Word*. Based on her own experiences teaching socially marginalized students in Portland, Oregon, Christensen's book is an argument for an expanded writing curriculum, an incorporation of the personal that more readily addresses the needs of students for whom literary analysis and esoteric discussions have little meaning. The secondary level's emphasis on critical writing leaves behind students whose economic and cultural backgrounds make topics outside their experience seem worthless. It is better, she argues, to give such students a forum for self-expression, a way of touching writing's foundational purpose: to clarify one's thinking, and then to speak that thought.

There is nothing touchy-feely about Christensen's preference for poetry, personal essays, reader responses, or letters addressing social issues. "I want to be clear," she writes. "Bringing student issues into the room does not mean giving up teaching the core ideas and skills of the class; it means using the energy of their connections to drive us through the content" (5). It is skills, not content, that is the first order of business in writing; the student who needs to learn structure, research, grammar, and voice can do so in writing experiences drawn from across the writing continuum, in the poem or personal essay no less than the literary critique. Writing drawn from personal experience for students in at-risk environments takes composition off the dusty shelf and into the streets, enabling these students to find purpose in expression. As Christensen explains, "More often students shared their fears. Violence was erupting around them and they felt out of control. They needed to share that fear" (6) It's the same argument George Hillocks, Jr., makes in *Teaching Writing as a Reflective Practice*:

> Not surprisingly, when given choices of what to study, [teacher] Deborah [Stern] reports that [students] usually choose to study issues that concern them, "sex and violence" for example. With Deborah's guidance, they choose texts that they will read as a group and texts they will read individually. They copy the lyrics of rap songs and bring them to class for study. When they write extended definitions of violence, they discuss examples from their own lives, from the rap songs they admire and from the newspaper stories they have collected. The fact that students have choices does not mean that Deborah has relinquished control. On the contrary, students make choices within a carefully thought-out rationale that begins with what she wants for her students: "to have some tools to think about the chaos of their lives. Sex and violence sometimes seems beyond their control. If we look at it deeply, at least they may have something to help them understand what's going on and what choices they have." (66)

Having taught her own students the power of writing, Christensen found a natural transition from poetry to the college entrance essay, where self-expression more directly addressed an educational goal. The transition inevitably involved the students in social justice issues, as Christensen brought in films, ads, news reports, and other media that played a role in her student's disempowerment. They were encouraged to "unlearn the myths" of their culture (36), researching and critiquing the public forum where others spoke louder than her students had been allowed. These are deconstructive acts, a form of analysis requiring extensive research, the development of criteria, and an ability to contrast differing levels of thought. (Deconstruction is discussed as one of five analytic approaches in Chapter 7.)

Christensen draws from a range of writings to spark her students' compositions, and there are compelling materials to work with. Multicultural and social justice anthologies abound (I have worked happily with *Crossing Cultures: Readings for Composition* in my Literature, Culture and Identity course). HBO has broadcast a series of Russell Simmons' poetry slams, and PBS produced a series of MTV-like poetry videos, *The United States of Poetry*. Bowling Green University's *Popular Culture Reader* includes two compelling essays, "The Peril of the Yellow Menace," and "From Plantation to Police Station: Black Stereotypes in Popular Culture." And filmmaker Marlon Riggs compiled a two-part history of black stereotypes in *Ethnic Notions* and *Color Adjustment*.

As much as I prize Christensen's work for her insight into writing as a social act, I also appreciate the universality of her message. All writing is personal, the poem no less than the evaluation, and enabling students to see that connects them with the power of words. If they leave our schools not knowing that, we have failed them, our profession, and much of what the writers we admire wrote for.

I know this in my bones, and I know this because I have seen it work.

Jennifer Martinez joined my newspaper staff her senior year, an immensely hardworking student I had taught three years previously in freshman honors (you can find her "Valley Fair" commentary on the accompanying CD). During the third year of the newspaper's publication, I wanted to up the ante, making what the staff wrote vital to themselves, the school, and the community. I'd been considering ways we might address social justice issues, something particularly important for a school dominated by upper middle-class white students. I thought such articles would help them as much as the causes they addressed.

I live in California's Silicon Valley, an increasingly two-tiered class culture that—the dotcom bubble burst notwithstanding—has placed some of the most expensive housing communities in the nation next to the most economically depressed. Into this chasm have slipped *los jornaleros*, the day laborers. Predominantly illegal Mexican migrants, the day laborers serve a clientele that will pay more for a personal shopper than a construction worker. Los jornaleros are cheap to hire, and because they have no papers, they don't quibble over wages. If they do get papers (our staff bought fake green cards at a local shopping center for $100), they can work in the fields, picking strawberries, apples, artichokes, or anything else that grows on the migrant circuit from San Diego to Seattle. They're here because corporations from Wal-Mart to Tyson bring them in, unregistered contractors bring them in by the truckload, and middle class families (like some of those at our school) hire them. I thought it was a story worth telling

As I explained the idea, I noticed Jennifer tearing up, watching me intensely. I stopped talking and turned to her. "You okay?"

Her eyes focused on me as she nodded and said, "That's my father you're describing." And she explained how her father had come up through the migrant circuit, enduring the fieldwork, creating an overwhelming desire to get through high school, eventually working his way to and through college, marrying, and raising his only daughter, the focus of his future. Jennifer wanted to be on the investigating team.

And inspired by her father, Jennifer requested my help in applying to Stanford. You could have counted on one foot how many students had entered Stanford from our school in recent years, and as good a student as Jennifer was, her quest was daunting. But I agreed, and over the next three months, as the team interviewed workers, lawyers, politicians, parents, students, a United Farm Workers spokesperson, and local charities, Jennifer and I also worked on her college essay. She decided to tell her father's story, how her hope was to carry on his example, to choose—no matter how intimidating the prospect—to hope for the best education. She was meticulous and professional in her interviews; she wrote and rewrote her college essay. After three months, we published the article in December and a few days later she mailed her application to Stanford.

That investigation of migrant workers in Silicon Valley—"Money and Migrants"—beat out 718 high school stories in a nationwide contest judged by the *Los Angeles Times*, earning Second Place for Team Investigative articles. A subsequent investigative piece on the relation between student buying habits and sweatshop labor—"The Dangers of Distance"—was selected by Quill and Scroll as the best out of 219 international entries for Team Investigative. The article compelled the School to end its association with the company that supplied part of the students' uniform.

And the first Monday morning in April, Jennifer carried into my classroom a framed copy of her acceptance letter from Stanford.

All writing is personal.

# *Student Samples*

*Suggestive:* "Texas-Shaped Tortillas" by Jenny McNatt

"Only a pinch," he chuckles

as I clumsily dump flour onto the smooth surface.

His hands, tired and worn, roll over the cool sticky dough

Time has taken away the elasticity of his body.

His eyes sag as he concentrates on the perfect tortilla.

I watch with quiet awe as he flips the dough from hand to hand;

it slowly takes a circular shape.

Looking down at my Texas-shaped mess, I realize the hidden art in what he is doing.

For once I forget about my life back home,

filled with instant messaging and crowded shopping malls.

Instead, I focus on an age-old tradition passed on for generations.

The black cast iron pan hisses as it comes into contact with the dough.

Pockets of air rise up, signaling it's time to flip it over.

I cringe as I burn the tips of my fingers unintentionally.

"Careful, Mija."

The words comfort me like a warm blanket on a rainy day.

A pain strikes me as I realize that moments like these will not last.

His unsteady balance and powdery white hair remind me that he will eventually pass on,

and all I will have are memories like these and Texas-shaped tortillas.

*Informative*: "A Rambling Romp through Tulip History" by Laleh Jalilian

Your name is weird.

As a shy, tender youngster of eight, I got this a lot from my classmates. After all, "Laleh" isn't the most common name in the world and certainly isn't the easiest for Americans to pronounce. I suppose this is why my name has had strange variations, like "Lala," or "Leila," and even once, "Loola." Come on, buddy, can't you see the "-eh" at the end?!

I think it was these weird pronunciations of my name that had me constantly asking my parents why I was named "Laleh." Each time, my parents would tell me that my classmates were uninformed. Not in a bad way, of course. They just didn't understand the meaning of my name. Though who could blame them? How were students in America supposed to know the meaning of an Iranian word? After all, I am Persian, and my name, "Laleh," means "tulip," which is the symbol of freedom in Iran.

I suppose this got me wondering to how this delicate flower had been given such a significant meaning. But the tulip hasn't always been associated with freedom. In fact, at one point, the tulip was considered a declaration of love from the "perfect lover," and to this day throughout Europe, this flower is an offering a young man makes to his beloved. Solid red tulips indicate an irresistible love, since by offering the tulip, the young man is saying, "like the redness of this flower, I am on fire with love." Yellow tulips represent a hopeless love that has no chance for reconciliation, while varicolored tulips are highly flattering, for they are for "beautiful eyes." Forget the rose! Give me a tulip!

But how the tulip actually became connected with love, I did not know. It was later that I discovered that the answers to all of my questions lie deep in ancient Persian literature, and in most of my bedtime stories. You see, when I was little, my father read me the stories of the Persian writer Ferdowsi to help me go to sleep. One of the stories I remember was taken from an ancient Persian legend, which recounts that a Persian youth named Farhad fell deeply in love with a maiden named Shirin. When Shirin did not accept Farhad's love for her, he went out into the desert to die from his broken heart. Each drop of blood that fell from him into the sand turned into a beautiful tulip.

Despite this beautiful tale, I still prefer the tulip as a symbol of freedom rather than love. Being named after such a noble concept has a great effect on you, though at times, I'm torn whether or not I should set my goldfish free from the oppressing bonds of the tank. And let's not even start on my cat's collar. In any case, whenever I walk down the streets of Tehran, the capital of Iran, and see paintings of tulips on the walls of buildings, I somehow understand why my parents gave me such a name: they were students living during revolutionary times.

But to an ordinary tourist, the tulip would look highly out of place in a country in the Middle East. After all, when most people think of tulips, Holland instantly comes to mind. Ask anyone to name things that are "Dutch," and you'll get tulips, windmills, and wooden shoes, generally in that order. But it's a misconception that tulips and other bulbous flowers are native to Holland; nothing could be further from the truth, since almost no bulbous plants are native to this part of the world. Tulips were, in fact, first cultivated as early as 3000 BC in areas belonging to (surprise, surprise) the once great Persian Empire. Tulips can be seen on the walls of the great city of Persepolis, and if I have not already established this, tulips have enjoyed a long and rich cultural history in Persia.

But they have also had a rich history in Europe and especially in Holland, since today, they are the symbol of the country. While making a flight stop at Amsterdam, my mom and I had five hours to kill, so like all women do when they have extra time, we shopped. But when I went to buy postcards to send to my friends (just to make sure they knew I visited Amsterdam), I was perplexed as to why every single postcard had pictures of huge fields of tulips. I didn't know it at the time, but of Holland's 47,150 acres of flower bulb farms, nearly half are planted with tulip bulbs, approximately 23,412 acres.

Apparently, the "Tulipomania" that once seized the Dutch has not disappeared, though it certainly has receded since 1593, when botanist Carolus Clusius brought the first tulip bulbs over to Holland. At first, the tulip was such a rarity that only the wealthy could afford them, and consequently, the tulip became a wealthy status symbol. A buying mania evolved! By 1624, one single tulip bulb could sell for $2250. Let me give you an idea what this sum could buy at the time: two loads of wheat, four loads of rye, four fat oxen, five pigs, twelve sheep, two hogsheads of wine, four barrels of beer, two barrels of butter, a thousand pounds of cheese, one complete bed, one suit of clothes, one silver tankard—and a sizable wagon to carry it all off!

Evidently, this was the flower that drove men mad. I always think it fascinating how material possessions like gold and money drive people to do crazy things, though I never really expected people to lose their heads over a flower. By then, people switched over to selling rare variet- ies of tulips by weight, which they measured in grain (it later dawned on me that this was the same unit of measure used by goldsmiths). The Tulip Craze reached its zenith between 1634 and 1637, and people consistently abandoned jobs, businesses, wives, homes and lovers to become tulip growers. But by 1637, disaster. Tulip trading crashed, throwing Holland into utter financial ruin. I don't know whether this was just or simply un- fortunate, though after this momentous event, the tulip bulb never really became cheap.

I suppose that you could compare their crash with the Stock Market Crash of 1929 in America. Undoubtedly, thousands of Dutch went hun- gry, and it was during these times that tulip bulbs began to be consumed. First, they had to be fried, and once the bulbs were well done, they were eaten with oil and vinegar. I've never actually tried this, but it seriously does not sound bad. After all, there are some people who still eat tulip bulbs of certain varieties; the Japanese make flour out of them.

So I guess having my name isn't really bad after all. I represent love in Europe, freedom in Iran, and people eat me all over the world today. Plus, I'm a pretty important factor in the Dutch economy. Not a bad his- tory for the tulip. Not bad at all.

Your name is weird.

What does it mean?


*Critical*: "Half-Baked Beauty" by Christina English

"I tan because I love it," gushed supermodel Christy Turlington in a 1993 interview with *New Body* magazine.

Why does Turlington—international symbol of fashion and beauty— along with millions of other Americans value tanning so much?

Until the nineteenth century, suntans symbolized something else. Pale, colorless skin was a quality afforded only by the elite upper class. Tans were attributed to the poor, workers who spent all their time out- side, under the sun, laboring. Queen Elizabeth I and other aristocrats used white face paint and painted thin blue lines of lead or arsenic paint on their foreheads in an effort to increase their pallid appearance.

However, during the Industrial Revolution, the tables turned. The poor moved inside factories to work, and thus away from the sun. Soon, paleness became associated with the industrial lower class. Conversely, the increase of machinery and technology facilitated travel, and wealth was displayed by tans achieved by spending time in exotic lands near the ocean.

But in the 1920's tanning evolved into more than a status symbol—it became a fashion statement. French fashion designer Coco Chanel introduced tanned models along with her innovative, revealing style of clothing. After that, tans became an accessory to the new, skin-baring fashions. Medically, the 1920's marked the start of the prescription of tanning as a cure for various health ailments, which ultimately led to the belief that tans symbolize health and vitality.

The popularity of tanning climbed in the 1950's and became more prevalent with the use of baby oil and silver metallic UV reflectors. In 1975, the indoor tanning booth for cosmetic purposes opened in Germany. Today, twenty-two million Americans go to tanning salons each year in an attempt to achieve the coveted "healthy glowing tan."

But whoever said tans were healthy?

Today, thanks to modern medicine, the likelihood of finding a dermatologist telling you tans are healthy is slim. In fact, the expected response is that the only thing tans are is visible proof that your skin is being damaged. To achieve this modern form of beauty, tanning salon customers lie down on a Plexiglas surface of a clamshell-like tanning bed, while surrounding lights tan their bodies. These lights are really UVA rays that are emitted through the glass, however. UVB rays were used until recently when the medical world realized that these "tanning rays" cause burning and that the radiation increases the risk of skin cancer. While UVB rays (shortwave ultraviolet rays) burn the outer layer of skin, UVA rays (long wave ultraviolet rays) penetrate more deeply and can weaken the skin's connective tissue. This weakening leads to premature aging in the form of wrinkles and sagging skin. Note: And this is supposed to be "attractive"?

Regardless of the source of ultraviolet rays, long-term exposure contributes to the risk of three kinds of skin cancer: basal cell, squamous cell, and melanoma. Skin cancer has more adverse effects than most people realize. It is not always as simple as "cutting it out." Chemotherapy and radiation are sometimes necessary, and scarring is almost always the result. If the cancer occurs on a visible area of the body, such as the face, scarring could blight the "perfect" appearance that the tanner has been trying to achieve.

And still, skin is not the only organ at risk when exposed to UV rays. Studies show that too much exposure to UVA rays can damage the retina, burn the cornea, and, over years, change the structure of an eye lens so that it begins to cloud and form a cataract. If left untreated, cataracts ultimately cause blindness. Note: blindness has never been considered sexy.

Against common belief, simply keeping one's eyes closed is not enough to protect against dangerous UVA rays. At least in the sun, it's easy to be aware of burning eyelids. While relaxing inside a tanning booth, however, it's much more difficult to stay conscious of the condition of your eyes.

Despite all these seemingly obvious deterrents, the vast majority of us ignore the fact that skin cancer is the largest growing epidemic in the United States. The physical "epidemic" of premature aging should not be overlooked either. This brings us back to the age-old question of what price humans will pay to achieve ideal beauty.

Would you ignore the warning labels on a bottle of toxic chemicals? Probably not. Would you ignore the warning labels on a piece of dangerous machinery? Highly unlikely. Then why would you voluntarily subject yourself to the sun's damaging rays, or its artificial counterparts, all in the pursuit of superficial appearance? Tan at your own risk.

---

Chapter 3 goes to the bedrock of a varied writing program, explaining how to teach inductive thinking as a prelude to composing. Subsequent chapters explain how the inductive approach enables students to gather and organize material, structuring it in a variety of formats.

# Unit II:
# Teaching Inductively

*"[The job of the writer is to] pierce this rotten diction and fasten words again to visible things."*
—Ralph Waldo Emerson

# The Matrix of Meaning:
# Induction

---

**Focus**: Teaching induction lays the foundation for further instruction in writing, reading, and analysis. Making students aware of the dialogue between specifics and abstractions clarifies for them how writing reflects the action of thought.

---

**Sections:**
- It's a Mystery: Teaching Induction
- Seven Days of Rain: Induction and Analysis
- The "So What?" Factor
- Paraphrase and Commentary
- Levels of Questioning
- Lesson Ideas

*Parts of speech are metaphors, because the whole of nature is a metaphor of the human mind....Our dealing with sensible objects is a constant exercise in the necessary lessons of difference, of likeness, of order, of being and seeming, of progressive arrangement; of ascent from particular to general; of combination to one end of manifold forces.*

—Ralph Waldo Emerson, *Nature*

*I am convinced that a very large measure of what educators mean by "teaching students to think" is in reality making them conscious of abstracting but is, unfortunately, not viewed this way.*

—James Moffett, *Teaching the Universe of Discourse*

*Ground your writings in the concrete discussion of particular works. Focus on the specific problems of form, design, and content that they raise. You will always discover that in the process of describing and analyzing particular works, you will arrive at more general conclusions than you anticipated.*

—Henry M. Sayre, *Writing about Art*

 I begin this lesson by asking the students to stand up.

"I'm going to narrate a scenario," I tell them, "and when you hear something that applies to you, sit down. Let's say that you get a writing assignment, and it's due in two weeks, so of course you wait until the night before it's due to begin."

A half dozen students slip into their seats. I continue.

"You finish your instant messaging for the night, set a big pot of coffee and a liter bottle of Coke beside your computer, and you begin. You sit in front of a blank screen for about an hour." More students sit down. "Then, with great pain, you crank out an opening paragraph—which most likely contains your thesis—and it sounds like crap, but, hey, it's now after midnight, the coffee's half gone, you've started into the liter bottle of Coke, and this thing is due in eight hours, so on you go."

The seated students are beginning to outnumber the standing ones.

"You move on to your first body paragraph and squeeze it out. It doesn't sound much better than your opening, but now the Coke's gone, the coffee is down to the dregs, the clock has chimed 1 A.M., and you're starting not to care WHAT it sounds like." A number of students like the sound of that, so they shake their heads once and are seated.

"As the night wears on, so do you, and eventually you crank out the second and third points, and, finally, your conclusion, and maybe it's the lateness of the hour, perhaps it's the sugar or caffeine talking, but your paper is starting to sound pretty good as you finish. And that's when you reread your opening and realize it sounds nothing like your conclusion." Big smiles by now, and if any students had been standing before, that last sentence finishes them off. Only once did a single student, like the cheese, stand alone. She looked at me meekly and said, "I just get my sister to write my papers."

And then I tell them about induction, the action of moving from specific evidence to general statements, from the concrete to the abstract. When we solve a problem, I explain, we progress through three stages: gathering evidence, making inductions from that evidence, and then arriving at a conclusion. In other words, the thesis, or focus, of our thinking is what we arrive at, not what we begin with. There is nothing wrong with a paper structured so that the main point is stated in the beginning, but, thinking this means the thesis is written *first*, students try to crank out initially what is actually the conclusion of their thinking. This explains why so many endings sound better than openings: the writer figured out her focus as she wrote. This also explains why students labor to produce a thesis and points and then desperately pore through a text to find a quote that will fit the argument; the result is a quote uncomfortably shoehorned into the discussion. When a student asks me to help her find quotes to support a thesis and points, I ask, "First, tell me how you got a thesis and points without quotes."

In my thirteenth year of teaching, I published an article in *English Journal*, "The First Shall Be Last: Writing the Essay Backwards." The tongue-in-cheek title summarized my recent observations about writing: locked into the deductive structure of the five-paragraph essay, students stumbled as they struggled to produce thesis, points, and examples, in that order. But during timed writings, I noticed that successful students didn't tackle the thesis first. Instead, they gathered material, made notes, developed generalized observations and then produced a conclusion; they didn't write a thesis until they'd arrived at it through preliminary work. They were recreating the inductive act of thinking, which enabled them to know what they were going to say before they started to say it. They were writing their essays backwards.

My subsequent assault on five-paragraph essays in critical writing took place on two fronts. First, as traditional instruction encouraged students to discard whatever structure their material led them to, students were forced instead to use a structure that didn't always fit their material. Second, the dominance of the five-paragraph essay in the classroom ignored a larger point: writing is not about reproducing a predetermined structure, it is about creating meaning. By focusing on an inductive approach, I argued, we could show students how to compose a paper more clearly, thereby making them aware of a paper's ultimate purpose: to bring clarity to a discussion or an experience, to wring from facts and incidents the essence of their meaning.

Writing yields meaning, and when we approach the task inductively, we enable students to see how what they write connects them to the world outside the classroom. In helping them find meaning, we clarify for them how writing is purposeful, not just the fulfilling of a course assignment.

Much of our mental activity is aimed at finding meaning in what we do. Meaning eludes pinpoint definition, yet it is the substance of our behavior, the marrow in the bones of our identities. We profess meaning in rituals, in declarations to intimates, or in communal activities. Hence, meaning is the glue that connects our daily, repetitive acts. When all our moments are boiled down to their essences, meaning is what remains. It is our validation. It is what we increasingly trot out of the cupboard as we age, the thing that explains why we did what we did when we were younger, and what enables us to face growing older. It is what some call the soul or the spirit, as Joseph Heller does in a passage from Catch-22. Yossarian contemplates the lifeless body of a soldier:

> It was easy to read the message in Snowden's entrails. Man was matter, that was Snowden's secret. Drop him out a window and he'll fall. Set fire to him and he'll burn. Bury him and he'll rot like other kinds of garbage. The spirit gone, man is garbage. That was Snowden's secret. (383)

Sans meaning, man is garbage.

Ultimately, teaching that does not convey that meaning-making is the point of writing is also garbage. As important as preparing our students for college is, it is not our primary goal. We are facilitators, adults whose purpose—whose meaning—is to interact with children at key moments in their lives and help them make sense of what they experience. If we do this well, we give them skills that aid them long after they graduate, recalling our lessons like ripples in the wake of a ship. And if we do this poorly, what they recall are lessons that provide pleasant, or unpleasant, memories, but offer no direction for navigating the shoals of life after high school. To believe that writing plays no part in such preparation is ludicrous. It is, like all art, a reflective exercise, the distinguishing action in our species that allows us to communicate with unborn descendants and hear the voices of ancestors.

In the sci-fi film *The Matrix*, Keanu Reeves's character wakes up, literally, into a new reality. Like the freed slave of Plato's cave, he is forced to re-orient his thinking, so that he can transcend his circumstances and discern the reality behind the perceived reality. This is the metaphor of meaning: what we see is only surface; without finding what connects, what under-girds all things, we live moment to moment only, lacking vision. Much as sailors once used the North Star as a guide, making meaning is the act of finding a higher truth that enables us to navigate the world in which we function. Making meaning, then, is the ultimate dialogue between the specific and the general because truth is not located in one or the other, but in their interaction. This is insight, the epiphany that occurs when we see how isolated elements are united and how disparate elements connect.

This dialogue of meaning is the essence of how we perceive our environment. It is the principle behind George Seurat's *La Grande Jatte*, in

*Georges Seurat, French, 1859–1891, A Sunday on La-Grande Jatte–1884, 1884–86, oil on canvas, 81³/4 x 121¹/4 in. (207.5 x 308.1 cm), Helen Birch Bartlett Memorial Collection, 1926.224. Reproduction, The Art Institute of Chicago.*

which he applies his theory of pointillism (the placement of colors not on top of each other, but in points situated side by side) so that color and figure (think "meaning") emerge from the dialogue of dots. It is why vanilla ice cream has one taste, and orange sherbet another but, when put together, produce a distinctly different flavor. And, with all apologies to the Fab Four, it's why The Beatles wrote more dynamic material as a group than when they went solo. Their sound was not produced by four individuals, but by four individuals in dialogue.

Hence, to declare that the whole is greater than the sum of its parts is to state a formula for meaning: "whole" is the ineffable essence that cannot be defined and yet exists. The ancients spoke of four elements—earth, wind, fire, and water—but later added a fifth, ether, which connected the other four. Meaning is the ether of our thinking, the unseeable that is nevertheless felt, the residue of thought. It is, to paraphrase a line from the 1965 film *A Thousand Clowns*, what makes us human beings and not chairs.

And it is what our students must discern when they write.

## *It's a Mystery: Teaching Induction*

*Captain Ernest Pappas frowned in concentration as he stood before Vermeer's "Mistress and Maid" in the Frick's plush West Gallery and was asked to describe the painting.... Though he hadn't so carefully analyzed a painting before, Mr. Pappas immediately saw how it related to his detective work in Queens: "Crimes—and art—can be solved by looking at the little details."*

—Ellen Byron, *To Master the Art of Solving Crimes, Cops Study Vermeer*

*"There is no mystery, my dear madam," said he, smiling. "The left arm of your jacket is spattered with mud in no less than seven places. The marks are perfectly fresh. There is no vehicle save a dog-cart which throws up mud in that way, and then only when you sit on the left-hand side of the driver."*

—Arthur Conan Doyle, *The Adventure of the Speckled Band*

When teaching induction, I compare the process to a murder mystery. Agatha Christie strews her Hercule Poirot tales with clues that the reader must gather to determine who the murderer is. This is induction.

I begin the class by walking over to a selected student, gently pushing her head onto the desk and declaring, "Stacey has passed on." After a respectful silence, I continue. "Now, none of you would look at Stacey's poor, mangled, blood-exhausted body and declare, 'Omigod, Mr. House killed Stacey,' for the simple reason that you initially have no evidence. Instead, you'd look around the body for clues. Finding purple pen marks, you'd say, 'Wow, these are marks from a purple pen, just like the one Mr. House uses.' Looking further, you might notice a pile of half-graded papers and declare, 'Hey, these are the papers Mr. House was supposed to give back to us today.' Eventually, all your clues would point to me, and only then would you declare, 'I accuse Mr. House of killing Stacey.'" Outside of those students who insist they suspected me before they had the clues, everyone gets the point.

I continue this metaphorical explanation of induction as mystery by illustrating the idea with a short narrative mystery ("Hot Fun in the Summertime") and a visual crime ("Gang of Four"). These are fun drills that reinforce the nature of induction: from clues (evidence) we arrive at a conclusion (thesis statement).

---

### *Hot Fun in the Summertime*

The Fourth of July bash was in full swing by the time the Johnsons arrived well into the evening. Mike greeted them at the door.

"Come in, come in," he said, waving Candace and Paul inside. The Johnsons, clearly fatigued, stepped into the foyer. "What kept you?"

Candace handed Mike a wrapped bowl of potato salad, sighing: "Traffic. It must have taken two hours to move a mile, all the while the sun blazing down." Mike noticed the reddened skin on her upper left arm. "I thought Paul was going to kill somebody, slamming on the breaks, honking his horn," she declared.

"The only thing I want to kill now is a bottle of wine," said Paul through gritted teeth, moving toward the living room.

Candace and Paul joined the other couples for the festivities. As the summer sun set, piles of dirty plates and lipstick-tinged glasses filled the kitchen sink. Later, when someone knocked at the front door, Mike headed toward it, wondering who else he'd invited. But when he opened the door, there stood two highway patrolmen.

The taller one of the two spoke, referring to a notepad: "You have a car outside registered to a Paul Johnson. Is he here?"

"Yes," answered Mike. "Is there a problem?"

"Witnesses at a hit and run got down the license plate of Mr. Johnson's car. We noticed it while patrolling the area. Can we see Mr. Johnson please?'

"Please wait here," said Mike and found Paul and Candace, who

cont.

seemed to know why Mike was fetching them. When he saw the patrolmen, Paul nodded once and stepped toward them.

"I'm Paul Johnson. I guess you're looking for me."

"That's right, Mr. Johnson," said the patrolman. "We're booking you for suspicion on a hit and run that occurred this afternoon near Maple and Randall Street. Please step outside."

Paul nodded again and moved forward, when Candace grabbed the patrolman's arm and said, "Officer, you can't arrest my husband. I know he didn't do it."

## HOW COULD CANDACE KNOW THE TRUTH?

*Answer*: Because Candace was the driver. Her sunburn was on the left arm, possible only if she were in the driver's seat.

---

## Gang of Four

Burglars broke a window and entered the home of Samuel F. Whippersnapper, a coin collector, and rifled his collection. He grappled with them and was shot and fataly wounded in the course of the struggle. He had time, however, to call the police, who stopped a car with these four suspects in it and brought them to the station house, together with the coat, which was the property of the murderer and contained stolen coins in a pocket.

Whippersnapper died clutching the button which is shown. The police were satisfied that the other objects sketched, which were found at Whippersnapper's, belonged to the burglars. From the above facts and an examination of the evidence and the four suspects, can you decide who shot Whippersnapper?

I then move from the world of detective fiction to the more mainstream realm of facts. *TIME, Newsweek, Harper's,* and other magazines run columns of statistics that, when paired, invite inductive conclusions, to wit:

**311:** U.S. Border Patrol agents stationed along the 3987-mile border between the continental U.S. and Canada.

**7761:** Border Patrol agents along the 1933-mile border between the U.S. and Mexico. (27)

Students suggest a number of inductions from these facts, such as, "Apparently, we don't trust Mexico" to "More Mexicans want to enter the United States for economic reasons than Canadians," or "It seems like we don't have anything Canadians want." I present another pair of facts from *Time*:

**$42.4 billion:** Estimated amount that will be spent on weddings this year, with an average cost of $18,874 per wedding.

**$19.1 billion:** Estimated amount that will be spent on wedding *gifts,* with an average of $85 per gift. (27)

Some witty child usually notes that if she only gets $85 worth of gifts from every person she invites to her $18,000 wedding, then marriage isn't a cost-effective proposition. Others comment that we seemingly value weddings more than other cultural acts (like the down payment on a house). Both observations work, which is part of the point: I'm less interested in right answers than in my students' abilities to defend their answers with evidence and logic.

I then broaden the discussion by shifting into other disciplines, so at this point I bring in visuals. Norman Rockwell's paintings are self-contained narratives, the parts of each work interacting to produce a story. For instance, the surprised look on the face of the young boy in the painting to the right suggests he has experienced a disturbing revelation. The Santa costume in one hand and the paper in the other (which we might induce to be a letter mailed to Santa that has inexplicably wound up in this dresser) imply he has found out Santa is a myth. Both the height of the dresser and the pipe atop it suggest this is his father's set of drawers, so the boy must assume his father plays Santa.

In the more nostalgic painting a boy and a man we assume to be his father are seated on the running board of an automobile. The "State U" pennant on the suitcase and the books atop it imply the boy is going away to college, a conclusion reinforced by the clean, if slightly ill-fitting, suit he wears. By contrast, the father is attired in working clothes, the sweat band around his forehead suggesting that he toils outside, perhaps as a farmer. This is reinforced and commented on by the two hats he holds, one for work (his) and one for fashion (his son's). Their expressions are studies in contrast. The boy, sitting upright and smiling expectantly, appears to look for the train that will take him away; the father, looking in the opposite direction, is hunched over, his wrinkled brow and gnarled hands suggesting weariness. Theirs is a crossroad moment: the years of labor father has put in have led to both his dream and his sorrow: the instant his son will leave for his own, better, existence.

Approaching texts inductively, we interact with them as historians search artifacts and primary documents for evidence to produce generalizations. Discussing this point, I produce a series of World War I and II recruiting posters, much like the following.

"Look at this poster and tell me what it suggests about the values of the culture producing it," I tell the students. Kids have a field day with this. The copy reading, "Gee, I wish I were a man" suggests a number of cultural values: men are more important in society than women; men are expected to be protectors of their country; women

recognize their inferiority in the culture of the 1940s but have resigned themselves to it. The woman's provocative stance, the unregulationlike display of the V-neck, and the phrase toward the bottom—"Be a man and do it"—are suggestive, as if to imply that available women are the rewards of service to one's nation, or that women's role is, sirenlike, to seduce the man into doing his duty.

These exercises can be applied to a variety of media, including film, music, and most appropriately, advertising. Indeed, ads and public relations messages abound with material for induction, both on the surface (denotation) and the hidden agenda (connotation). Students are both more media savvy and naïve than adults, and deconstructing ads is engaging and surprising for them. But the activity reinforces the message that induction is a universal skill, not something practiced only within the four walls of the classroom. And that's the point. Induction is such a central part of our thinking that we don't—to be more accurate—teach it as much as make students aware how frequently they use it (metacognition). When they choose a college, shop for clothes, size up partners at a dance, select a film from a video store, they are engaging in inductive thinking. Induction is the way we solve problems, the method we employ to navigate from one decision to the next.

Having once illustrated for students how induction is the foundation of thinking, we are now prepared to teach how they can use it to write.

## *Seven Days of Rain:*
## *Induction and Analysis*

In the course of this book, I will explain how induction is central to all writing, but for now let's focus on the area of writing in which we most frequently require induction: analysis. On a colored board on the wall of my room, I have written the following: Evidence, Inductions, Conclusion. This is a shorthand formula for the analytic process: first, close read the text and circle important words, phrases, or figures of speech; second, write down inductions about specific pieces of evidence; third, summarize what your inductions suggest the focus of the text is.

At this point, students need to be aware of the difference between denotation and connotation, as knowing the latter aids them in determining what they should pay attention to in a passage. When Ralph Ellison declares in the opening pages of *Invisible Man*, "Like the bodiless heads you sometimes see in circus sideshows, it is as though I have been surrounded by mirrors of hard, distorting glass," he provides images that pique our interest. A circus sideshow connotes a showcase of freaks, intimating here how the narrator feels he is perceived by others; similarly, mirrors suggest self-reflection, an idea given further weight when the narrator describes them as "distorting glass." Isolating images is foundational in analysis; the concreteness of sensorial writing is easy to spot, and images invariably suggest connections to more abstract feelings or ideas. I also teach haiku in this context as its compressed, imagistic language depends on connotation, its meaning revealed only when we move beyond the literal to the figurative. When the Japanese poet Basho writes, "Mountains and garden / they enter the room, / the summer," he evokes the majesty and beauty of nature in the first line, personifies it in the second, and underscores its grandeur and power in the final line ("autumn" or "winter" would have closed the poem with a much different feeling).

Having taught induction as a thinking skill, I test student understanding of the process via analysis (the subject of this exercise and further explored in chapter seven) and in composing (the focus of chapter four). Poems provide quick immersions into the act of inducing, and Gary Young's "Seven Days of Rain" is an effective intro for a lesson on induction.

### "Seven Days of Rain"

After seven days of rain the creek begins
to fall below the ferns and the crumbling
rock above the waterline. The silt
settles out slowly and trout
rise again for flies. Steam
lifts itself from the roof and bent
limbs of the redwood and pine. The storm
has passed and I am finally free
to work indoors without fear
of the rising waters. I unpack
boxes and trunks, arrange photographs
into a livable landscape. What can't be used
or thrown away, I release to the archeology
of closets—diplomas, letters from those
now dead, and at last, a tin box passed
down four generations to me. My mother's
mementos: a diary, brittle pressed flowers
and snapshots that could be anyone.
In a corner of the box, folded neatly
against a bag of foreign coins,
a length of heavy yellow lace still shows
the flesh-colored smudges of my mother's makeup.
Now that she is gone, this lace will
age for her, and I do not need
to lift it to my face and inhale the breath
that greeted me with each embrace

> to know there is something in all of us,
> anger, remorse, or love, that refuses always
> to pass entirely away.

I read through the poem once and direct students to reread it several times more on their own until they have marked up figures of speech, sound devices, rhetorical devices, or anything else they find important. In this first stage, students are gathering their evidence, not yet asking what is relevant. Ala the clustering exercise explained in chapter four, it is important that students not reject words or passages they're uncertain about. They will, of course, wind up circling much more evidence than they will use in a final paper, but that's part of the process; in subsequent stages, they'll winnow out the less relevant examples. For now they're building a reservoir of possible material.

It doesn't take long before they begin to note patterns in the images or recurrent ideas. These are the first inductions, and I encourage students to write them in the margins. They share these with the class, and within a few minutes, we have a number of inductions which I have written on the board. Again, we are not rejecting these observations as yet, merely gathering as many as the class produces.

After ten to fifteen minutes of listing inductions, we move to the final stage of the process. Reviewing the list on the board, we note patterns and similarities among our inductions, and the discussion begins to focus on a few key ideas. In this way, we are selecting out the most compelling inductions (which will show up in revised form as points) and discarding the less noteworthy. Finally, we try to synthesize these generalizations into one overall statement: a thesis. In practice, one lesson looked like this:

## Evidence

As students made random observations about varied literary techniques, phrases, or ideas that struck them, they noted the following:

- The poem contains a number of personifications: "Steam lifts itself," "this lace will age for her," "something in all of us...that refuses," "the breath that greeted me."

- The poem contains a number of alliterative passages: "mother's makeup," "silt settles out slowly," "livable landscape," "mother's mementos," "still shows"; there is also a great play of assonance and consonance, such as "days of rain," "creek begins," "lace will age," "greeted me."

- The poem opens with and contains a number of nature images.

- Several images evoke the past: "mementos," "snapshots," "diplomas," "photographs," "diary," "brittle pressed flowers." "Archeology," and "down four generations" reinforce this theme.

- Structurally, the narrative begins in the woods and then moves indoors.

- The poem is primarily imagistic but concludes with an induction.

- The poem begins en medias res.

- Images of destruction or loss—"crumbling rock," "lace will age," "bent limbs," "letters from those now dead," "brittle pressed flowers," "storm," "fear of the rising water," "she is gone"—mix with images of life: "trout rise again," "steam lifts itself," "I am finally free," "I unpack," "I release," "inhale the breath that greeted me with each embrace," "something…that refuses…to pass entirely away." Additionally, the title "Seven Days of Rain" suggests both the seven days of creation and The Flood, events of creation.

- A number of images suggest a kind of containment: "unpack," "boxes," "trunks," "closets," "tin box."

At this stage, students appreciate that focusing on gathering evidence gives them a starting point: "If I can read it [the poem] two or three times and start to look at diction, figurative language, and sounds," noted Mairead, "it's not overwhelming. You have a checklist; you can pick it apart line by line."

## Inductions

The students continue citing examples until they find as many as they can. But even as they list these, they automatically begin to leap to the next level, connecting isolated passages. Based on some of the observations listed above, they make the following inductions:

- Organic images connect animal, human, and, finally, spiritual dimensions, suggesting that nature and the human are not merely parallel forces, but bound at the root. This seems reinforced in images that wed the human and the natural—"a livable landscape"—and the organic with the inorganic—"flesh-colored smudges on lace."

- Entropic images mix with suggestions of rebirth. The opening description of rain suggests both destruction and generation. "The storm has passed," observes the speaker, "and I am finally free." The inanimate "yellow lace" is "smudged" with "flesh-colored" make-up and emits the "breath" of a dead relative. Finally, the things of the past are themselves "arranged" and "unpacked," "used" once again or "thrown away," suggesting a restoration of order after the chaos of the storm.

- The poem often seems a meditation on death and rebirth, from the abrupt, perhaps Genesis-inspired opening—"After seven days of rain"—to the closing assertion that "something refuses always to entirely pass away."

- As the poem moves from out- to indoors, it seems also to move from the exterior world of the speaker to the interior, intimating that, now "free," the speaker can begin the task or organizing his world of memories and mementos, setting straight the unaddressed issues the storm forced him away from.

- Intimations of the past are hooked to the present, particularly as the speaker opens his mother's tin box and feels her life in the presence of her mementos. This parallels previously mentioned themes of the connected elements of life and the interaction between man and nature. In this context, the reference to "archeology" suggests both a storing and unearthing of objects that connect past and present.

- After the abundance of images, the poem closes with a number of abstractions—"anger, remorse, or love"—suggesting the events of the storm and its aftermath have produced a meditation—an induction—wherein the speaker not only connects all life, but connects its contraries as well. In this way, he intimates that the storm, for all the "fear of the rising water" it brings, is a necessary prelude to rebirth. Water both destroys and gives life, the universal theme. Stasis is the enemy: life is change.

## Conclusion

Just as the students don't use all their evidence to form their inductions, they don't use all their inductions to make their final statements. What is needed at this stage is to find a focus suggested by their inductions. As with any interpretation, there is rarely a single answer, so students focus on a statement that ties up their key inductions. By this time, they appreciate that developing the thesis last makes their task easier. "When you start with a thesis," commented Tania, "you're kind of grasping at straws. This way you can construct a thesis that you know you can back up because you know you have the evidence."

They note how many of the inductions reveal the poem's dissection of life's interconnectedness. Cast as a narrative, the poem moves spatially and temporally toward a resolution, the speaker detailing movement from the post-storm environment to a "housecleaning" wherein order is restored. Finally, the poem reconciles what appear to be opposites or contradictions, suggesting that the surface deceives: below, all things connect.

Having explicated the poem by first listing a number of examples that support a variety of inductions, all of which lead to a central statement, one student sketches the following outline:

**Thesis**: Gary Young argues that life results from the interaction of order and chaos.

> *Point One:* The poem's opening describes a post-chaotic state where life is slowly restored.
>
> > Examples: Quote and discuss the opening image of the storm and nature's response.
>
> *Point Two*: As the narrator's fear calms, he begins to restore order in his interior world.
>
> > Examples: Quote and discuss passages detailing the speaker's ordering of items in his home.
>
> *Point Three:* As the speaker concludes his narrative, he reflects on the connection between seemingly opposing emotions.
>
> > Examples: Quote and discuss the poem's final lines, explaining how these abstractions echo the similar parallels between life in the natural world and the speaker's home.

This is only one of a number of thesis statements the students generate. Equally defensible alternatives include, "Gary Young illustrates that death is a necessary condition for rebirth," and "In 'Seven Days of Rain,' Young insists that, in an essential way, all life, organic and inorganic, is connected."

The important idea is that a thinking process is involved in our reading of this, or any, literary piece. Though the analysis we later write moves from general to specific comments, the thinking process we engage in during our analysis is the reverse, and by consciously following this process, we increase our ability to grasp the inner workings of the text. When we attempt to start our writing with the final statement, we short-circuit the process, shutting down the brain that is unable to state what it has not arrived at. Writing backwards—consciously reproducing the inductive process—we can more clearly state how the poem works

# *The "So What?" Factor:*
# *Using Induction to Teach Commentary*

Admit it. At some moment in your grading history, you've posed a pen over an example a student has dropped into his analysis without commentary, sitting there like a lone breakfast egg on a plate. There is no commentary, no explanation of what the quote suggests. You press pen to paper and write, "So what?"

"So what?" is what we think when we want to ask, "What does it mean?" We applaud the presence of the quote, but we despair that the student has elicited no meaning from it, has failed to explain why that quote is significant and how it supports the larger argument. What we want is the inductive leap, the distillation of meaning from that quote. This is the commentary, the heart of the paper, the statement that connects the specifics of the examples with the abstract argument of the thesis and points.

The following box includes examples of specifics transformed into inductive statements, into "so what?" observations. I use this sheet when I want to illustrate to students the dialogue between the specific and the general, the concrete and the abstract. I also provide a variety of specifics to make clear that induction works with any kind of writing. Once they grasp the difference, and connection, between the two levels of thought, they understand both the point of analysis and the perspective that makes writing more than a rehearsing of abstract statements or a list of details. The two work in dialogue, no matter the form of writing.

| Type of Specific | Specifics | So What? The Inductive Leap |
|---|---|---|
| **Background information** | While the Progressive Era saw the rise of America's first millionaires, as well as billionaires, it also saw the development of the Lower East Side in New York City, the most populated and poorest section of the world. | The Progressive Era's economic extremes prove it to be the first time a true class system developed in America. |
| **Textual quote** | By another impulse she took off the formal cap that confined her hair; and down it fell upon her shoulders, dark and rich, with at once a shadow and a light, in its abundance, and imparting the charm of softness to her features. (Hawthorne 171) | In this passage from *The Scarlet Letter* the act of unpinning her hair suggests that Hester feels free, even sensual, within the forest, where civilization does not restrain her. |
| **Textual passage** | When Waverley Jong returns home after running from her mother, she is received quietly, without attention, as her parents ignore her. | Despite Waverley's skill as a chess player in *The Joy Luck Club*, the true winner in the larger game of |

*cont.*

| | | life is her mother, who knows how to defeat an opponent with silence. |
|---|---|---|
| **Poetic passage** | 'tis an unweeded garden that grows to seed, things rank and gross in nature possess it merely" (*Hamlet* 1.2.135–137) | Echoing much of the other garden imagery of the play, Hamlet describes his world as nature uncontrolled, unrestrained, wherein death and sexuality so dominate that man is victimized by his environment |
| **Secondary source** | Doctorow locates Disneyland in "a town somewhere between Buchenwald and Belsen" and subjects it to a long and fierce mock-sociological analysis. (Foley 90) | Barbara Foley suggests that Disneyland is central to *The Book of Daniel*, and that Doctorow's comparison of it to Nazi concentration camps is intended to make us aware that, far from an innocuous environment, it is a metaphor for corruption in the postmodern world. |

# *Paraphrase and Commentary*

In critical writing, students struggle to explain the significance of their examples. This is a failure of induction. This inability to explain the "So What?" Factor is related to student confusion about the difference between paraphrase and commentary. I use the following two handouts to clarify the distinction, drawing from works we have recently read.

# Paraphrase

*The following three passages are followed by examples of para-phrase, not commentary. The observations are not analytical; instead, they merely restate the passage in other words. Paraphrase is inadequate as insight because it does little more than tell us what we already know from reading the quote, instead of telling us what the quote means.*

## From *The Chosen* by Chaim Potok

The hydrangea bush on our lawn glowed in the sunlight, and I stared at it. I had never really paid any attention to it before. Now it seemed suddenly luminous and alive. (Potok 93)

> Reuven comes home and sees the bush in front of his house in a new way. He stresses that this is different from the way he saw the bush before.

## From *The Joy Luck Club* by Amy Tan

My mother didn't treat me this way because she didn't love me. She would say this biting back her tongue, so she wouldn't wish for something that was no longer hers. (Tan 45)

> Lindo Jong says that her mother did actually love her but couldn't express that love.

## From *Twelfth Night* by William Shakespeare

> If music be the food of love, play on,
> Give me excess of it; that surfeiting,
> The appetite may sicken, and so die.
>                    (1.1.1–3)

Count Orsino is miserably unhappy because Viola does not feel about him the way he feels about her.

# Commentary

## • *Isolate the key word, phrase, or image*

## • *Comment on its significance; induce its meaning*

*Commentary is analysis, making an induction about a particular passage. Rather than restate what the author has written (paraphrase), commentary explains what the author **means**. The easiest way to comment on a passage is to find a key word, phrase, or image and explain how its connotations provide insight into what the passage signifies. Boldfaced words in the passages below become the focus of the following commentaries.*

### From *The Chosen* by Chaim Potok

The hydrangea bush on our lawn **glowed** in the **sunlight**, and I stared at it. I had never really paid any attention to it before. Now it seemed suddenly **luminous** and alive. (Potok 93).

> Potok fills this passage with images of light, playing on the book's theme of vision and insight. Returning to his home after his eye operation, Reuven's new ability to see is reflected in a world that, despite his bandaged eye, "glowed in the sunlight," a world so newly vibrant that it becomes "luminous," a contrast to the darkness of the eye ward.

### From *The Joy Luck Club* by Amy Tan

My mother didn't treat me this way because she didn't love me. She would say this **biting back her tongue**, so she wouldn't wish for something that was no longer hers. (Tan 45)

> Raised in a culture that discourages emotional expression, Lindo Jong learns from her mother to repress her emotions. She symbolizes her mother's repression by noting the woman's "biting back her tongue," effectively censoring any expression of love.

### From *Twelfth Night* by William Shakespeare

If music be the **food of love**, play on,
Give me **excess** of it; that **surfeiting**,
The **appetite** may sicken, and so die.
(1.1.1–3)

> Employing a metaphor that compares love to food, Orsino requests an "excess" of music not for pleasure but so that he may glut himself ("surfeiting") on love and thus kill his "appetite" for more love.

# *Levels of Questioning*

Benjamin Bloom's taxonomy of critical thinking encouraged teachers to promote higher levels of thought by asking questions aimed at more than recall (what I would call evidence or specifics). Questions eliciting interpretation or evaluation move students inductively from concrete examples to higher levels of abstraction. Level 1 questions aim to gather specific information. Level 2 questions require inductive leaps from level one information; this is the level of interpretation: tying the facts of the text into a pattern of meaning. And level 3 questions apply our level two understanding of the text to the world beyond it and analyze how the theme of the text touches on universal issues. Such questions can generate effective discussions.

| Level 1 Questions | • Stated explicitly in the text.<br>• Who, what, when, and where questions.<br>• Work on the factual level, establishing evidence.<br>*Examples*:<br>-In *Ellen Foster*, what illness does Ellen's mother suffer from?<br>-Of what faith is Shylock? |
|---|---|
| *Level 2 Questions* | • Implied in the text<br>• How and why questions<br>• Interpret and analyze<br>*Examples*:<br>-Why does Ophelia's cooperation with her father disturb Hamlet?<br>-What is the significance of the scarlet letter? |
| *Level 3 Questions* | • Going beyond the text to apply its themes to parallel situations.<br>• Analytic questions.<br>• Work on the level of analysis, synthesis and/or evaluation, using the text as a guide to explore larger issues.<br>*Examples*:<br>-What does Shakespeare suggest about young lovers in *The Merchant of Venice*?<br>-What does Bradbury want to say about all civilizations as he follows the rise and fall of Mars?<br>-Are the lessons regarding man's innate evil in *The Lord of the Flies* applicable to our own era? |

# *Lesson Ideas*

- **Art:** Norman Rockwell's paintings, among others, can be downloaded from websites and placed on overheads. Single panel cartoons—like the "Far Side" comics of humorist Gary Larsen—are also good for inductive exercises.

- **Room List:** For this exercise, ask students to make a list of items in their rooms. Then, removing the names, copy or put on an overhead sheet selected lists. Students in the class then make inductions about the occupant of this room based on its contents. Use the list of one student below as a sample.

  - Posters of Mia Hamm and Brandi Chastain on the beige walls; also, photos of Nick Carter and Brad Pitt.

  - Bedspread with various Winnie the Pooh characters on it.

  - A variety of CDs, including titles by N'Sync, the Backstreet Boys, and Britney Spears.

  - Rolltop desk with papers and pens scattered on it; a Random House Dictionary, Third Edition; an IBM computer with speakers out of which downloaded music is playing; textbooks; two novels by Stephen King and three by J. K. Rowling.

  - Clothes are strewn across the floor, including sweat socks and several large t-shirts, a pair of hiking boots, a pair of running shoes, and a Boston College sweatshirt.

  - On the window sill are several framed photographs, most of teenage girls, one of a girl and her family, and two of a longhaired cat.

- **Creating Questions**: Distribute the "Levels of Questioning" handout, explaining the different kinds of questions. Then, in conjunction with a reading assignment, instruct students to create two level 1, two level 2, and two level 3 questions. Next class, students ask these questions of their peers, conducting the discussion of the reading themselves.

- **Landscapes:** Cutting up old calendars or posters, place a series of landscape photos around the room. Direct students to take into account the natural resources in the pictures and determine what the livelihood and lifestyle of the local residents might be.

- **Advertising:** Tell students to bring to class a number of ads from a specific magazine. Then, sharing their ads with the class (but not the name of the magazine), encourage other students to induce what the target audience of the magazine is.

- **Movie Posters:** Bring in movie posters and pin them up around the room (you can also use ads from a magazine or newspaper). Students then induce the movie's target audience.

- **Mysteries:** Books like *Two-Minute Mysteries* and *Crime and Puzzlement* (the source of "Gang of Four") provide puzzles that require inductive thinking.

- **Facts:** In addition to *TIME,* magazines such as *Newsweek, US News and World Report,* and *Harper's* "Harper's Index" list facts that prompt inductive responses.

- **Shoes:** If you and your students are brave, have them take off and place their shoes in the center of the room. Then, randomly selecting a single shoe, hold it aloft and ask students to induce the personality of its owner.

- **History's Mysteries:** This PBS series is a one-hour show featuring four investigations into historical questions. The researchers move through time and space to work their way back to the root of a question posed by a curious viewer.

- **Fun with Fables:** The nature of a fable's construction makes it inductive—an anecdote rounded off with a moral. Aesop's fables, which are available on the Internet, illustrate the inductive act and provide models for inductive exercises. Have students create their own fables based on personal experiences, explaining how they learned the lesson their story illustrates.

—·—

The inductive process begins with specifics, the building blocks of writing. Chapter 4 explains a number of ways to gather materials we subsequently work into patterns of meaning.

# Rummaging the Cupboard: Gathering

---

**Focus**: In the dialogue of writing, gathering specifics is the initial step in the inductive process. Thus, students need to know what specifics—writing's building blocks—to look for. Subsequently, they need to know the varied ways of gathering those specifics.

---

Sections:
- The World Emerges from Little Details: The Building Blocks of Writing
- How to Gather
- Creating Sections
- Close Reading: How to Make Notes and Gather Info
- Note Taking
- The Art of the Interview
- Dialogue and Gathering: An Illustrative Conversation
- Student Samples
- Lesson Ideas

*And then she [Virginia Woolf] would set us down and interrogate us. I remember once she said, "What has happened to you this morning?" And I would reply, "Nothing." She would say, "C'mon, c'mon. What woke you up?" and I would reply, "It was the sun coming through our bedroom window." "What sort of sun?" she would say. "A kindly sun? Angry sun?" We would answer that in some way. Then she was fascinated by the detail of how we dressed. Of course, what she was doing was gathering copy.*

—Nigel Nicolson, *nephew of Virginia Woolf*

*Always details provoke more ideas than any generality could furnish.*
—Carson McCullers

*You assemble scraps of description such as appearances,
actions, moods, details of setting or clothing. You provide bits
of relevant historical information about the subject's ancestry,
career, past life, typical milieus. You might intersperse snatches
of dialogue among these to illustrate a relationship, activity,
or state of mind. Each piece of information is connotative
and evokes in the reader a reaction to the larger unit that it
suggests, like thinking about the genius of Leonardo da Vinci
by looking at a reproduction of Mona Lisa's smile.*

—Lynn Z. Bloom, *Fact and Artifact: Writing Nonfiction*

*Sometimes a scrap of paper or a photograph suggested further
investigation....I went through attics, discovered forgotten
suitcases of drawings and letters, met distant cousins who
offered watercolors and paintings, picked through dumps,
and haunted museum libraries. I scoured newspaper archives
in Boston, New York, Chicago and the Library of Congress.
Though by the time I began my book, much had been discarded,
my grandmother, fortunately, rarely threw anything out,
and so I accumulated an abundance of material—scrapbooks,
family photographs, sketchbooks: in biographical terms, a
treasure trove.*

—Honor Moore, *Twelve Years and Counting: Writing
Biography*

 At the Edison Laboratory in Orange, New Jersey, tourists stand before a table overflowing with a hodgepodge of natural materials: animal horns, the felt of rabbits, a hippopotamus hide, and dried seaweed. Edison called it "the junk pile," a collection of unrelated materials his assistants played with in conjunction with their experiments. From such play emerged materials useful for experimentation.

The analogy to writing struck me immediately. Ray Bradbury described the writing process as proceeding from "mulch," his word for the gathering of materials that he "dumped" into his brain—comic books, toys, news articles, conversations, observations—that interact until they produce the germ of an idea.

If induction is a dialogue between specifics and abstractions, gathering is the act of first acquiring those specifics. Later will come the generalizations and observations that specifics produce, but initially students need to gather the basic materi-

*Photography courtesy of Eastern National, Copyright 2005.*

als that will pin down their arguments, give flesh to their descriptions, and provide pictures for their narratives.

We can call this brainstorming, prewriting, listing, or research, but it needs to be taught as a specific and independent activity. My experience is that students give the gathering process short shrift because it sounds like another unnecessary step in the writing process. But a lesson in induction makes clear that without specifics, writing lacks dimension and credibility. Abstractions clarify while specifics exemplify. Abstractions provide a view from the mountain top, but specifics reveal the foundations of the slope.

Teaching gathering as a specific process benefits students who struggle with abstractions, and who aren't clear how to generate ideas. While making observations intimidates such students, recalling incidents, remembering conversations, writing down sensorial details, or asking questions of a friend are manageable actions. The act of gathering such material invariably generates ideas and observations that students can utilize as they begin to write.

As educator Dr. Gabrielle Rico argues when she writes about clustering, it is important to temporarily shut down that part of the brain that wants to censor, reject, or discard material long before we've decided what we want to do with it. Writers need one segment in the writing process where weighty ideas are pushed to the side as they gather foundational material. I tell students to look at this act as a preparation similar to what goes into cooking: before the cake exists, we place on the counter eggs, sifted flour, a cup of sugar, tabs of butter, and teaspoon of vanilla. The cake will rise, I tell them; for now, open the cupboard doors and rummage.

# *The World Emerges from Little Details: The Building Blocks of Writing*

*Don't say the old lady screamed. Bring her on and let her scream.*

—Mark Twain

*The commonplace is miraculous if rightly seen, if recognized.*

—Charles Simic

*Blue Car* writer and director Karen Moncrieff's film about a teenage girl's struggle to survive late adolescence features a classroom scene between Meg and her English teacher, Mr. Auster. When Auster presses Meg for details on a poem she is writing about her parents' separation, she isn't sure what he's seeking.

"Was there a particular time you felt bad," he asks, "or you just felt bad in general? So what happened when your dad left? Was it day or night?"

When she responds, "Night," Auster pushes for more.

"Did he say goodbye to you when he left? Ms. Denning, I want you to write about that day. In detail. Write about the weather. Write about what you were wearing. What you were thinking. Be specific. A whole world emerges from little details."

Meg is still uncertain what he's asking for, so Auster leans back in his chair and provides an example.

"When we buried my son, I'd forgotten to put in my contact lenses. And I stood over him, and before they closed the coffin—trying to fix him in my memory, I could see the red from his sweater and his blue pants and there was a scab on his forehead that, um, it hadn't healed—it was from a bicycle accident—and I could feel that scab when I kissed him, but when I looked at him, he was...well, he was out of focus."

He looks at Meg. "So when your dad left, what were you doing?"

"I don't remember," says Meg.

"Okay, forget that I'm here. Close your eyes." She does. "Where are you standing?"

"By my window. In my room."

"Did your dad leave in a van or a taxi or—"

"A car."

"A car. What color was the car?"

"Blue."

"Okay." Auster picks up a fountain pen and hands it over the table to Meg. "Go on."

Moncrieff has captured the essence of instruction in this scene: drawing out of students the details of their world they have forgotten or dismissed as unimportant. They invariably stare at blank sheets of paper or computer screens, unclear what they should write. The inevitable student response to the instruction to brainstorm is, "What should we brainstorm?" My response is, "Anecdotes, quotes, descriptive details, and facts." I call these the building blocks, the components, of all writing. From these foundation pieces, writing emerges. Each type of writing will emphasize or require different building blocks: anecdotes and descriptive details dominate suggestive pieces, quotes and anecdotes are the cornerstones of informational writing, and quotes and facts are essential in critical writing. Indeed, like DNA structure, writing isn't characterized by the exclusive use of any of these as much as their combination and amounts. These, then, are the elements of gathering, the component parts students need before they can structure or style their material.

## Anecdotes

"Every picture tells a story, don't it?" asked Rod Stewart, suggesting the pervasiveness of narrative. Have you ever sat through a low-grade movie until the ending? Of course you have. And why? It's the plot, stupid. We love stories. We can bore our students into a stupor with information, but the minute we say, "That reminds me of something that happened once," they look up. Plot compels, creating a tension that needs resolution. Friends hold our attention when they tell us they've got a story about someone we know.

"Narrative is a key structure in almost every sort of writing," argues George Hillocks, Jr. in *Teaching Writing as Reflective Practice*. "Research reports provide a narrative of what the research of the subjects of observation did. Closely argued court decisions often provide detailed narratives of the events leading up to the need for a decision. Aristotle's *Nicomachean Ethics* present brief narratives with details carefully chosen to illustrate distinctions between true virtues and seeming virtues. Even business reports and manuals include narratives. For qualitative researchers, narrative is an important research tool. Indeed, many qualitative researchers strive to include the kinds of detail that make the resulting documents empathic."

I illustrate the effects of narrative in class by telling my students the following anecdote.

> I once entered the lobby of the St. Francis Hotel in San Francisco and seated myself in a large chair. While enjoying the illusion of being rich, I watched three men in trench coats enter the lobby, all of them wearing shades, all of them carrying newspapers, and one of them holding a briefcase. They sat down across from me and in unison unfolded their newspapers and began to read, keeping their sunglasses on. After nearly fifteen minutes, again in unison, the three folded up their newspapers, rose, and departed through the front door. And left behind the briefcase.

This story never fails to create silence. Students stop taking notes, their eyes locking on me. When I pause at this point, someone demands, "What happened?"

"I don't know," I respond. "I made it up. But the point is, you're all focused on me now, and every one of you wants me to continue, which is more than I can say about your attention when I'm lecturing." Anecdotes grab us; our breathing slows down slightly when a tale begins. Anecdotes light up writing, divert us, and illustrate what we mean in ways information can't. They are essential.

## Description

Alfred North Whitehead wrote that "we think in generalities, but live in details." Descriptive detail is painting with words, using imagery to pin down the abstract statement and give it weight. It is what teachers mean when they urge students to show, not tell. As Rebekah Caplan of the Bay Area Writing Project explains, the abstraction of "The pizza was delicious" conveys little, but providing detail does: "Mushed into the creamy orange of golden oil, the pepperoni sat, tiny bowls of grease rimmed in crusty black." The first sentence tells, the second shows. Setting and characterization demand detail, which makes it more the province of the suggestive and the informative, but the critical is also served by description of a concert performance (in a music review) or the narration of Huck's behavior on the raft in a literary analysis. Description is what gives poetry its power, and bad student poetry is often characterized by its absence. The student who writes ineffectual verse often chooses the abstract over the specific detail. When one of my students composes a lament along the lines of, "I don't know why he left / He said he loved me / Now I wonder what I'll do with all this free time," I respond, "I don't want to hear the complaint; I want to know where you were when you found out it was over, what you said, how you were dressed, what he acted like as he spoke to you." I want to see the breakup. Describing the war in Serbia in "Every Hell is Different: Notes on War Writing," Christopher Merrill explained how he accumulated his materials:

> In my terror I took notes, not because I expected to survive, but because the act of writing calmed me down. I recorded almost every conversation, story, and joke. I described my surroundings in minute detail. I timed the intervals between the rare outgoing pop of a Bosnian grenade and the ensuing blizzard of Serbian shells. Thus by the time we went to bed, in makeshift conditions, I had a fairly complete set of notes from one day of life in a basement under fire. (Forche 102–103)

## Quotes

The most common phrase in a circle of gossip is, "What'd he say?"

We want to hear the voice, the exact words. Long novelistic passages intimidate readers, but turn the page and spot a column of dialogue, and we're tempted to jump ahead. Newspapers run "Man on the Street" columns which garner interest for no other reason than we are curious what people say. Quotes bring authenticity to writing; they move discussion from the blandness of "Some people believe…." to the credence of "Scientist Frederick Lewis asserts…." They validate, which is their appeal in critical writing when we seek corroboration from other perspectives. And they give us the human presence. When we read quotes, we travel from the general to the specific, from the news report of the disastrous hurricane to the voice of a disaster victim who sounds a little like us. Literature abounds with voices, from Holden Caulfield's despair to Celie's calculated resistance to Blanche DuBois's elitism. The specificity of the voice creates authenticity.

## Facts

Factual information is the math in the message. It is the distillation of abstraction into the graspable specific. Our historical knowledge takes on perspective when we hear of the genocide of six million Jews, the desperation the Great Depression engendered becomes palpable when we learn the era's nationwide unemployment rate was 25%, and we are sobered learning the average age of American soldiers dying in Vietnam was nineteen. Like all specifics, facts change what is vague into that which we can grasp. Like quotes they suggest authenticity, and like description they provide focus. The jumbling of experience becomes ordered when facts are developed. Facts cook down the porridge of information into a clear broth.

My colleague Joe Poirot created a shorthand acronym to teach his students the basic writing components: FADS (facts, anecdotes, detail, speech).

# *How to Gather*

*The generic term research suffers from conceptual synecdoche in that, for many, the part has become mistaken for the whole. The single species of empirical research is treated as the entire genus.*

—James Moffett, *Teaching the Universe of Discourse*

*As strange as it my sound, all memoir is a process of researching one's own life. By that I mean rethinking, of course; I also mean reimagining and perhaps revising—because to see the past anew is often to view it, even at great distances, more clearly. But in the context of these remarks, I mean the*

> *word research to imply just that—research, a diligent and systematic inquiry into a subject (in this case yourself) in order, as even the most basic dictionaries will say, "to discover or revise facts, theories, or opinions."*
>
> —Michael Pearson, *Researching Your Own Life*

> *Research and writing are absolutely integrated.*
>
> —Brenda Shapiro, *feature writer*

We must rescue the term "research" from the academics who have so tainted it that we usually associate the activity with towering book stacks lodged deep in the bowels of the library. Like too much of teaching, research is an activity students associate with busy work, something to be done for papers no one (often including the teacher) really cares about. The reality is that research—like the observations and inductive thinking of writing—is as common to our living as breathing. Whenever we ask questions, seek info to make a decision, search out differing perspectives, or watch an activity closely, we are researching. This is nothing more than the gathering of information. As such, we do it when we listen to others, when we observe behavior, when we participate in an action, when we watch a movie, listen to a song, or play with a CD-ROM. All these actions produce materials (anecdotes, quotes, descriptive detail, and facts) that become the building blocks of writing.

A disadvantage, then, of any writing program that focuses predominantly on one type of writing is that it restricts students to a small field of research. Hence, when literary analysis dominates the curriculum, we simultaneously exclude and devalue the use of memories, interviewing, and material that does not come from books. This is hardly preparing our students for college in the twenty-first century, or any life outside of high school. Just as it is important to help students understand what they can brainstorm, it is also helpful to identify for them the ways they can gather material.

Research should be perceived as what it is: a rich submerging into material and a stimulating part of writing that comes before the structuring, focus, and stylizing of expression. But it is important, as Hillocks argues, to note the place of inquiry in gathering information. Gathering info per se is no guarantee of successful writing. Material must be sought in the service of something other than meeting a writing deadline. When we gather material in response to a stimulus or problem, we operate from a curiosity that compels us to seek out information to form ideas. Put another way, we begin the gathering process with inquiry, compelled by questions. Hillocks believes that

> inquiry has been excluded from writing courses except for the "research paper" which, in many high schools at least, is really only an exercise

in copying from library sources, not inquiry at all in the sense I intend here. Textbooks have largely ignored it, only admonishing students to collect data or brainstorm, suggesting that there is no need for hands-on inquiry. (95)

In other words, research is most compelling when it seeks to explain what we do not know.

Of the seven types of gathering activities listed below, writing programs tend to exclude all but the researching of prepared materials. But if college-prep testing requires more extensive writing, if colleges themselves insist on more written facility, and if we are to connect writing with experiences outside the classroom, then we need to instruct our students in all the ways they can interact with and experience their world.

## Clustering

### *Memory as resource*

San Jose State professor Gabrielle Rico was attracted to research of the 1950s and 1960s that suggested the two hemispheres of the brain did not imitate each other. Instead, they performed distinctly different operations. Out of her investigations emerged the term "clustering," an activity aimed at getting students to shut down the analytical, logic-based left hemisphere and encourage the more associative, metaphorical right hemisphere. Here, she reasoned, were lodged the memories, images and metaphorical connections that give writing its richness, that produce the building blocks of anecdotes, quotes, descriptive details, and facts. Though Rico may not have intended the commentary, her work suggested that education had too highly favored the left hemisphere, requiring students to structure and analyze material before they even had it in hand. Indeed, the only resistance I have had from teaching clustering comes from students so wedded to structuring material before they have it, that they find it tough to shut down the left hemisphere. There is hope, I assure them, from their addiction. Rico's method is disarmingly simple. Students receive a kind of prompt—a word, a phrase, an image—as they sit in front of a blank piece of paper. They write the prompt in a circle in the center of the sheet. They then create more circles on the page, filling them with words or short phrases inspired by the prompt, and connected by lines that flow back to the center circle. The important qualification of clustering is that students must not "think" in the conventional way. In other words, they must not bring up a word, phrase, or idea and immediately judge its appropriateness for their composition; they must not censor their ideas. Instead, they must place within each circle words as they come, making a mess of the page with lines, words and circles, never deleting or rejecting, only letting ideas flow. Rico's book, *Writing the Natural Way*, is available online. Also, Inspiration software (www. inspiration.

com) sells software that enables students to create clusters on a computer and then, with a click, convert them to outlines.

## Close reading

### *Isolating passages and quotes*

Close reading is nothing more than marking up a text, but it is a gathering activity because readers identify passages for possible inclusion in later writing. In effect, students interact with the material by circling key words and phrases, placing question marks beside confusing passages, isolating recurring motifs, or composing short chapter summaries. This interaction heightens awareness of what the student is reading, while focusing on textual strategies. Close reading is essential for literary analysis, particularly if students are drawing examples from a novel: sifting through 300 pages of unmarked text for quotes and examples later is time-consuming. Teachers can encourage close reading by requiring dialectical notebooks, wherein students record and then respond to selected passages from their reading.

---

**Close Reading:**
**How to Make Notes and Gather Info**

Close reading is gathering materials from a text, a kind of research-as-you-go. The benefits are many. A closely read chapter can be reviewed quickly before class in preparation for a reading quiz; a book that has been marked is easier to find examples for as you prepare your essay; finally, the very act of marking up a text enables the reader to more closely focus on it and retain key ideas and passages. Students unable to mark up a text because it's not theirs can use sticky notes instead or keep a dialectical journal. None of the following ideas is written in stone, but students needing a starting point can use them as guidelines.

- Highlight or underline passages that reveal crucial information, show changes in character, or trace the development of character. You might also mark them with a "C" for character or "T" for theme.
- React to the text: make notations in the margins as you read passages that are disturbing or noteworthy.
- Place a question mark (?) in the margin if you don't understand what the passage means.
- Put an exclamation mark (!) in the margin to indicate something surprising or unusual.
- Consider using these symbols: * emphasizes a statement already underlined or denotes a recurring idea; + indicates something you want to remember.

---

Cont.

- Use sticky notes for marking or cross-referencing ideas, or for easy access to specific pages in the text. Use a variety of colors for different purposes.
- A smiling face shows that you agree or like an idea.
- A frowning face shows disagreement or dislike.
- Circle key words or phrases.
- Underline vocabulary words you don't know. Jot down a brief definition in the margin, especially if the word is critical to your understanding of the passage.
- When you finish a chapter or section, write a two or three sentence summary at the beginning.

## Note taking

### Listening

As with close reading, note taking mystifies students, unable to distinguish between writing nothing and jotting down everything. Cornell University's note taking strategy encourages students to see relations between different kinds of notes by using an organizational pattern. Students can respond to cues given by the teacher (keywords or phrases; ideas written on the board) that they place in one column, and then listen for information that fleshes out or explains the ideas. Students should also record examples and specifics to the right in an adjoining column. Finally, and very importantly, Cornell notes require students to summarize their gathering by identifying main ideas. In this, not only do students record key information, they begin organizing it into distinct patterns.

### Note Taking

Cornell notes require students to organize material as they listen rather than assemble a jumble of data. In the first column, students write key ideas, words, or questions they encounter during the lecture; to the right, they elaborate on any of these, providing specific details, examples, or information. When the lecture concludes, students summarize the focus and main points in the summary box at bottom. Having followed this format, students have inductively begun to compile the outline of a report: focal ideas (summary), sections (main ideas and questions), and specifics (elaboration and examples). Teachers should consider allowing a few minutes at the end of a lecture for students to compile and, perhaps, share their conclusions.

*Course* _____      *Date* _____

| Main ideas and questions | Elaboration and examples _____ |
| --- | --- |
| _____ | _____ |
| _____ | _____ |
| _____ | _____ |
| _____ | _____ |
| _____ | _____ |
| _____ | _____ |
| _____ | _____ |
| _____ | _____ |
| _____ | _____ |
| _____ | _____ |
| _____ | _____ |
| _____ | _____ |
| _____ | _____ |
| _____ | _____ |
| _____ | _____ |

*Conclusions and summaries* _____

_____

_____

## Observation

### *You are there*

Teachers practice "you are there" writing when they send students outside to record their observations, but there's no need to stop at the campus. At least once in my writing program, I tell students to visit and describe a locale. This is up for grabs. Students have gone to the mall, the beach, a friend's house, a rave, a museum, a delicatessen, a park, a grandparents' home. My requirement is that they pick a place they can actually visit before writing it up; they're not allowed to rely on memory (though if they wish to recall a vacation visit, they are allowed to work from photographs or film). The purpose is to focus them on gathering details. They must take a notepad with them and spend at least an hour at the location, looking for items the average visitor would overlook. Observation sharpens our sensorial thinking, forcing students to look beyond the surface and consider how the everyday world reveals itself in subtle ways. Doing this, they are performing the most basic of inductive activities, detailing how the concrete suggests meaning.

## Hands-on

### Field research

Field research is an underused but valuable kind of gathering. Like observation, students take in sensorial detail, but field research requires participation, the experience of participating in the studied behavior lending credibility to the final report. Lessons are enhanced when teachers create sensory experiences for students, whether that is listening to music, viewing a film, handling an object, or tasting food. Sensorial impressions are vibrant, providing memorable fodder for discussion. Tangible material widens our experience of the subject matter. A discussion of *The Great Gatsby* takes on depth when students hear Chicago jazz, watch Valentino in *The Sheik*, leaf through a collection of movie magazines and read the ads, wind up a gramophone, or visit a car museum to see a Bugatti. The traditional museum, for instance, allows observation, as museum goers move from object to object; by contrast, a living museum like Plimoth Plantation in Massachusetts places the visitor in the middle of a colonial village, able to speak with persons who recreate the speech, customs, and observations of a seventeenth-century colonist. While observation demands the senses, field research engages the mind.

## Interviewing

### Oral sources

Interviewing is the most interactive of researching activities. Like musical improvisation, the interviewer must be attentive to the current of the dialogue, pursue questions as they pop up, and respond to the mood and tenor of the conversation. Interviews require preparation: advance research on the topic enables the interviewer to ask questions that probe more deeply. Interviews also demand listening skills because interviewers must respond to the mood and info of the moment. Moving machinelike through a list of questions does not constitute an interview; questions need to be prepared in advance, but the interviewer should listen for ideas or statements he hadn't anticipated and follow up on them. Teachers looking for models can often find Q & A formats in a variety of magazines or they can record Charlie Rose interviews from public television, tape James Lipton's *Inside the Actor's Studio* from the Bravo channel or obtain tapes from National Public Radio where the mastery and pleasure of the interview is apparent in Terry Gross's *Fresh Air* segments or Scott Simon and Liane Hansen's *Weekend Edition*.

---

# The Art of the Interview

The interview is a conversation. In essence it is a dialogue. Reduced to mere fact finding, the interview rarely reveals; it merely services. More than other forms of research, it calls upon communication skills, upon remembering that the source is capricious and whimsical, responsive only so far as the interviewer knows how to draw her out. The art of the interview, therefore, lies only in part in what the interviewer asks; it lies as much in how the interview is conducted.

### The Tips:

*Research*: First, prepare for the interview by researching the background of your interviewee. Learn what you can about the subject or about the subject's field. This does more than enable you to prepare good questions; your knowledge assures the interviewee that you cared enough to learn about him or his subject matter.

*Questions*: Write good, open-ended questions that avoid those that elicit "yes/no" responses. Also, don't bother with those that indicate you haven't a clue what to ask, i.e., "So how do you feel about this?"; "Anything you'd like to add?" Prepare questions that invite the subject to speak for some length, asking for anecdotes: "Was there an event that first made this clear to you?" or details: "What was going on around you while this unfolded?" or commentary: "How would you characterize the audience's reaction?"

*The Tone*: Don't approach your interviewee with anything less than respect and appreciation for the reality that he doesn't owe you an interview. Introduce yourself and shake hands, explain what you wish to interview for, and ask if there's an appropriate time you can meet. This is your first chance to make the interviewee feel at ease and listened to as well as establish the demeanor of the interview to follow.

*Prepared Materials*: Showing up at an interview without adequate materials signals to your subject that you don't value his time and didn't think enough of the interview to prepare adequately for it. Always have a notebook (sheets of paper are clumsy and unprofessional), at least two pens (one might run out), and a tape recorder. Test the tape recorder in advance for distance and quality of sound, and make certain it has fresh batteries. You should still take notes in the event your recorder fails to operate.

*Converse*: The interview itself should sound like anything but. It should be a conversation. This is important: the more relaxed and "listened to" your interviewee feels, the more he will open up and reveal his personality. Don't stick your face in your notes as you write; make frequent eye contact, smile as appropriate, and provide encouraging gestures that indicate you're listening. And share yourself. I call this technique "priming the pump," wherein you elicit a memory or comment by providing samples of your own. Not only does this make you look accessible, it can spark ideas for your subject to react to. In other words, not all your remarks should be questions; talk to your subject. And follow up tantalizing tidbits of info: don't follow your list of questions so closely that you miss important information. If your interviewee provides bio background and happens to mention that he spent a short time in jail for embezzlement, Lord help you if you simply proceed to the next question. Not only would you miss a chance to get something interesting, you'd convince your interviewee you see this as an assignment only, not a conversation.

### Sources

Students benefit from hearing good interviews, and a number of examples are out there. Ted Koppel of *Nightline* asks probing questions without sounding pedantic or confrontational, as does Jim Lehrer of *The Jim Lehrer News Hour.* For a wider range of fare, PBS's Charlie Rose is masterful in doing background research on his subjects, talking with them, and "priming the pump." NPR abounds with excellent interviewers, none less so than Terry Gross, whose *Fresh Air* afternoon program has an arts orientation that appeals to kids. NPR also sells tapes of Gross's work and that of other interviewers, available at their website, NPR.org. A number of magazines conduct question/response interviews, but one of the best is *Rolling Stone*, which does in-depth interviews every few issues. And James Lipton's "Inside the Actor's Studio" reveals that interviews are conversations: witty, creative and revealing.

### Third-person

#### *Prepared materials*

At last we arrive at the province where most educational research dwells, but even here, educators can further acquaint students with a wide range of available sources. As important as secondary texts are, they should be supplemented with articles from newspapers, speeches, magazines and periodicals. And in our computer age, research assignments need to keep up with the Internet. Teachers are wary—justifiably—of letting students download any Internet source, yet they can simply set up requirements for web use. I tell my students that only college- or library-based sites are acceptable; anything published by an individual is suspect. Additionally, many scholarly essays are available online through EBSCO Host or Gale Research, and community libraries are increasingly making these available through their own online websites. Thus, teaching students how to use the Internet not only increases their range of resources, it sharpens their ability to distinguish between credible and incredible sources. Finally, CD-ROMs offer a range of audio and visual materials that supplement researched work. Teachers acquainted with a collection of CD-ROMs can aid their own teaching as well as offer another source for their students.

## *Dialogue and Gathering: An Illustrative Dialogue*

Around September of each year, students begin seeking help on college essays. Though I can't give them all the help I'd like, I work with a few more intensely, conducting dialogues (a la the *Blue Car* sequence) with them to dig up anecdotes, quotes, facts or details they can use. Students have invariably referred to this process as one of the most helpful in their high school experience, in part because it unleashes memories they'd long forgotten, in part because it helps them produce better essays, and in part because the action models the gathering fundamentals I've taught them.

Drawing off interview techniques we've covered in various courses, my aim is to pull out ideas that will distinguish these essays from the reams of mundane and formulaic submissions admissions officers wade through. And as the following example illustrates, this necessitates asking a lot of questions that lead into dead ends and fruitless cul de sacs, dredging up material that won't pan out. But that's part of the process. Gathering is, like the scientific method, an open-ended inquiry; the writer does not impose purpose or structure on ideas in their infancy.

Emma Richter graduated from Georgiana Bruce Kirby Preparatory School in 2005. When she first approached me at the beginning of her senior year, Emma knew she wanted to write about her interest in science when she applied to Brown, but she wasn't sure how to proceed. The excerpts that follow come from a second conversation conducted in October.

**Jeff House:** I think what you saw yesterday is that I really want to get specifics, more and more anecdotes—specific details are what [college admissions officers are] going to remember. Basically, any generalities aren't going to help you, abstractions and stuff like that. These admissions officers, you know, read hundreds of these things a day, so what you want are those specific moments, even the little unique ones that may not sound like a big deal but they give a sense of your personality.

**Emma Richter:** Mmn, hmm.

JH: Much of the essay is, isn't, uh—the details of your life academically are on the other sheets, the essay is a chance for your voice to come through.

ER: Mmn, hmm.

JH: So, even though you might be focused on a topic, as you are, about your interest in science, what's gonna be more interesting to them is your personality. If that doesn't come through, then you really haven't succeeded in the essay, ok? So what I wanna do is help you pull out the stuff that's gonna be not only distinct to Emma, but is gonna help you kinda develop that voice.

ER: Do you think I can still use some of what I've, like, written up?

JH: Yes! Definitely, um, I'd try to expand on it. So—

ER: Yeah.

JH: So, first thing I'm gonna ask you, did you have a chance to ask your parents about—

ER: Well, first I asked my dad. When we lived in Hungary, I was in preschool, for a year, my dad and I would always go on these, quote, "wild boar hunts" —

JH: [Laughs]

ER: So, like, we'd always go out and looking at—of course we never found wild boar—

JH: Uh, that's good.

ER: But we would just go out in the woods, but so I always had, there was definitely, you know, an emphasis on the natural world, and then when I talked to my mom this morning, she was saying how, well, I was living in Maryland, and my public school in Maryland did have, you know, a strong emphasis on science, especially in third grade. We were doing all kinds of things, we had guest speakers coming in, like we did some chromatography, fingerprinting, kind of DNA science thing like that, and we had someone from the CIA come in and talk, and, so, because we were right on the border with Washington—

JH: People from the CIA came to speak?

ER: There, yeah, there was some, I don't remember exactly what it was, that's what she said, but I was a curious child. I might have not displayed something really specific. I mean I know we always did little science fairs in second and third grade, which was like every class did a different kind of project.

JH: Uh huh. Take me back to the wild boar hunt—this intrigues me. Obviously this is something your father must have named.

ER: I don't know—I would agree too.

JH: You don't remember the name of the forest?

ER: I could find out. We were living in Budapest and I remember very little. I remember a lot more from living in Moscow: that was kindergarten and first grade. This was just, I lived in NY and I had one or two years of preschool and then a year of preschool in Hungary, and then we moved back to New York, so I was living in Hungary, I don't remember very much, but I do remember these treks.

JH: So you had forests outside of Budapest?

ER: We'd always go on hikes. My dad and I always liked going on hikes, but we called it a "wild boar hunt." I thought it would be so exciting to actually see a wild boar.

JH: So you thought you were actually looking for wild boar?

ER: There was always that dynamic that maybe we would see a wild boar, maybe we heard a story of someone spotting one. They probably existed in this forest. We went on these hunts; my dad would always call me "eagle eyes" because I could always spot things really well.

JH: Like what? What kinds of things were you really good at?

ER: If we were looking for something—spray paint on trees marking things in forests—and I would always spot that and if we were looking at the landscape, I was very observant and I could always see things; it was kind of like that was one of my nicknames.

JH: So do you remember the sensation or the feeling you had? Was this exciting for you to go out, and was it being in nature or actually looking at things that intrigued you?

ER: Probably both. I think I really always, being a city kid, I always loved going to Central Park. It was like this wealth of opportunities. It's a huge park. It was the most amazing place. You can be in the middle of it and feel you are out in the country because you have these huge rocks that are there. I would always climb the rocks, and there would be the grassy fields and the sculptures and the big Alice in Wonderland sculpture. I would always climb on Alice. There were all the familiar landmarks, and the Carousel that was too fast, it was the fastest carousel in the world.

JH: So one of the things that is hitting me is that you are a very curious person and that you have a very exploratory nature. Would that be accurate?

ER: Yeah.

JH: Talk about that.

ER: They definitely go together.

JH: Yeah, they would. How has that manifest itself in your life? In what ways would you see yourself displaying those qualities?

ER: The way I had been raised definitely fostered that interest in the world and lots of different cultures. I am a pretty worldly person just from traveling so much. Even as an infant my first trip was going to Greece and Russia, and then when I was four to five, to Thailand, Italy, Tokyo.

JH: What was the context? Why were you moving to these places?

ER: We didn't necessarily move; the only places abroad we lived were Budapest and Moscow; the rest of this was just travel.

JH: This comes from your parents.

ER: My parents really liked travel, and my dad definitely was very interested in languages in college and learned to speak Russian fluently. The reason we moved to Moscow was, he was working with AID, so we were right next to the embassy. I don't know as much about it, but for my dad it was a really good opportunity for him because he could speak Russian, and when he was in college he did a lot of tour leading and taking groups to Russia. He would travel. My mother always liked travel because during college she lived in Greece for a year, and she's an art historian and became an art historian/librarian at NYU and had this appreciation for other cultures. And always would go and look at museums. Every time we were traveling, it was never just a vacation. We were doing something educational, we were going to museums, visiting archaeological sites, so—

JH: So, you were raised by parents—the world was like a school, this was the place you looked at, you observed.

ER: [Nodding] I have memories of many different cultural ties and lots of different museums, and I have seen a lot of famous pieces of art. It is something we continue because we enjoy having this worldly sense.

JH: What I see in you is again that kind of driving curiosity which I think is more unique than maybe even you understand. Most kids learn for the sake of getting the grade.

ER: I really like the idea of learning for the sake of learning, and I was looking for that in colleges: working against each other, working collaboratively or at least in the way—

JH: It sounds like the grade is incidental.

ER: I feel good when I get good grades, but it's never been about doing better than someone else, but I feel good for my standards.

JH: So put this into context, then: a lot of what we've been discussing is your interest in science, so the science is just a natural outgrowth of the way you were raised, you were just curious about the world. You talked to me yesterday about the dolphins and your cruel trick of stopping up the blowholes. A sadistic trainer—

ER: [Laughing] They don't care, the dolphins don't mind, it's one of their trained responses. He was a really funny guy.

JH: How old were you when you did this?

ER: This was the summer after fifth grade, but by that point I had skipped a grade. I skipped fourth grade. The good class was already full, and I was in the fourth-fifth split, but the education was better. The idea of doing fourth grade again would be like repeating third grade.

JH: So, this incident with the dolphins was a summer camp?

ER: This was a summer camp. It was my first full summer in Santa Cruz (we moved here the summer before). My friend from Maryland came and we did this week-long camp together called "Ocean Explorers" and—

JH: And you had a sadomasochistic trainer—

ER: [Laughing] No, the emphases are different for each of the week-long programs. There is "Masterful Marine Mammals," "Fins, Furs, and Flippers." That was the first I did. That one had the special emphasis on staying in the lab, and you get to go behind the scenes in the research part, and you get to do some of the behavioral things with the dolphins. Then the trainers would call them up onto the pads, and you weigh them, and help give a medical exam to their harbor seal, Sprout, and a lot of different things, and all these programs give you an idea of what it's like to be a marine biologist, like what do people do in the fish kitchen, and—

JH: What's the fish kitchen?

ER: Where they chop all the fish to feed all the animals.

JH: Did you chop fish?

ER: I might have chopped a bit of fish.

JH: Sounds like, and tell me if I'm wrong, but part of the appeal of this is hands on.

ER: Definitely. I am a very hands-on and auditory person. I really need to have things explained to me. When I speak I use a lot of gestures. Someone had me once try to tell a story without gesturing and I had such issues.

JH: Mm, mm.

ER: Having, doing something yourself makes it a lot easier to learn it. So having these experiences where I was getting to do things with this animal. Some of the days we went to Ano Nuevo and saw the elephant seals; we went to Monterey Bay Aquarium. Throughout all these programs there are a lot of different programs and activities, kayaking—

JH: Science for you isn't really an abstraction; in many ways it's an extension of the wild boar hunt. I mean you are actually there in the element doing something, you're not just reading a textbook.

ER: I do think most people will say this—textbooks, unless I have a really exciting textbook, it's not going to thrill me as much as actually doing something and listening to someone speak about it and then trying it yourself. Learning a method through actual repetition, through actually doing it, you'll learn it a lot better than reading about it.

JH: That sounds like, to me, one of your distinguishing characteristics. For you there's a real tactile sense, you interact with the world, again it's not a cerebral activity. You get a certain pleasure out of the physical contact, the manipulation, the interacting. Would that be fair to say?

ER: Yes, definitely. I do like that a lot. I've been volunteering there for more than a year now at the Seymour Center.

JH: What's the Seymour Center?

ER: Long Marine Lab built the Seymour Center, which is an educational facility. It has a small aquarium and a touch tank that's become the home base for the Ocean Explorers.

JH: "Touch tank"—what's that?

ER: It's a tank, open at the top and there are lots of different marine organisms that people can actually feel and hold—

JH: That's just right up your alley, isn't it?

ER: [Nodding] That's what I volunteer at; I work in a touch tank. That's one of the things I do.

JH: What things are in there?

ER: There are sea stars. I love the idea of showing someone a marine organism they have never heard of, and by seeing this now, they might. If I show them a sea star and tell them about how amazing the creature is. Telling someone about a sea star and making them realize how cool it is.

JH: Give me a specific: do you recall any moment when, working with children, when you gave them something? Do you remember anything?

ER: I enjoy working with children, especially because they are so open to whatever it is. Sometimes they are scary, and I have had several little kids who are really just afraid to touch it.

JH: What do you do with a kid like that?

ER: Sometimes putting the animal into terms they can relate with: "It's really just soft and squishy, it doesn't hurt, it's ok." Like little hermit crabs. There are some kids who are "Right on, I want to hold that." Usually the little kids are a little more hesitant. I've even had some adults who just don't know anything about the field, and that's fine, but if I could tell someone about one of the organisms that would prevent them from buying a dried sea star, or doing something that's a horrible practice, that's really doing the job. They basically put them out of water and kill them. But seeing the actual organisms alive, in an area where people can touch them and learn about them, it's a real tactile experience. It's real. We have our filtered Monterey Bay water in the tank—it's cold, after a while my hands are completely numb. I don't even notice it. We keep our organisms under the water, and I can show them the sea stars; we have some anemones over here and urchins and sea cucumbers over here and different kelps and hermit crabs.

JH: And people can touch all this?

ER: And people can touch all this. You should come to the Seymour Center!

JH: Maybe I will.

ER: I work every other Saturday.

JH: This seems to touch on some other aspect I've had a sense of, in what little time I've known you. You have this kind of a social emphasis, you relate some of this to causes, senses of justice, you're not just the "Frankenstein" scientist out there playing with nature; this kind of reinforces some values for you, is this right?

ER: Yes, I think so. Also the fact that I have a lawyer father, for things to have reasons. I grew up watching TV shows like *Star Trek, Seinfeld, Law and Order*. I love *CSI*. In terms of the social aspect, too, I am definitely a social person. I put a lot of emphasis on talking to people and personal contact. I am not shy and I will go up and—that's why I am pretty good for a leadership position as well, because I don't have a problem with talking to people and introducing myself. In Maryland, in my third grade class there was this girl named Aijan, and she was from Kazakhstan, and it was not like I could speak a lot of Russian, and I would incorporate her into what we were doing. She could speak some English, not very good English. We were friends and I would help her out. I took her ice skating for the first time. She had never been ice skating before, and I taught her how to ice skate. I am definitely a people person. I am always moderating conflicts and kind of like the middle person who people will come to with their problems and talk to me. It's kind of what I wrote my reflective essay on in tenth grade. People will come for advice; even with situations I can't even relate to, I can still put myself in a position to understand it.

JH: You can identify and find sympathy with lots of things. There's a term that Edwin Wilson uses, biophilia, love of life. Even with living things, he talks about how we want to surround ourselves with plants, or with pets or stuff because there is a sense of connectedness. I guess I get two dominant things about you: you just feel connected to so many things; you are not threatened by the world as far as I can tell. And then, two, I keep going to that sense of curiosity. I love the image of you climbing up on Alice, because one of the phrases in the *Wonderland* book is "curiouser and curiouser," which may be interesting to work into your essay. That sense that that's just your driving thing; you're not threatened by the world, you're absolutely curious about it, and it just keeps reinforced in you this sense of connectedness. You're talking about connecting up your essay, and maybe this is one of the central themes of your life. You don't perceive the world as a dangerous thing or something that needs to be dominated; you really want to understand it because you become enriched by it; and at all levels, that biophilia, that sense of everything that's alive, is attractive to you and just pulls you in. Does that sound like a fair description?

ER: Yeah. That's definitely...I think having these very worldly experiences when I was younger, very young, and continuing it...we continue to travel, but not to the same extent. In the summer before eighth grade we went to Greece, the summer after tenth grade we went to France, and this last summer I went to Ireland, and that was the first time I traveled with friends—my mom came as well—but it was my Celtic Band that went—

JH: Celtic Band—what are you talking about?

ER: This is another of my musical interests. I really like Celtic music. Quite a few years ago I became involved with the Community Music School of Santa Cruz. One of my good friends played the Irish Harp, and she took lessons from this woman, who had this music school, and she was a really established musician (her husband plays cello); she plays lots of wind instruments, harp, and guitar. They have this whole community of people that did all this Celtic music. They had been hosting this little kids' Celtic camp for children for several years. The first year I started hearing about—I...she actually came to the school and taught at Celtic band, which was this really sad attempt to do something, and at the last rehearsal before the performance, I came in and said "Oh it's cool" and she said, "Here, you'll play bones." So of course I'm not playing the bones the real way, I'm just hitting them together.

JH: And "bones" are?

ER: They're bones, basically, long and skinny. The way you're supposed to play them is you put one on your hand like this [demonstrating], and you hit them in a certain way. You clack them together. There's a few different ways of playing them. Of course I didn't have time to actually learn to play them, so I just played them like this—

JH: Mm, mm.

ER: After that, the summer of seventh grade was the first summer they had a teen Celtic camp, and it was an overnight camp for a week in the summer up in the boonies, like the hippy boonies; you play music, hang out. Ever since then, every summer I've done that. There was this Wednesday band at Louden Nelson, and basically a bunch of people who got together to play music. This director of the Music School was the director of the band. And we would play and learn tunes. Maybe the culminating event was playing at Sunshine Villa. Several of my friends had been involved in this, and they had been in it for a little while, and in tenth grade I joined it at the beginning of the year because they needed a piano player. It's not like the piano is especially a Celtic instrument because you just play chords. But for me it was something I could definitely do, and I had been going to these Celtic camps, and I had the opportunity to join the band. At that point the band became closed, because we decided we want to make a CD. So we worked that year toward making a CD. Tovah and Rachel and others, Caitlin, are in it. At the end of the year we made a CD. We actually have it; we cringe when we listen to it. It was this horrible hot day; we did it in Tovah and Rachel's living room in Ben Lomond. It was late May, we had to tune between each tune, and everyone's fingers were slipping on the instruments. It sounds pretty good, considering the conditions; it was just disgusting. We were crammed into their living room, sixteen of us, with cellos, harps, flutes, all the recording equipment. Then we decided over the next year, "Why don't we try to plan a trip to Ireland because that would be so cool to go and even play in Ireland; that would be so cool."

JH: Yes, it would.

ER: A lot of people asked, well, how would we get the money to do it, how would we go? Not everyone wanted to go. I became, people would have to admit, I was the spokesperson for the group. A lot of the group— they were genius musicians, but they don't like talking, they've got that musician syndrome. Our band teacher wanted to name us "Too Young to Marry."

JH: Two things are striking me: one, do you want to focus on your science, as—certainly an aspect you want to communicate to your college, that you have an area of interest. As I am listening to you, the overriding thing is that curiosity, again. You have been involved in so many things that science is one outgrowth of a lot of just that basic curiosity. I am wondering if maybe you'd consider focusing your essay more—rather than on a discipline—on just that quality that you have. I think you could bring in all these different, very unique experiences which I think flesh out a picture of you as just driven by this. Colleges are looking for people who want to learn. You've just driven yourself. Two, in terms of structure—and this can be tricky, but I'd be curious if you'd be interested in doing it—if there's some way of capturing your speaking voice, almost writing the essay like it's one side of a conversation, like you're talking about these things, in that a lot of this stuff comes up like you're in this tangent.

ER: [Laughs] I go on so long.

JH: No, but listen, listen. Capture your voice. The way that you…maybe you set it up as part of a dialogue, I don't know, like me doing it here. You'll be going along and all of a sudden you'll trip onto something, like the way you mentioned the Celtic band. I could see your paper going, like, "I didn't tell you about Celtic band," "I didn't tell you about —." Almost like you are capturing your own voice in speaking, but in the course of this kind of monologue, bit by bit, all these things about you come out. Do you get a sense of what I'm saying? I'm thinking about those "50 Essays that Work"; they just were not that formalistic kind of stuff: "I've always done well in team sports"….I'd like to really capture that voice that you have, the way you speak. You have that constant detail and moving in and out of stuff and that tangential stuff, which I think would get your personality across, and you have done so many things. In some ways your parents gave you this kind of opportunity, but you just sucked it up; you wanted that stuff, you were driven by that. I would think seriously about maybe approaching with those two things and not focusing on the science so much….

ER: I do talk about it. On the application there are several—in this first essay question, I am talking about science and music, and I have some very specific connections and, for example, Woods Hole program—I want to foster a connection between Brown undergrads and Woods Hole. We have a friend who works there and I am talking with him. I am interested in marine biology, and it's short. In music, I'm saying Providence has all these ties to my music; my great grandmother taught piano in Rhode Island for 65 years.

JH: Better write that down.

ER: I have. Then there's an essay: "Please write in general order of importance your activities." I have something that constitutes this. Then there's the big essay.

JH: It sounds like you might cover the academic stuff in the earlier essays. So an essay that focuses on that would be redundant. I keep coming back to that point that the essay is your personality. By the time they get to that personal essay, they have read through everything else in the form: they know your SAT, GPA, your awards, they know you are an academic student of high achievement, but so are a lot of other kids. What the essay is, is an opportunity to say, "This is who I am; this is my personality; this is what I am like." And that is where they're going to say, "Oh, yeah, this kid would be great on our campus." Between the kids who are achievers—because their whole life is just that, and they react to the test, and they fill out all the homework like they're supposed to, and that's kind of a dull kid and not that interesting. You have a different orientation, and that's what you want to bring out.

ER: That's reminding me of *The Chosen:* you don't want to have just this mind without a soul. Oh, the end of *The Chosen.*

JH: Bring that in too. When you talk about sixteen kids in a hot house in Ben Lomond on a July day, constantly retuning their instruments—that's a visual image I think should be here. When you talk about traveling to Ireland, and you're in this senior center and you've got three people in the audience—that's a visual image. When you talk about covering the blowhole on the dolphin, that's a visual image. You looking for wild boar, that's a visual image. Every one of those will do two things: it will create an image that is unique—no one else sat in a room with fifteen other people retuning instruments—

ER: Except for the other people in the band who are probably applying to Brown.

JH: We'll worry about them later. Do you understand? What will distinguish you is what you've done. That's where the stories and anecdotes come in, the driving curiosity behind them.

ER: Originally I was thinking of doing something like this, but I got overwhelmed by the scale of it and how to tie it all in such a short essay. I get really bothered when I am not coherent.

JH: You can use this to your advantage. First, you will have a theme: curiosity. Second, you will have a kind of structure in that we are watching your mind going through these things, but third, it also brings out your personality.

ER: How much of it should be examples, and how much be reflecting on it?

JH: I would do a lot of it on the examples. I would make them a cornerstone of your paper, and your commentary intersperses or connects them.

ER: I was thinking of doing something like this. I'll just see where it goes.

JH: I think your speaking voice is your personality, and it will be much more interesting to read than the very formal academese that most kids will turn in. Even at a place like Brown, which is a little more off-center, you are still going to get a lot of kids who are going to say "I prize my education: Mom and Dad sent me to Exeter." [Brown admissions officers] don't care about that—they get those by the millions. This is the chance to sound like a human being.

ER: I'll work with it. Right now I am between the stages of formal essay and not, because we are doing this in English Honors. Is it supposed to have structure? Not?

JH: This has structure. This is one of the misnomers that if it does not have a five paragraph count orientation, it doesn't have structure; that's a crock. Of course this has structure. That kind of musing tangential thought is a structure. We'll work on how to shape it so it isn't completely amorphous—it isn't just a list of stuff. It will have some kind of structure. There's a cute way, and a very effective way to capture that voice.

ER: I'm a pretty good creative writer, if I can get into it. At the beginning of my essay I had that voice in that example—it's hard to write about yourself.

JH: Yes, I know, but you don't got no choice. Treat it like—in poetry, it's called a dramatic monologue. T. S. Eliot, Robert Browning did this par excellence. Where the speaker in just kind of rambling on reveals all this about himself. Browning is brilliant at this—dramatic monologues—where in the course of speaking, it's a kind of irony. The speaker thinks he is conveying something to his audience, but in point of fact, the subtext is conveying something else. You could write it like you're talking about your experiences, but the subtext which connects this is that this kid is just alive, and wants to learn, and it isn't even learning, it's just the way she breathes.

ER: I think that this ties me to Brown a lot because Brown has this open curriculum.

JH: [Nodding] Brown violates the disciplines in many ways.

ER: Of course you don't want to write an essay which is like "The reason I like Brown is because of the Open Curriculum." If I can really tie it in and say that because of the Open Curriculum, and because I am a strong student and have so many interests in so many areas, I can really take advantage of it.

JH: You in your voice can sound like the Brown student. So at the end, you want Brown not to stop your education or derail it: Brown is an extension of the way you have lived your entire life.

ER: Yes, a natural extension.

JH: Because it facilitates that openness; you break down the boundaries. In many ways that's why I don't want to see you focus on just science. I don't think that's what your life is about. Science is one of the many ways that you express that curiosity and that kind of connectedness.

ER: I'll work on my draft.

Emma's resulting essay, "Wild Boar Hunts," interweaves anecdotal material and abstract summaries. She chose to italicize the abstract sections to heighten the different levels of the essay, an interwoven structure that works nicely.

## *Wild Boar Hunts* by Emma Richter

When I was four, my father and I would go on "wild boar hunts" near the Palvolgyi caves in Budapest. We never caught any boar, but we never questioned their presence. When I was seven, we traveled from my Moscow home to Africa. Wearing Egyptian headwear, I learned to ride a camel, and because of my size, I could scamper through the tunnels of the Great Pyramid of Giza.

*Curiosity has always connected me to the world.*

At age nine a Tokyo Fish Market vendor offered me a morsel of raw tuna. It would have been rude to refuse. I climbed the Acropolis at twelve, sweating and panting under the Athenian sun.

*The world was my first classroom.*

Standing in Van Gogh's room at Cloitre Saint Paul, I shared the barren space—a bed, a chair, and a window looking over fields of sunflowers—he saw in his last years. And last summer, at sixteen, I sat on the side of an Irish highway with my Celtic band waiting for someone to fix our flat tire. We sat, singing, in the long grass.

*I prefer first-hand, tactile experiences.*

At ten I climbed into a pool where Puka, the dolphin, waited. Billy, the one-armed dolphin trainer, and I gave commands, including the one I preferred avoiding: with my hand on Puka's blowhole, Billy whistled, and Puka shot up a spray. Billy called out, laughing, "You've got dolphin boogers on your hand!" Since this encounter, I have deepened my love for the scientific process. I thrill to the hunt: long hours tweaking variables, late nights mixing solutions in my school's biology lab, lengthy e-mails seeking genetically modified cells for experimentation, and nerve-wracking examinations by experts.

When I was thirteen, I undertook a Science Fair Project proposing onion DNA as a "sunblock." Needing proper equipment to quantify my results, I knocked on the door of a UCSC chemist I had never met, a bit nervous, but prepared to explain my experiment. She smiled and ushered me in.

*Curiosity is the force that drives my ambition in science and my passion for music.*

Sitting on my father's shoulders in a packed Red Square, I listened to cannons blasting to the "1812 Overture," inspiring the crowd to support Yeltsin against a coup. On another occasion, I stood alone on the stage. It was the beginning of the Bay Opera's second act of *Tosca*. I proudly sang my solo as the Shepherd. I was eleven. Like travel, music joins in me the traditions of continents, religions, cultures and time periods. As I sing, I feel connected.

Because my experiences have given me an appreciation for diversity, taught me the effects of complex variables, and blended my voice with others, I desire a community that cherishes collaborative thinking about the world and my generation's role in it. I would be honored to extend my curiosity at Brown, and while I expect I will not find wild boars in Providence either, I will still thrill to the hunt.

# *Student Samples*

### *My Grandparents' House* by Katie Van Domelen

The front door is in the back of the house.

Don't ask me why. It just is. I guess that means there's no real back door. Sometimes, when our car pulls up the crackling gravel driveway and rolls over the black cord that triggers a doorbell, I wonder about that back door/front door conundrum. In the end I satisfy myself by concentrating on the farm outside my backseat window.

I can't see half of it, but I know it by memory. Nothing ever changes out here. In the northwest corner, towering blackberry bushes droop with dark, juicy fruit beginning to fall on the ground, painting it in deep purple colors. In my mind's ear I can hear the gentle echoing creak of the tree swing as it gnaws away at the twisted old oak branch in the northeast corner, near the old sheep pasture where a few still graze. Right in between the two, straight north, a short distance out into the sea of cattails, the ground gets a little squelchy and becomes a pond that's home to a host of frogs. Oak trees fence that side of the house off from the blackberries and the pond.

As our car turns the corner into the driveway, I can just make out the orchard of apple trees that hide the swing. Eastward an ancient barn with warped boards and rust door handles backs up against the orchard, facing an almost identical one across a wide path that leads into the horse pasture. They hide the same treasures of rusty farm equipment, dusty boxes, and spider webs, a mouse's paradise and a young explorer's adventure. The horse pasture itself lays empty unless it's being rented out. On the inside of the gate my cousins planted an assortment of vegetables, which they grow with great care.

Grandma and Grandpa are standing outside to meet us when we finally park. They hug us and help with the luggage, and eventually we all get ushered inside. From behind me I hear the screen door click shut. My nose is immediately assaulted with smells of cooking. A soft chewy batch of my grandma's famous chocolate chip cookies is sitting out on the counter cooling, and I can smell dinner wafting out of a covered pot. Aunt Teresa, Uncle Bud, Tyler, and Sara are already there. My eyes follow the sound of scratching from pool table chalk and finally rest on Tyler standing impatiently in the corner, waiting for my grandpa to shoot. The sharp clicking of polished balls punctuates greetings between beaming faces.

Soon my grandma puts us to work setting shiny white plates on the folding table outside on her screened porch. Behind the table and beyond the screen, a broad grassy square lies bordered with towering trees that wall off the road. This is where the front door should be. Going back inside to load up with plates and food, I look around at the house. I can't see past the door into the bedrooms and staircase, but I can see the kitchen and all the women bustling about with pans and plates and food, bumping into each other occasionally. My brother and sister sit at the table on the other side of the counter, immersed in playing with Legos and dolls. The men are talking and laughing boisterously, making a show of skill at the pool table. In the background jazz music drifts out of the living room from my grandpa's old records and undertones the conversation.

My reverie doesn't last; in a flash plates are shoved into my hands ("idle hands are the devil's tools"), and I walk back out to the porch smiling. All too soon the night grows late, spoons clatter into bowls previously full of homemade ice cream, now licked clean. I crawl upstairs, drag my feet to the room I share with my brother and sister and reluctantly get ready for bed. An hour later I'm snuggled under my blankets, listening to the heavy wooden door close with a muted whine. I lie on the bed with the windows open, smelling the country musk of hay and dirt. Soon frogs and crickets strike up a lullaby I could swear was just for me.

Downstairs someone laughs.

Outside the wind sweeps down the old road towards the cemetery.

## *Aaron and Arianna* by Kelsey Miller

Aaron said, "I'm not your favorite cousin, am I?"

I thought, "Of course you're not."

Everyone knows Arianna is my favorite.

Arianna has long curly hair. She lets me play with it too.

She drinks Slurpees with me and we pretend it's medicine when it melts.

Ari knows what a credit card is, and she is the smartest girl I know.

She sings her warm-ups from singing class and tells me she'll be famous.

But I was only five, so I shook my head and muttered, "No, Ari is."

If Aaron asked me again today,

I would think, "Of course you are."

I chose the wrong cousin, Aaron.

Everyone knows you're my favorite.

You listen to me when I talk and you understand me.

Ari talks to me once or twice each year and asks me how tall I am now.

You and I talk every day and you ask me how my day was.

You drink coke with me while we watch a movie.

When Ari came to visit, she smoked while I waited for her in the park.

Ari left, but you stayed with me, Aaron.

She stopped going to school and instead followed her friends blindly.

But you are in college now, and you have friends who think for themselves.

You never followed the crowd, but Ari followed the wrong one.

But I'm only sixteen, so I would just nod my head and mutter, "Yes, you are."

## *Grandpa Gordon* by Natalie Christopherson

Grandpa Gordon smoked. The freckles and sunspots on his bald head were lingering evidence of so many summers on the beach in Mexico. He would sail the Sunfish off the sand-spit into the bay, and I saw black and white pictures of the bathroom he made from a refrigerator box. That was before they put in the green wooden port-a-potty. I stayed on the beach with Christie, and we stuffed our swimsuits with oranges to pretend we had big boobs, while my grandpa sailed around the bay. The sail was painted with a rainbow.

The grand piano was black and took up most of the living room. It looked like it belonged in a mansion somewhere with roomy halls, cold marble floors and crystal chandeliers. But there it sat, plopped in the middle of the brown carpet on 12 court. Next to it sat scratchy orange chairs, a faded tan sofa and an old wooden coffee table in front of a brick fireplace.

We would sit around the crowded dining room table at Thanksgiving, smooshed between the window and the opposite wall, which made it impossible to get up to pee. I reveled in the confusion and fullness of these occasions, a contrast to the small white table where the three of us sat at home.

My grandpa always sat at the head of the table on Thanksgiving. Everyone held hands as his steady voice said grace: "We give thanks for this food and this chance to be together." His hands shook as he brought the food to his mouth.

There was one bathroom in the house, and with everyone there at the holidays it was constantly occupied. "Take your time," my grandpa would say. After dinner he'd smoke his cigarette out on the cement back steps; that was before my grandma fell and they put up the iron railing. By the time he sat down to play the piano it would be getting late. Everyone gathered around and I'd hug my knees and listen to the conversation that filled the warm room as my grandpa's stubby fingers found their rhythms.

He died around Easter. The Kaiser doctors wouldn't do bypass surgery, and they sent him home. He died the next day with one hundred percent blockage in one artery and eighty percent in the other.

My grandma kept his ashes on the mantle next to the piano for months. Before he died she had never spent a night alone in her life. She decided she wanted him to rest forever in the ocean, so we went out on the boat to scatter the ashes.

We picked pink camellias in the backyard in the rain and put them in a plastic bag. It kept raining as the boat sailed out of the harbor. I crumpled the petals in my fingers before watching them hit the waves. My uncle sat at the head of the table that Thanksgiving.

Now we go and visit the plaque on the Palace Verdes Cliffs that reads "Gordon Todd." It's right there next to all the other names. I always wondered who these people were and who put the wilted flowers next to their names. The metal of the plaques is almost completely green from the ocean spray.

The ladder to the attic at my grandma's house folds down into the hallway. I go up there sometimes for her because her hips can't handle the steps. Lots of cardboard boxes litter the floor, and the air is stiflingly warm. The door to the left leads into a little room, my grandpa's dark room. Everything is still in the drawers, the photo paper and bottles of developing chemicals. There's a lamp with a red cover over it, and if all the boxes and dust were moved out, it would be just like it was the last time he was in there. The photographs have collected a layer of dust but they show the same image. I try not to move anything.

Now my grandma wants to sell the piano. We all tell her not to, but nobody plays it anymore.

# *Lesson Ideas*

- **Generating Questions**. Make a list of "Odd Jobs" (clothing inspector, Mammoth Caves tour guide, food taster, rodent hunter, etc.) on an overhead. Break students into small groups, each selecting a different job from the list. Give them five minutes to generate a list of questions they'd ask the worker. After each groups shares its questions with the class, ask students outside the group if there are additional questions they could come up with.

- **Observation**. Send students to a specific location on campus to jot down all they see. Once they've returned to class, generate a list on the board of all their observational details, encouraging them to recall details others missed.

- **Campus Issues**. Discuss a current issue on campus. Then ask students to generate a list of all the sources they could research to find out more about the issue.

- **Interviews**. Bringing in tapes of media interviews (i.e., Charlie Rose, Larry King, Terry Gross, Ted Koppel) or printed interviews (from *Rolling Stone*, *Seventeen*, a local paper), have students critique the questions, comparing and contrasting interviewing techniques.

- **Stories**. Students love to tell stories. Have them respond to prompts ("My Most Embarrassing/Exciting/Memorable/Funny Moment") and share with their peers. Then tell them to write a short version of the tale, focusing on specific and telling details.

- **Connections**. Brenda Miller suggests this activity in her "A Braided Heart" essay from *Writing Creative Nonfiction*: "Take three disparate objects, at random, from your purse, your backpack, your shelves. Set them in front of you and begin writing, allowing fifteen minutes for each object. See if there is a common image or theme you can use to bind these together." (24)

- **Shel Silverstein**. For a delightful diversion, track down Shel Silverstein's "Sarah Cynthia Sylvia Stout," a cautionary song that, in advising children to "always take the garbage out," enumerates a long list of trash that Sarah Stout fails to haul away from her home, thereby ensuring her "awful end." A disturbing example of the power of specifics.

———·———

Having gathered a wide range of materials, students now face the task of organizing their specifics into a clear structure. Chapter 5 explains how to teach structure via a selection of structure types.

# The First Shall Be Last:
# Structuring

---

**Focus**: Structure clarifies how the separate parts of a composition relate to one another. As a result, it cannot be predetermined; it must arise from the material organically. Hence, writing programs must teach a range of structures to complement a wide range of writing experiences.

---

**Sections:**
- Writing's Three Parts
- Specificity: The Importance of Detail
- Creating Sections
- Focus: The Golden Thread
- Connectors
- Song and Structure
- Structure Types
- Student Samples
- Lesson Ideas

*In the beginning, the earth was without form and void.*
—Genesis 1:1

*The pattern which connects is a metapattern. It is a pattern of patterns. It is that metapattern which defines the vast generalizations that, indeed, it is patterns which connect....In truth, the right way to begin to think about the pattern which connects is to think of it as primarily a dance of interacting parts.*

—Gregory Bateson, *Mind and Nature*

*The most powerful form in incantation, however, comes from*

*one's own written words—sheer words themselves in clusters,*
*clumps, lists, strings, sentences. The advice here from the*
*writer seems to be, "When mute or in doubt, start generating*
*words on the page; then through examining what you have*
*produced automatically or semi-automatically, you may*
*discern a pattern or theme in the seeming written chaos."*

—Janet Emig, *The Web of Meaning*

 Speaking to a class of Beats a half century ago at the California School of fine Arts in San Francisco, social scientist Gregory Bateson pulled a freshly baked crab from a paper bag and placed it on the classroom table.

"I want you to produce arguments which will convince me that this object is the remains of a living thing," Bateson addressed the Beats. The artists pondered, one eventually suggesting that the sea creature was symmetrical.

"You mean it's *composed,* like a painting," noted Bateson. The art analogy was deliberate, as Bateson noted when he wrote the incident up in *Mind and Nature:* "The anatomy of the crab is repetitive and rhythmical. It is, like music, repetitive with modulation." (7) Coaxing his class, Bateson posed the question he presented years later to his readers: "What pattern connects the crab to the lobster and the orchid to the primrose and all the four of them to me?" (7)

What Bateson pushed his students to recognize was the significance of patterning, of meaning, created via structure. From the raw materials of experience we categorize sensory data and memories until they interlock like genetic codes, their arrangement itself signifying more than the individual parts. We discard and snip away at what we find until the elements fit together. It is that *fitting* we see, not the parts of which it is composed. Thus, teaching structure is helping students see that the arranging of parts is a specific and conscious action.

The first thing to note, then, is that structuring is a choice: writers select/create the format that enhances their material. Listing is not writing; structure embodies, we might say reveals or forms, how the ideas evolve and are revealed.

As an editor on my college paper, I received advice about page design from my adviser: a bad layout calls attention to itself; a good one enables us to instead focus on the content of the page. So it is with writing. Awkward transitions, shoehorned formats, count-the-sentences structures appear as artificial as they are, redirecting the reader's attention from what we are saying to how we are structuring it. Structure should be the inevitable way to present our gatherings. Hence, it should not be the first item of business. Structures imposed before the writing process begins often force students to fit their materials into a predestined format, regardless of the fit. Such instruction discourages students from selecting the format appropriate for their material; instead, they rely on the teacher to tell them what the final product should look like. The goal of writing is to encourage students to choose the most effective forms of expression, not rely on teachers to dictate those forms. Unless we intend to accompany them to college, we thus fail them.

Students little understand structure if they encounter only one form of it. Instead, exposing them to a variety of formats enables them to see the role of structure as a tool of clarity. It doesn't take much to explain this idea: most pop songs are made up of three verses and two choruses, most films move chronologically from an earlier point to a later, magazines divide their content into subsections, houses are designed to accommodate particular flows of activity, a wardrobe is comprised of individual elements that must harmonize into a whole, dinners are coordinated affairs of complementary courses, and concerts follow prescribed formats. No mathematical proposition, no legal argument, no scientific principle, no political speech is devoid of structure. It is what keeps us from chaos. It is what gives beauty to the star and the snowflake. It is not the mere property of a writing assignment; it is the fingerprint of the universe.

## *Writing's Three Parts*

In his redefinition of the short story nearly two centuries ago, Edgar Allan Poe wrote that all the elements of a tale must cohere to produce a single effect. As a literary critic, Poe was rowing against the tide. In contrast to his focused compositions, successful writers of the early 1800s wrote leisurely narratives that combined observation and description in varying arrangements of plot which meandered where the author's whimsy directed. Poe's near contemporary, Washington Irving, wrote delectably detailed passages; in "The Legend of Sleepy Hollow," the author takes lovely detours from the plot, as when he describes the fixings of an autumnal feast in detail that rivals a seventeenth-century Dutch still life. The description makes us salivate, but it doesn't advance the plot. Focus was not his intent

But we are Poe's descendants. All elements within effective writing—specifics, sections, and focus—create a seamless whole. The poem, the literary analysis, the play and the novel, the newspaper article and the editorial, the personal essay and the interview—all writing is composed of these three parts. Identifying the sections each kind of writing is comprised of, and then determining their relationship, we give writing the structure that blends the dialogue of specifics and abstraction into a unified presentation. All writing, then, consists of these parts: a focus, sections that work together to flesh out that focus, specifics that illustrate those main and sub ideas.

## Building Structure

The key strategy in structuring writing is starting from the ground up: collecting our specifics, gathering them into sections, and using those sections to suggest a focus. In other words, though our finished composition may begin with a central idea, such a focus is not the start of our thinking, but the result of it. This indicates the importance of prewriting: we first organize our material, working inductively from specifics to general observations, before we begin the paper.

**1. The Foundation:** *Specifics*: anecdotes, quotes, details, and facts are the foundations of well-structured writing. Without these concrete basics, the thinking in our writing is based on nothing and lacks support.

**2. General Support:** *Sections:* Specifics must be organized into groups for clarity. We do this when we detect patterns in our collection of specifics. These categories place the concrete specifics into abstract generalities (inductive leaps) so that the reader begins to see how the specifics relate to each other to generate meaning.

**3: The Cap:** *Focus*: What concrete specifics and their categories support is the focus of the work. This can be a single idea, an emotion, effect, statement, argument, or thesis. The roof cannot exist without support from the walls and flooring, nor can it be built first, but must be placed upon an already established foundation and walls.

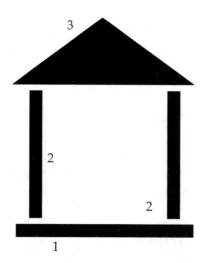

## Specifics

*Anecdotes*: Short stories or narratives

*Quotes*: Word-for-word statements.

*Descriptive detail*: Concrete images that appeal to the senses.

*Facts*: Mathematical or scientific statements.

## Sections

*Points*: Abstract statements used to support a thesis or argument.

*Chapters, scenes, stanzas*: Groupings that separate plot or thematic developments.

*Paragraphs*: Smaller groupings that link sub-ideas or themes.

*Subsections*: Groupings that divide larger works into smaller, thematic units.

*Steps*: Stages of a process.

## Focal Point

*Thesis* (implied or stated): Used in critical writing, a thesis is an analytic statement regarding a selected topic.

*Argument*: Used in persuasive writing from editorials to advertising, an argument is similar to a thesis, but it has the additional task of encouraging action on the reader's part.

*Theme*: Used predominantly in suggestive and informative pieces, a theme is less explicit than a thesis; it is better understood as the author's attitude towards a topic.

*Tone, mood, or atmosphere*: Used in suggestive writing, these foci are less intellectual than emotional, less oriented toward a clear statement than a feeling.

Thus, the writing process involves moving inductively from specifics to generalization, from the concrete to the abstract. Once we have gathered our materials, we can shape them into a structure appropriate to our purposes.

# *Specificity: The Importance of Detail*

*No truth except in things*

—William Carlos Williams

*Specifying is an act of analysis; relating, an act of synthesis.*

—James Moffett, *Teaching the Universe of Discourse*

Photographers know the importance of cropping, the removal of competing material until the eye is focused on the essential. As a police reporter in Las Vegas, working for the *Review-Journal*, I learned the literary equivalent of cropping. A journalistic lead—the condensing of the story's highlights into a quick opening—requires the selection of the most important parts of the story, and the subsequent paragraphs contain only those images and phrases that succinctly, and precisely, convey the essential meaning. Similarly, photojournalists carve through a sea of faces and movement to find the image that has the greatest impact.

Focused journalism produces sharp, clean writing, and it is no accident that many stylists began as reporters: Ernest Hemingway, John Steinbeck, Joan Didion, Tom Wolfe, Sherwood Anderson, and Theodore Dreiser among others. Charles Dickens, whose detailed prose helped move the novel from sentimentalism to realism, first wrote for London's penny dreadfuls, scouring the city's landmark settings and backstreets. A friend later illustrated Dickens's penchant for focusing. Once, in the company of the eminent Victorian, he strode down London's Strand. When the duo reached the end of the street, Dickens stopped, then turned to his walking companion and listed a wealth of items he'd spied in the shop windows as they walked. The novelist had an eye for detail.

Detail is what distinguishes good writing by separating it out from the muck of the mundane and the trite. Each of us recollects someone whose manner, dress, words stuck in the craw of our cranium, but the effective writer collects those images that recreate the picture drawn on the writer's inner eye. In *Syn and Syntax*, Constance Hale speaks of the power of nouns, encouraging writers to choose those which create the indelible mark, the fingerprint of personality. Hale quotes *New Yorker* writer Whitney Balliett's description of jazz legend Dizzy Gillespie:

> Gillespie, who is not a clotheshorse, was wearing a Sherlock Holmes hat, and houndstooth jacket, rumpled striped brown pants, a navy-blue T-shirt, and a couple of medallions suspended from a long gold neck chain. He hasn't changed much in the last ten years. He has a medium-length grayish Afro, and he looks grizzly. His huge and celebrated cheeks are broadsides in repose and spinnakers in action, and he has a scimitar smile and a thousand tiny, even teeth. He likes to smile and roll

his eyes in mock surprise, but most of the time his eyes are narrowed; they take in much and send out little, and when he puts on his dark-rimmed, two-tone glasses they disappear. (16)

As Balliett's passage illustrates, concision does not mean restriction or reduction so that the writing barely breathes. Imagery and detail tumble out of his paragraph, but each is carefully selected, creating a plate of nuggets, not a wash of sediment.

Effective writing, then, begins with specifics, from the focus on diction to the gathering of anecdotes, details, quotes, and facts. Woven together seamlessly, specifics elevate composition from the prosaic to the poetic, but it is not the exclusive property of fiction. The best informative writing pays attention to specifics, which is illustrated in the work of Wolfe, Didion, Ron Rosenbaum, Richard Rhodes, Pico Iyer, and John McPhee. Similarly, critical writing in the hands of conscious stylists delights as well as it analyzes, as illustrated in the scientific compositions of Stephen Jay Gould and Lewis Thomas, in the travel writing of Bill Bryson and Tim Cahill, the nature observations of Wendell Berry and Annie Dillard, the sports writing of Steve Rushin, the business commentary of Ken Auletta. Their attention to detail creates writing that transcends the subject matter and reveals its connection to our own selves. They carve clear paths through dense forests, letting light play with shade until we see the familiar as if for the first time.

Specifics suggest the presence of bone beneath the skin.

# Sections: Organizing Your Marbles

Specifics are the building blocks of writing, the raw material we organize into a pattern that suggests meaning. The arrangement and interaction of these specifics is what produces the end product. Flour is a component of baking, but depending on what combination of other components it is mixed with—milk, baking soda, yeast, salt, butter, hot water, dried fruit, or nuts—it produces different breads or pastries. What writing specifics we choose, and how we arrange them, determines the poem, essay, article, critique, or novel we end up with.

This collection of marbles is a kind of toy, but as a toy, it can be divided into smaller collections. Depending on our criteria for classification, we could divide this group of marbles in several ways:

- By color
- By size

- By function within the game
- By design
- By worth or value

As we determine our sections, we determine their relationship, which suggests how they are to be presented. We may divide a narrative into simple, chronological steps or we can alternate past and present events, mixing in flashbacks; we might eschew narrative completely in a poem, instead choosing to organize its stanzas around an idea that develops in complexity as new information is introduced; a reportorial piece is often organized around topical sections, elements of history, background, personalities or narrative working toward a dramatic finish. Essays can similarly be divided in a number of ways beyond the five-paragraph structure, and critical essays are suitable for a range of structures. It is worth noting that the term "points" often confuses students (and more than a few teachers) when applied to analytic essays. Though points are technically abstract statements that defend a thesis, students understand them more clearly if we define them as statements that make clear the division of their papers.

Sections are the categories our specifics form. Bateson would define them as the patterns that arise when we look at the similarities and differences of our specifics. Ultimately, we may well discard some specifics that do not fit into categories, just as we may not use all the categories we create. The selection of what sections and what specifics we ultimately select is governed by the overall purpose of our writing. And we determine that purpose when we decide what our focus is.

## *Focus: The Golden Thread*

*In all my stories, there is one idea running through them like an iron rod, and to which all other ideas are referred and subordinated.*

—Nathaniel Hawthorne

*I had to keep my eye on the single strands that came in and out of focus, filaments that glinted differently depending on where they had been. At the same time, I had to keep my eye focused on the single image that held them all together. As William Stafford wrote a few weeks before he died, "There's a thread you follow. It goes among / things that change. But it doesn't change."*

—Brenda Miller, *"A Braided Heart: Shaping the Lyric Essay"*

> *The material suggests what's going on. You've got to let the*
> *material develop your thesis and, as you work, the piece takes*
> *on shape*

—Brenda Shapiro, a feature writer

Songwriter Carole King tells of her collaboration with a novice song-writer who came to her with a conglomeration of lines and images for a song, but no focus:

> They were great phrases, but they had no thread. I said, "Charlotte,
> what do you wanna say?" She says, "Omigod! Omigod! I never thought
> about that. You've changed my life. I actually have to have a point! I
> have to *say* something."

The focus is a text's dominant impact. It's what King's friend means when she says a song has to have a point. It's what we require students to unveil when we ask what the author meant, the mood that emerges from a song or movie, the call to action we feel compelled to initiate after reading a persuasive piece. It can be as baldly obvious as a stated thesis or as subtly suggestive as a Pink Floyd song, but without it a piece of writing rambles and divagates without purpose. The focus is what separates the memoir from a diary account, a reporter's article from his notebooks, or a critical research paper from a list of Bartlett's quotations. If we have written well, the focus is what we ultimately hope the reader takes away from our work.

As a police reporter for the *Las Vegas Review-Journal,* I worked for a managing editor who took a certain pleasure in redlining the copy of new recruits. But he knew structure, and he introduced me to the concept of the golden thread. The golden thread referred to any idea that permeated and connected a work, so that a word, phrase, or image repeated at key spots drew the reader back to the focus. It reminds the reader of your intent and, like bread crumbs trailing through a Grimms's forest, points the way back to what began the discussion.

The golden thread can be as explicit as the thesis and topic sentences of a conventional critical essay or it can be as implicit as the recurrent images of a poem. When Hamlet repeatedly speaks of disease, illness, and decay, Marcellus connects the figurative language via a central metaphor: "Something is rotten in the state of Denmark" (I.iv.90). In a reportorial piece, the golden thread is felt as sections are linked by concepts or ideas that reinforce the main idea.

The golden thread, then, is a conscious repetition of a key word, phrase, or idea throughout a work so as to tighten its focus. Having determined, as King's friend did, what our point is, what we want to say, the golden thread is our repeated signal to the reader what that point is what the focus of our paper is.

# Connectors: Threading the Parts Together

Connecting words and sentences are the sinews that knit together the sectional bones. The relationship between individual sections and components is made clear via connectors that trace the development of a theme or argument. Like punctuation, connectors become road signs that guide the reader through the twists and shifts of a writer's journey.

But it should be noted that experimental forms of writing—much modernist poetry or articles employing episodic or pastiche structures—rely on implied connectors. Such work suggests, rather than states, the relationship of the parts. The absence of explicit connectors serves writers working on a level beyond the merely informative; they often seek to reproduce the writer's own engagement with the subject matter—fractured or impressionistic—or argue that the subject matter itself is so disparate as to defy easy categorization. In such cases, the lack of connectors is not bad writing, but a deliberate suggestion of the discussion's complexity.

But even the most experimental of pieces relies on juxtapositions that imply a relationship, and though its connections are not explicitly conveyed, the arrangement of the sections reveals a deliberate construction. Clearly, beginning writers are served when taught more explicit ways to connect sections, but they also benefit from exposure to more experimental forms. Forced to consider ways to convey the more difficult discussions, students must confront their own inner logic and clarify how their ideas relate.

## Introductions

Introductions serve two goals: provide perspective and hook the reader. The more explicit/critical the writing the greater emphasis in the intro on providing perspective; the more implicit/suggestive the stronger the emphasis on getting the reader's attention. Thus, as with all writing, the creation of the intro depends on the intent and structure of the overall work.

Hook intros—attention getters—draw the reader in. Though they should at least suggest the overview of the piece, their orientation is toward forceful or compelling expression.

### Dictionary definition

This is a war horse, so commonly used that I personally counsel my students against it as it has approached cliché status. Still, used sparingly and effectively, a dictionary opening can work.

When Daniel Webster defined Machiavellian as "characterized by unscrupulous cunning," he hadn't even met Uriah Heep.

## Quotation

The voice contained in a good quote establishes a personal ι

"I tan because I love it," gushed supermodel Christy Turlington in a 1993 interview with *New Body* magazine. Why does Turlington—international symbol of fashion and beauty—along with millions of other Americans value tanning so much?"

—Christina English, "Half-Baked Beauty"

## Anecdote

Stories are innately good hooks, and an anecdote catches a reader's attention better than most openers.

When I was twelve, I graduated from being a boxer to being a spreader. As my grandpa stood behind me, reaching over to guide my hand, he taught me how to spread the ravioli filling. His dark Sicilian hands, dirty and coarse from years of boning and cutting meat in an old sausage factory, gripped my hands firmly, but gently. "Do it like this, Rachel. There you go. Hey, look at my little Rachel, she's spreadin' the filling! There you go, babe! Ha, ha, she's got it."

—Rachel Field, "Ravioli"

## Descriptive

Setting the scene evokes a mood or tone that invites the reader in.

A few seventh grade girls wearing extremely short Blue Asphalt jean shorts speedily exit out of Wet Seal, silver braces reflecting off the light coming from the sky windows above, their lips glossed with the crimson tint of Bonne Bell's Strawberry Lip Smacker and frosty pearl Champagne Cover Girl eye shadow smeared carelessly along their lids. Anyone within earshot can hear their deeply involved, and never-ending, pointless argument over which 'N SYNC member is the "hottest." A Caucasian man in his early twenties slowly struts a wannabe "ghetto" walk by Bath and Body Works, dark-denim baggy pants sagging low to the mall floor to reveal his Tommy Hilfiger boxers (not to mention a deficiency in his strut); his metallic silver Oakley sunglasses don't complement the dark midnight black wig toppled messily on his head, which could also be mistaken for a middle-aged man's toupee. Somehow the Offspring's "Pretty Fly (for a white guy)" enters my head. A security guard follows close behind.
—Jennifer Martinez, "Valley Fair"

### Question

Questions provoke, confronting the reader with a puzzle requiring solution.

> "Man Pulls Tractor with Nipple Piercings." Picturing this grotesque ritual, only one word comes to mind: ouch. Why do we pierce our bodies? What does it symbolize in our society? Why can't I get my nipples pierced?
> —Sarah Nadler, "Needles and Skin"

### Phrasing

A turn of phrase, use of a pun, or playing with words: clever phrasing engages and entertains the reader.

> I met the Bean Counters in preschool.
>
> They introduced me to the Bean Tray.
>
> It was a simple concept. On the Bean Tray were two bowls, one filled with black beans, the other with white. Each day, we took turns at the Bean Tray Table. It was here that we learned to count—we counted beans.
>
> —Jennifer Chapski, "Bean Soup for the Soul"

> At eight years of age, I was not a typical human child. In fact, the truth of the matter is that I wasn't human at all—I was a unicorn.
>
> —Christie Miller, "Unicorns"

### En medias res

Dropping the reader into the middle of an action creates questions needing resolution. I advise writers using this technique to start with the climactic moment of a narrative and then back up to fill in the details.

> The nervous tension filling the arena hovers like a cloud of fog in the cool morning air. My entire body is shaking, not so much shivering from the frosty chill in the ice rink as quivering with nerves. I look out at the ice, a shimmering white sheet, glistening with cool water, its rock-hard surface, cruel and unforgiving when a jump is miscalculated and a helpless skater falls hard to the ground.
> —Becca White, "Skating"

Critical essays need not avoid hook intros, but their openings more clearly and quickly outline the scope and focus of the discussion. The focus is clearly stated—as in a thesis—and usually clarified before the body of discussion begins. I do not personally favor restricting critical intros to a set number of sentences or insisting on a specific placement of a thesis. Papers of three to seven pages generally work with one to three paragraph introductions, but as with all composition, the structure should proceed naturally from the materials rather than be indiscriminately imposed by formula. I've seen students begin an essay with a thesis in the first sentence and then briefly summarize the scope of the argument; I've read papers in which the thesis is withheld until the conclusion, the writer outlining the argument that makes the thesis appear inevitable; and students have written papers for me utilizing the "funnel" opening, wherein a general overview of the topic is narrowed down to a specific thesis. Each of these approaches works. Teach them all and encourage students to vary openings according to the internal logic of the writing.

## Conclusions

A conclusion is the rounding off of the reading experience. It can, like the hook opening, engage the reader with a final snap, or, as in the critical essay, produce a snapshot of information that is key to the discussion. What it should never be is repetitive or boring. In particular, critical pieces should avoid merely recapitulating the thesis and points in the final paragraph. Though it is important to draw the reader back to the focus, critical essays should employ closings more effective than simple repetition. All the techniques used in hook intros, for example, can work in the conclusions of critical, informative, and suggestive works alike. The conclusion of a critical essay can employ a kind of reverse funnel. For instance, a discussion on the nature of sin in Puritan culture as seen in Nathaniel Hawthorne's *The Scarlet Letter* might conclude with a comment on the nature of sin in American culture today. An analysis of Holden Caulfield's struggle to engage adulthood might close with an observation about the universal challenge of leaving childhood behind. Such conclusions, working like level three questions, provide a perspective for the paper's discussion, enabling the reader to see why this topic is of value beyond the work itself.

I also teach cyclical structures, wherein the conclusion of a work refers back to an image or idea in the opening. This technique makes for a clean rounding off of the discussion. For examples, see "A Rambling Romp through Tulip History" and "Bean Soup for the Soul" found in the student sample section of the accompanying CD-ROM.

# Transitions

## Transitional Words and Phrases

| | |
|---|---|
| Addition | again, also, and, and then, besides, equally important, finally, first, further, furthermore, in addition, in the first place, last, moreover, next, second, still, too |
| Cause and effect | as a result, for this reason, therefore, hence, consequently, accordingly |
| Comparison | also, in the same way, likewise, similarly |
| Concession | granted, naturally, of course |
| Contrast | although, and yet, at the same time, but at the same time, despite that, even so, even though, for all that, however, in contrast, otherwise, regardless, still, though, yet |
| Conclusion | in short, to conclude, in brief, on the whole, in summary, to sum up |
| Emphasis | certainly, indeed, in fact, of course |
| Example or illustration | after all, as an illustration, even, for example, for instance, in conclusion, indeed, in fact, in other words, in short, it is true, of course, namely, specifically, that is, to illustrate, thus, truly |
| Repeating an idea just stated | in other words, that is, to repeat, again |
| Repeating an idea more precisely | to be exact, to be specific, to be precise, more specifically, more precisely |
| Summary | all in all, altogether, as has been said, finally, in brief, in conclusion, in other words, in particular, in short, in simpler terms, in summary, on the whole, that is, therefore, to put it differently, to summarize |
| Time and sequence | after a while, afterward, again, also, and then, as long as, at last, at length, at that time, before, besides, earlier, eventually, finally, formerly, further, furthermore, in addition, in the first place, in the past, last, lately, meanwhile, moreover, next, now, presently, second, shortly, simultaneously, since, so far, soon, still, subsequently, then, thereafter, too, until, until now, when |

Unless a writer is employing abrupt juxtapositions for a particular effect, he must guide the reader through the shifts in his thinking via clear signals. Transitional words and sentences make clear why we are moving from one section to the next, why we have arranged the sections in the order we have.

Critical writing frequently employs topic sentences to introduce sectional or subsectional shifts, announcing to the reader both the scope of the discussion to be and its relation to the previous section. Informative writings often rely on transitional topic sentences, though not as stringently as in critical writing; suggestive writing more frequently relies on simple juxtaposition of sections and paragraphs.

Within a sentence, transitional words indicate how thought is shaded, how it moves from one vantage to another to tease out detail. Note how Nathaniel Hawthorne uses transitions to explore the contrasts of thought Dimmesdale experiences in this passage from *The Scarlet Letter:*

> The Minister, **on the other hand,** had never gone through an experience calculated to lead him beyond the scope of generally received laws; **although**, in a single instance, he had so fearfully transgressed one of the most sacred of them. **But** this had been a sin of passion, **not** of principle, **nor** even purpose. **Since** that wretched epoch, he had watched, with morbid zeal and minuteness, **not** his acts —for those it was easy to arrange—**but** each breath of emotion, **and** his every thought. (83)

The passage begins by contrasting Dimmesdale's flagging moral strength with Hester's ("on the other hand"), and the subsequent "although" emphasizes the disparity between the communally accepted laws and Dimmesdale's reckless transgression. The "But" that begins the next sentence serves to insist that this was no mere transgression; it was worse, a "sin of passion," and the subsequent "not" and "nor" drive the nail in further, noting that the transgression could not be partially acceptable as a "principle" or "purpose." In the final sentence, we see Dimmesdale's internal struggle, the "and" increasing the list of ways he examines himself (with "zeal" and "minuteness"). This internal query is further delineated as Hawthorne notes that Dimmesdale focuses "not" on externals—"his acts," because these can be easily created for appearance—"but" (a contrast to the viewing of acts), instead, his every "emotion," "and" (for further emphasis) "his every thought."

Hawthorne invites contrast and delineation by opposing transitional thoughts. His polar opposite, Ernest Hemingway, nevertheless enlisted transitions just as effectively to underscore not a contrast, but a kind of sameness created via repetition:

> Troops went by the house **and** down the road **and** the dust they raised powdered the leaves of the trees. The trunks of the trees **too** were dusty **and** the leaves fell early that year **and** we saw the troops marching along

the road **and** the dust rising **and** leaves, stirred by the breeze, falling **and** the soldiers marching **and** afterward the road bare **and** white except for the leaves. (3)

In this opening passage from *A Farewell to Arms*, Hemingway underscores the monotonous marching of troops, massed and anonymous, by the repeated use of "and," a coordinating conjunction that yokes together items of equal weight. There is no contrast here, no hierarchy of importance: all is a bludgeoning similarity. This fleshes out Hemingway's portrait of a country whose war has stripped it of life (note the repetition of "dust"), which is further underscored by the use of a "too" which emphasizes that even a symbol of life, the trees, looks no different from the inanimate countryside of dust covered houses and roads.

Transitions, then, carve out niches of thought and detail, as Hawthorne and Hemingway demonstrate, or join larger chunks of writing. The fastidious, careful writer finds in them a complement to the thought process itself.

# Take Note: Teaching Structure Through Song

Song is poetry set to music, a relationship underscored by the use of the term "lyric" in both genres. Their similarity is further underscored in their structural arrangements, the stanzas of poetry corresponding to the verses, chorus, and bridges of music. Their difference, however, lies in their popularity: song seeps into our world via film, radio, TV and CDs; poetry sneaks into the classroom. Perhaps the structure of poetry is most accessible if we understand the similar structures of music.

Popular music is a recent invention. Well into the twentieth century, orchestras entertained the masses with Sousa marches, classical passages, ballads, and perhaps a sprightly folk dance. But New York City's Tin Pan Alley borrowed from those forms and more to create short, lyric-based pieces. Drawing from the rich musical heritage of ethnic-drenched, turn-of-the-century Manhattan, Tin Pan Alley songwriters joined the Italian love of operatic arias and Northern European folk stylings to produce concentrated, repetitive pieces playable on the parlor piano. The popular song appealed to the rising urban middle class.

Its essence is an arrangement of verses and chorus, as in the popular "For Me and My Gal" composed by Edgar Leslie, E. Ray Goetz, and George W. Meyer in 1917:

**Verse 1:**   What a beautiful day, for a wedding in May,
See the people all stare, at the lovable pair.                          A
She's a vision of joy, he's the luckiest boy,
In his wedding array, hear him smilingly say

**Chorus:**   The bells are ringing for me and my gal,
             The birds are singing for me and my gal,
             Everybody's been knowing, to a wedding they're going,
             And for weeks they've been sewing,
                 ev'ry Susie and Sal,
                                                                          B

             They're congregating for me and my gal,
             The Parson's waiting for me and my gal,
             And sometime I'm going to build a little home for two,
             For three or four, or more;
             In Loveland, for me and my gal.

**Verse 2:**  See the relatives there, looking over the pair,
             They can tell at a glance, it's a loving romance,        A
             It's a wonderful sight, as the fam'lies unite,
                 Gee! it makes the boy proud, as he says to the crowd

**Chorus:**   The bells are ringing for me and my gal,
             The birds are singing for me and my gal,
             Everybody's been knowing, to a wedding
                 they're going,
                                                                          B

             And for weeks they've been sewing, ev'ry Susie and Sal,
             (To a wedding they'll be heading)
             They're congregating for me and my gal,
             The parson's waiting for me and my gal,
             And sometime I'm going to build a little home for two,
             For three or four, or more;
             In Loveland, for me and my gal.

This verse-chorus-verse-chorus structure has a shorthand notation: ABAB. We use the same shorthand when breaking down the structure of a poem:

"Sonnet 130"

| | |
|---|---|
| My mistress's eyes are nothing like the sun; | A |
| Coral is far more red than her lip's red; | B |
| If snow be white, why then her breasts are dun, | A |
| If hair be wires, black wires grow on her head. | B |
| I have seen roses damasked, red and white, | C |
| But no such roses see I in her cheeks; | D |
| In some perfumes there is more delight | C |
| Than the breath with which my mistress reeks. | D |
| I love to hear her speak, yet well I know, | E |
| Music hath a far more pleasing sound; | F |
| I grant I never saw a goddess go; | E |
| My mistress, when she walks, treads on the ground. | F |
| And yet, by heaven, I think my love as rare | G |
| As any she belied with false compare. | G |

—William Shakespeare

"Easter Wings"

| | |
|---|---|
| Lord, Who createdst man in wealth and store, | A |
| Though foolishly he lost the same, | B |
| Decaying more and more, | A |
| Till he became | B |
| Most poore: | A |
| | |
| With Thee | C |
| O let me rise, | D |
| As larks, harmoniously, | C |
| And sing this day Thy victories: | C |
| Then shall the fall further the flight in me. | C |
| | |
| My tender age in sorrow did beginne; | D |
| And still with sicknesses and shame | E |
| Thou didst so punish sinne, | D |
| That I became | E |
| Most thinne. | D |
| | |
| With Thee | C |
| Let me combine, | F |
| And feel this day Thy victorie; | C |
| For, if I imp my wing on Thine, | F |
| Affliction shall advance the flight in me. | C |

—George Herbert

The ABAB structure of the popular song has dominated mass culture from piano sheet music to Internet downloads, though specific eras modified it in accordance with changing tastes. As Tin Pan Alley songwriters melded their craft with jazz and Broadway melodies, tunesmiths like Cole Porter, Irving Berlin, and George and Ira Gershwin developed intro sections (traditionally, these openings are slower than the verses and chorus, with a different chord progression) and bridges (musical transitions between verse and chorus). As Broadway reached its peak during the post-World War II era, songwriting teams from Rodgers and Hammerstein to Lerner and Loewe experimented with and expanded the structure of the song. But by the mid-60s, the success of The Beatles, Bob Dylan, and a host of urban musicians encouraged young popsters to explore alternative structures as well. At their best, these musical experiments wed sophisticated formats with the conventions of pop music, as in "Suite: Judy Blue Eyes" by Stephen Stills, "Stairway to Heaven" by Led Zeppelin, or Beach Boy Brian Wilson's "Good Vibrations":

"Good Vibrations"

I, I love the colorful clothes she wears
And the way the sunlight plays upon her hair
I hear the sound of a gentle word                                    A
On the wind that lifts her perfume through the air

I'm pickin' up good vibrations
She's giving me excitations
I'm pickin' up good vibrations
(Oom bop bop good vibrations)
She's giving me excitations                                          B
Oom bop bop excitations)
Good good good good vibrations
(Oom bop bop)
She's giving me excitations
(Oom bop bop excitations)

Close my eyes
She's somehow closer now
Softly smile, I know she must be kind                                A
When I look in her eyes
She goes with me to a blossom world

I'm pickin' up good vibrations
She's giving me excitations
I'm pickin' up good vibrations
(Oom bop bop good vibrations)
She's giving me excitations
(Oom bop bop excitations)                                            B
Good good good good vibrations
(Oom bop bop)
She's giving me excitations
(Oom bop bop excitations)

I don't know where but she sends me there                            C
(Ah my my whole elations)

Gotta keep those lovin' good vibrations
A-happenin' with her
Gotta keep those lovin' good vibrations                              D
A-happenin' with her
Gotta keep those lovin' good vibrations
A-happenin'

I'm pickin' up good vibrations
She's giving me excitations

I'm pickin' up good vibrations
(Oom bop bop good vibrations)                                            B
She's giving me excitations
(Oom bop bop excitations)
Good good good good vibrations
(Oom bop bop)
She's giving me excitations
(Oom bop bop excitations)

Na na na na na
Na na na na na na na
(doo doo)
Na na na na na                                                          E
Na na na na na na na
(doo doo)

[musical exit]                                                          B

Wilson's song was revolutionary when it debuted on AM radios in 1967, eschewing the traditional AABA song structure for an ABABCDBED format that nevertheless held together, pushing the boundaries without sounding strained. Clearly, structure was the key to organizing such disparate musical passages, providing a focus that drew the sections together. But though popular music makes occasional forays into such advanced structures, the more traditional combination of verse and chorus still dominate. Select music from what your students listen to and use it to introduce or reinforce the way structure operates in their own musical worlds, and thereby illustrate how structure is the parlance of all language.

## *Structure*

*And what is form? Form is "achieved content."*

—James Wood

*The structure of a thing is the way it is put together. Anything that has a structure, then, must have parts, properties, or aspects which are somehow related to each other. In every structure we may distinguish the relation or relations, and the items related.*

—Suzanne Langer, *An Introduction to Symbolic Logic*

Students presented with a variety of structures can feel overwhelmed. For that reason, many English programs focus on one or two types. Such stripped down curricula make grading and instruction simpler, particularly when a single format is repeated over several units, even years.

But such a narrow focus has drawbacks. First, it does not teach students the concept of structuring, which, once understood, would enable them to organize their own thinking. They focus instead on reproducing a canned format rather than seeking the structure that would best communicate their ideas. This is important: ideas can be structured in numerous ways, so that students who see varied ways to represent their thinking find a single format frustrating and their expression stunted. If the single format they are predetermined to produce does not accommodate an approach they have developed, they must abandon their thinking or shoehorn their ideas into an ill-fitted format. A more developed teaching approach to structuring emphasizes the relationship between ideas, and students who understand how their ideas connect feel the need to select from a range of structural formats.

I teach four kinds of structure types, arranged by purpose. This illustrates that, though the components of writing are universals, their arrangement depends on the author's intent. And as the student essays on the accompanying CD show, writers often experiment with combinations of structures. Ultimately, the student exposed to a scope and sequence program of varied writing experiences is better able to create and adapt to a wide range of assignments. I present these types here by level of difficulty. A fully developed scope and sequence program presents a variety of structures over a series of levels, so that students are repeatedly reacquainted with the concept of structuring and learn how to expand their repertoire of types.

### By Sequence
Chronologic
Dialectic
Cause-effect

### By Order
Classification
Spatial
Associational
Illustrative

### By Similarity
Comparison
Continuum

### By Contrast
Interwoven
Episodic/fragmented
Pastiche

# *By Sequence*

## Chronologic
## Dialectic
## Cause-effect

Sequential formats are time based, meaning they detail stages or shifts. They trace a character's development or explain how an idea grows in importance. Such structures dominate suggestive pieces, which primarily utilize narratives and anecdotes. But they are also common in informative work, detailing history or a sequence of events. Finally, they aid writers of critical work when documenting the development of a character or idea.

Chronologic structures are among the easiest for a student to master, from the narratives of suggestive writing to the explication of an evolving idea in critical analysis. They are particularly accessible for writers of critical papers, as tracing a thematic or character development requires simply isolating the stages of that progression. Dynamic characters undergo change, and a sequential format explores the stages of that change. Literary themes often undergo development, lending themselves to a chronologic exploration of their evolution. A Shakespearean sonnet, for instance, often follows the structure of an argument, so that an idea stated in the opening quatrain is contrasted or expanded upon in the subsequent quatrains until it finds resolution in the couplet. Detailing the stages of this thematic development makes a compelling argument.

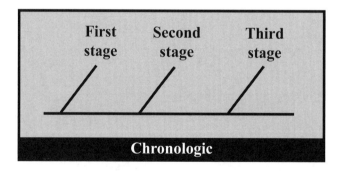

A dialectic structure is based on German philosopher Georg Hegel's explanation of the movement of history. Hegel suggested that an initial condition, a thesis, always creates an opposing condition, an antithesis. The opposing conditions struggle until they yield a kind of compromise, a synthesis. This is the key difference between a chronologic and a dialectic structure: in a dialectic argument, the final stage is a compromise or balance, so that the third stage borrows from the first two. A dialectic structure is particularly effective in analytic arguments when debates move beyond simple dichotomies into more complex areas of discussion.

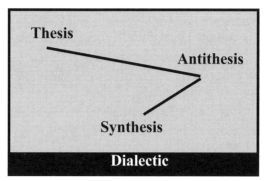

Finally, a cause-effect argument is based on a logical structure: a premise (if) and a conclusion (then). For instance, one might argue that *if* politicians continue to lie to voters, *then* voter turnout will continue to decline. Or, *if* teens begin smoking early in life, *then* quitting will be harder as they grow older. In this way, the writer argues that a final condition is the result of a previous one, so it becomes necessary to trace the movement of one state to the next. A cause-effect structure is useful in all kinds of writing, but it is particularly suitable to critical pieces.

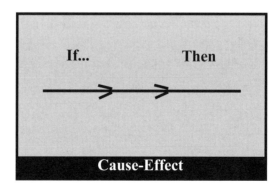

## Sample Outlines

### Chronologic

**Thesis**: The changing symbolism of the scaffold in *The Scarlet Letter* parallels the community's evolving attitude toward sin.

*Point 1*: Hester's public shaming on the scaffold as the novel opens reflects the community's belief that sin must be punished.

*Point 2*: At the novel's midpoint, Dimmesdale ascends the scaffold, where he is joined by Hester and Pearl, their strength soothing his private shame. In this way, the scaffold becomes a place where outcast sinners find community.

*Point 3*: Finally, as Dimmesdale publicly confesses on the scaffold at the novel's end, we see in the townspeople's refusal to condemn him a shift from judging external behaviors to focusing instead on the characters' hearts.

### Dialectic

**Thesis**: Forced into a sequence of different environments, Jane Eyre must confront her flaws in each location before she can find peace.

*Point 1:* Initially Jane is headstrong and independent, often to her own disadvantage.

*Point 2*: After a series of setbacks, Jane flowers under Rochester's love and begins to see herself as desirable.

*Point 3*: Forced to abandon her Romantic ideas after Rochester's confession, Jane retreats emotionally to the safety of St. John's home.

*Point 4*: Only when Jane learns to draw from all the influences in her life is she able to find peace with Rochester and within herself.

### Cause-Effect

**Thesis**: In *Lord of the Flies,* William Golding insists that if the trappings of civilization are removed, mankind will revert to evil.

*Point 1:* Despite their efforts to recreate civilization, the boys fail at building shelter, finding food or establishing a social order.

*Point 2:* As a result of their increasingly chaotic lifestyle, the boys abandon long-range planning for impulsive behaviors that lead to savagery.

## Media and More

Because of their plot-based nature, sequential examples are plentiful. In music, old English ballads like "Barbara Allan" and "Lord Randall" narrate events of former centuries; for a more recent example, download Gordon Lightfoot's "The Wreck of the Edmund Fitzgerald." The folk revival of the 1960s influenced the creation of narratives in pop music, the Beatles producing such fare as "She's Leaving Home," "Norwegian Wood," "Rocky Raccoon," and "The Ballad of John and Yoko."

Movies, plot structured as they are, provide manifold examples of sequential structures. Your students can cite a range of examples, but most Disney films are archetypical journey narratives, from *The Lion King* to *101 Dalmatians* and *Finding Nemo*. Televisions sitcoms and dramas are another rich source of sequential examples.

In *Fact and Artifact: Writing Nonfiction*, Lynn Z. Bloom explains a number of ways to write chronologic pieces, including flashbacks, telescoped events, or alterations between past and present.

The accompanying CD-ROM contains a selection of sequentially structured student work, including "Hola, Abuelo," "My Childhood Trauma," "Best Advice I Ever Heard," "Pretty in Pink," "Tink," "A New Beginning," and "Hospital Visit."

# *By Order*

**Classification**
**Spatial**
**Associational**
**Illustrative**

As students begin working with more abstract ideas, they find structures based on categorization more accessible. These formats identify patterns within a mass of information, arranging the sections by order of importance (classification), physical proximity (spatial), closeness of thought (associational), or metonymy (illustrative). Categorization formats break a concept into smaller parts so as to clarify how the relationship of those parts explains the character of the concept. In effect, these structures provide perspective by examining an idea or character's varied facets, the differing aspects enabling us to see the subject more fully, much like perspective gives depth to a painting

Classification is the most accessible of the ordered formats, the act simply of finding patterns within a mass of material (much like our earlier grouping of marbles). We classify material by finding a common thread among seemingly related items; teasing out that relationship elicits a focal point. We might, for example, look at a room of magazines, comic books, novels, and poetry books and discern that all are different kinds of reading material. We can then argue that the world of literature is divided into categories meant to reach an audience of varying interests.

The notion that connects our categories operates as a golden thread, the idea that is felt throughout the work. Because classification essays are more commonly used in critical writing, there the golden thread is typically stated directly, as with a thesis. But writings organized spatially or associatively can just as easily develop an implied focus,

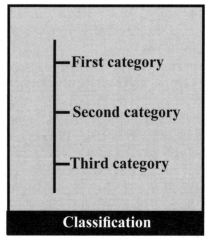

**First category**

**Second category**

**Third category**

**Classification**

so that the golden thread is sensed more than stated. This is the case when a spatial or associational format is used in suggestive writings, as in a memoir or travelogue. Spatially arranged writings may work toward a climax, but they just as easily work by accumulation, details massing like scenes in a tapestry until a full picture emerges.

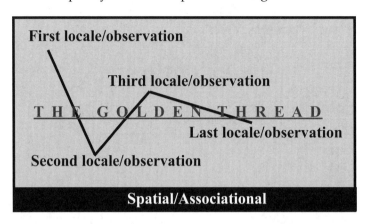

A work whose sections connect more by suggestion than direct statement are organized associatively, the connections more felt than declared. It is the golden thread that holds spatial and associational formats together, for such formats often work atmospherically, sounding more like musings as scenes or ideas seep into each other. They move from observation to observation (or locale to locale), connected by subtle transitions

Spatial structures work well for impressionistic writing, though they can also trace the geographical shifts of a novel for a critical essay (think how *To Kill a Mockingbird* expands geographically from Scout's home to the state of Alabama). It is not uncommon to find writing organized in associative formats in some informative work, but it tends to show up in more experimental writing. Students need to understand the importance of the connecting idea—the golden thread—in such work. When done poorly, categorization formats can sound like lists, and minus some sense of cumulative impact they are ineffectual.

Illustrative formats use a specific example that represents a larger whole. A story, quote, image, or setting is described as emblematic of a larger concept. In a memoir, for instance, a writer might narrate a visit with an ailing relation that developed a philosophy he would live by the rest of his life. A feature article might describe a day in the life of a college student to illustrate the

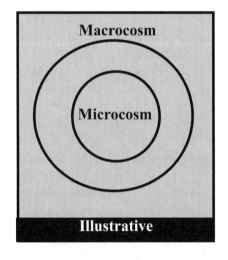

triumphs and travails all college students face. A concert reviewer could cite a moment in a performance that encapsulated the entire evening, and a critical analysis might select a scene from a novel to reveal how it serves as a microcosm for the work as a whole (as does the opening chapter of Ralph Ellison's *Invisible Man*). In this way, illustrative formats are quintessentially inductive writings, the author abstracting a larger idea from a smaller example.

## Sample Outlines

### Categorization

**Thesis**: Earthlings in *The Martian Chronicles* view the culture of Mars in differing ways.

*Point 1:* Many of the first earthlings are indifferent to the history of the Martians.

*Point 2:* Many in the second wave of earthlings are overtly antagonistic toward the Martians.

*Point 3:* Finally, later groups of earthlings become interested in the history and customs of the Martians as they become the new Martians.

### Associational

**Focus**: The items in my room reveal me as artistic and creative.

*Section 1:* My "music center" comprises two synthesizers and a recording deck.

*Section 2:* A variety of impressionist paintings adorns my walls.

*Section 3:* The wallpaper I selected harmonizes in color and theme with the room's furniture.

### Illustrative

**Focus**: McDonald's typifies the changing, fast-paced lifestyle of America.

*Observation 1:* McDonald's production line service reflects the way America has mechanized the work environment.

*Observation 2:* The increasing popularity of the drive-up window reflects our desire for speed over leisure time.

*Observation 3:* The preference of many Americans for the high fat and content of the McDonald's menu echoes our similarly growing interest in stimulating all our senses.

## Media and More

The Beatles again provide a number of songs using applicable formats. "Here, There and Everywhere" is structured by categories while

"Penny Lane" wonderfully illustrates the appeal of a spatially arranged work. The free form nature of John Lennon's later work employs associational structures, as in "Strawberry Fields Forever" and "Tomorrow Never Knows." Finally, Eleanor Rigby's life serves as a microcosm for "all the lonely people" in the song of the same name.

Documentaries often employ categorical structures, and good programs are available from such cable sources as The History Channel, The Learning Channel, Discovery, and A&E. Public television channels feature such documentary programs as *NOVA*, *Frontline*, and *American Experience*.

Student work on the accompanying CD-ROM employing categorical formats includes "My Grandparents' House," "Penafiel," "Apple's A-Peel," "Valley Fair," "Jane Eyre: A Balance of Extremes," "Half-Baked Beauty," "My Rose," "Singapore," and "Identity Begins with Communication."

## By Similarity

*Comparison*
*Continuum*

By comparing similar ideas, we make those ideas more definitive. Henry M. Sayre explains in *Writing about Art* that

> the object is not to list the similarities and differences between the two works for the sake of listing them, but, rather, to reveal, through comparison, important features and traits of the works that would otherwise be lost or obscure. More to the point, the comparison must have a point. (15)

Formats arranged by comparison or on a continuum explore the nuances and aspects of a concept so that we finish the discussion with a clearer notion about that concept. The properties of heat, for instance, make sense only when we have two differing states; by experiencing both hot and cold water, we begin to understand their individual properties as well as the concept of temperature. Such comparisons act like Shakespearean foils: the three father-son relationships in *Hamlet*, for instance, create a discourse on the nature of filial relationships. Structures that compare similarities revolve around a specific idea and give it depth by illustrating its various dimensions. Thus, the point of a comparison format is to clarify a specific concept by seeing it in two contexts.

A continuum has the same purpose but expands the range of contexts. For instance, we might understand the concept of democracy by comparing its development in Classical Athens, the Roman Republic, the court of Henry VIII, and its institution by America's Founding Fathers. Similarly, the nature of parent-child relationships can be explored

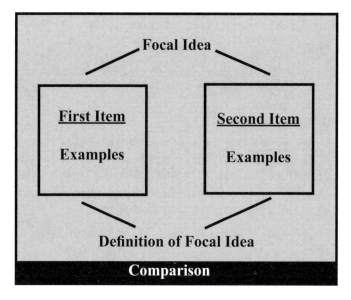

by comparing differing family interactions in *The Joy Luck Club* and *The Chosen*. In these instances, we explore the ideas along a continuum. We might, for instance, make a continuum about politics, placing radicals at the left end of a line, moving right past liberals, moderates, and on toward conservatives and, finally, fascists. This continuum clarifies how government's role is perceived by differing groups. For this reason, the comparison structure is the easiest for students to learn, but more sophisticated discussions employ a continuum.

It is important to teach that formats examining similarities aim toward clarifying a central idea (i.e., a golden thread), so that looking at differing treatments of that concept/thread deepens our knowledge of it. Weak structures ignore the point of comparing the sources, however, focusing instead on only the differences. For instance, writing that fathers in Hispanic culture are more strong-willed than American fathers in American culture

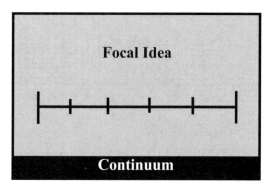

tells us only that there are differences between the two cultures; such an approach tells us nothing about the nature of fatherhood. Unless we use the contrasting information to clarify a specific concept, the argument is merely informative, not analytic. Appropriate for all kinds of writing, formats based on similarity are particularly effective in critical writing because of their nuanced analysis and logic.

## Sample Outlines

### Comparison

**Thesis**: While Sophocles and Shakespeare both wrote of the tragic nature of existence, their treatments reflect differing beliefs about mankind's place in the universe.

*Point 1:* Reflecting the ideas of Classical Greece, Sophocles saw man as limited by his circumstances and unable to surmount them.

*Point 2:* Shakespeare similarly saw man as limited by his circumstances, but reflecting the Renaissance belief in man's elevated place in the universe, his tragic heroes generate more sympathy, admired for their struggle rather than denigrated for their hubris.

### Continuum

**Thesis**: John Steinbeck explores the effects of capitalism on various levels of society in *The Grapes of Wrath.*

*Point 1:* The novel opens with images of centralized, and destructive, power, as bankers in the East destroy the land of the Midwest and dispossess the farmers.

*Point 2:* Steinbeck's portrayal of middle and lower class citizens draws more of our sympathies, as he suggests their kindness and compassion result from their disinterest in power and money.

*Point 3:* Finally, Steinbeck believes the dispossession of some workers encourages revolution, the unemployed and homeless fighting and gathering to gain control over their lives.

*Point 4:* Ultimately, the author argues that capitalism encourages abuse and destroys familial and communal bonds.

## Media and More

"Eleanor Rigby" and John Lennon's "In My Life" compare persons of similar backgrounds. Storylines that explore the effect of a single action on several persons or groups are studies in similarities, as in Arthur Miller's dissection of Puritan paranoia among Salem citizens in *The Crucible.* E.L. Doctorow uses the same technique in much of his historical fiction, most notably in the book, film, and play *Ragtime.*

Many contemporary films utilize comparison structures in more experimental ways, weaving around a single theme the stories of numerous characters who meet only briefly or not at all, as in *Thirteen Conversations About One Thing* or *Things You Can Tell Just By Looking at Her.*

Sample student writing includes "Patriotism: The Perils" and "Religion in *Jane Eyre.*"

# *By Contrast*

**Interwoven**

**Fragmented**

**Pastiche**

Writings that employ strongly contrasting sections attempt to create larger perspectives than the single focus of comparison structures. Comparison formats focus on a specific idea and its similar characteristics or behavior in a variety of contexts. Formats seeking a fuller perspective cast their nets wider, bringing in a range of seemingly disparate ideas. It is not unusual for such writings to employ starkly contrasting styles and sections, as John Steinbeck does with his alternating chapters in *The Grapes of Wrath*. Shifting between the personal story of the Joads and the larger study of Depression Era culture, Steinbeck heightens our awareness of the forces the Joads are contending with, simultaneously increasing our admiration for their fighting spirit. Similarly, such modernist poets as T. S. Eliot advance ideas via jarring juxtapositions, abruptly shifting content, locale, style, and/or tone. Because of their experimental nature, contrasting structures are more plentiful in suggestive work, but they are staples of postmodern journalism as well, from the rants of Hunter S. Thompson to the stylistic experiments of early Tom Wolfe.

Lynn Z. Bloom argues for the power and methodologies of contrasting structures in *Fact and Artifact: Writing Nonfiction*:

> When the elements are assembled in juxtaposition, they reflect and refract on one another to provide a more comprehensive meaning; the whole becomes greater than the sum of its parts. You might juxtapose contrasting elements such as evidence of your subject's stinginess and generosity. You might arrange fragments in chronological or historical order, proceeding from earliest to most recent or the reverse or shifting back and forth in time. (78)

Whereas the sections in other structures are identical in tone and style, those of the interwoven, fragmented, or pastiche variety are deliberately varied, forcing the reader to encounter a wider range of viewpoints and experiences. Because such viewpoints are sharply different, they force us into one of two responses. Having to reconcile views we formerly considered incompatible, we might realign our thinking, reconsidering the viability of ideas we once dismissed. Or—in a typically postmodern response—we might, forced to confront irreconcilables, retreat from the debate, perhaps believing the resolution is beyond us, perhaps believing no solution exists.

Brenda Miller recognizes the strength, and the universality, of such

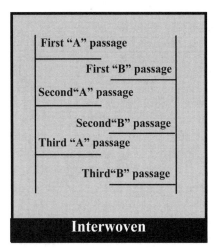

structures when she describes the lyric essay in "A Braided Heart: Shaping the Lyric Essay":

Writers like Seneca, Bacon, Sei Shonagon in the tenth century, Montaigne, hundreds of others: all could be said to write essays whose forms were inherently lyric; that is, they did not necessarily follow a linear, narrative line. Many excellent writers and thinkers have tried to pin down the lyric essay, defining it as a collage, a montage, a mosaic. It's been called disjunctive, paratactic, segmented, sectioned. All of these recognize in the lyric essay a tendency toward fragmentation that invites the reader into those gaps, that emphasizes what is unknown rather than the already articulated known.

The fragmented structure, a staple of modern poetry, eliminates transitions, juxtaposing sections with a dreamlike logic; indeed, the psychologically influenced surrealists favored fragmented discussions, suggesting they were closer to the foundation of human thought than the refined expressions of polished poetry or prose. This was an idea that Jack Kerouac and Allan Ginsberg popularized during the Beat movement of the 1950s. In much of his work, T.S. Eliot used fragmented structures to reflect the disjointed experiences of daily life as in "The Love Song of J. Alfred Prufrock." As that and other modern works evidence, fragmented structures shift in

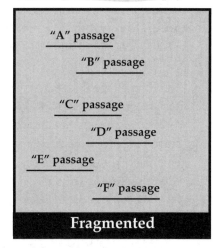

time and space, but the voice/style of the author remains largely consistent.

By contrast, the pastiche style is a mélange of varied voices and perspectives. The pastiche format is an extension of the interwoven, simply bringing in more than two contrasting sections. Tom Romano, in *Writing with Passion: Life Stories, Multiple Genres*, argues that multigenre papers force students to see a discussion from a variety of vantages and experience it in a number of ways, from the factual to the impressionistic. As Romano explains, such a construction may include passages of poetry, memoir, narrative, historical research, newspaper headlines, etc. Such bold shifts—characteristic of John Dos Passos in his *USA Trilogy*—jar us out of our familiar thinking, compelling us to probe more deeply for a universal connection.

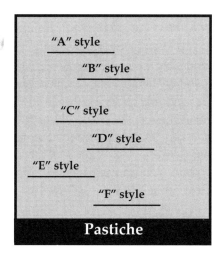

Despite the seeming difficulty of these structures, many students enjoy them, and some even excel at them. Though they may not be a department's choice for beginning writers, they nevertheless offer students additional approaches to a discussion, what William Faulkner might have referred to as thirteen ways of looking at a blackbird.

## Sample Outlines

### Interwoven

**Focus**: The ways boys and girls prepare for a dance.

*Section 1*: Set in a girl's bedroom, where a young woman and her friends are getting ready. Stylistic emphasis is on recording their conversations.

*Section 2*: Shift to the boys washing their car in the driveway. No conversation: we simply observe their behavior.

*Section 3*: Back to the girls, posing for pictures before the boys arrive.

*Section 4*: Shift again to the boys, gathering up corsages and piling into the car.

*Section 5*: The meeting of the two groups at the girls' house. The girls chatter; the boys look down and smile.

### Pastiche

**Focus**: Life at the mall.

*Section 1*: Employees arriving at the back doors of their stores. Focus on descriptive detail.

*Section 2*: A record of the music and announcements echoing through the mall before shoppers enter.

*Section 3*: In the offices of security guards, where the director reads announcements.

*Section 4*: Recorded snippets of conversation from entering shoppers.

*Section 5*: Detailed description of a homeless man outside the parking lot, holding a sign.

## Media and More

By the mid-1960s, The Beatles began writing songs whose verses and choruses were strong contrasts, including "We Can Work It Out," "Dr. Roberts," and "Lucy in the Sky with Diamonds." These experiments increased as the foursome experimented with more fragmented and pastichelike structures in "Happiness is a Warm Gun," "A Day in the Life," and the closing numbers on *Abbey Road*. The 1960s and 1970s were a heyday for experimental structures in rock music, from The Beach Boys's "Good Vibrations" to Led Zeppelin's "Stairway to Heaven," "A Quick One While He's Away" by The Who, and the infamous "Bohemian Rhapsody" by Queen.

Because contrasting structures abound in postmodern culture, experimental movies are plentiful. In addition to the films mentioned in the previous section, consider *Adaptation, Thirty Films about Glenn Gould, Possession, Traffic, Rashomon,* and *21 Grams,* among many others.

These experiments in perspective are common in the work of novelists like James Joyce (*Portrait of the Artist as a Young Man*), William Faulkner (*The Sound and the Fury*), Milan Kundera (*The Unbearable Lightness of Being*), and Toni Morrison (*Beloved*).

Sample student work utilizing experimental structures includes "Bean Soup for the Soul" and "It's All Relative."

# *Student Samples*

### *Bean Soup for the Soul* by Jennifer Chapski

> *What I must do is all that concerns me, not what the people think.*
>
> —Ralph Waldo Emerson, *Self-Reliance*

I met the Bean Counters in preschool.

They introduced me to the Bean Tray.

It was a simple concept. On the Bean Tray were two bowls, one filled with black beans, the other with white. Each day, we took turns at the Bean Tray Table. It was here that we learned to count: we counted beans. I, however, was a bright child. The envy of my peers, I could count to 100 effortlessly at the tender age of three. I thus deemed bean counting tedious and unnecessary.

I clearly articulated this point to my teachers; nevertheless, I was assigned the obligatory fifteen minutes—eternity to a three-year-old—with the Bean Tray. I had no intention of displeasing my teachers, so I counted 100 beans. I then counted the 100 beans backwards as I returned them to their designated bowls. That showed I knew how to count but left me with about ten minutes. I was bored, but I knew I would not be permitted to leave the Bean Tray. So, I decided to amuse myself by pretending to be a cook. I unknowingly proceeded to do the forbidden: I mixed the black and white beans together to make bean soup.

My teacher soon discovered my transgression, and I was duly punished. I had to separate the black and white beans I had mixed, picking each individual bean out of the giant Bean Bowl. I'd broken a cardinal rule: beans were for counting, not making soup.

**Bean Counter Theorem #1:** *Beans are that which cannot be divided for any purpose other than existing as beans. The bean is complete unto itself, and thus allows for no division or opposition.*

As the years progressed, I encountered several variants of the Bean Counter Theorem, for, as I have found, Bean Counters prevail in every aspect of life.

At my elementary school, there was no institution more intrinsic, more indispensable to daily existence than The Line. If the children were restricted to the confines of a perfectly straight line, teachers reasoned, childlike exuberance would be suppressed, thus minimizing disorder. As a result, everything we did was done in lines.

When the bell rang in the morning and school began, we were not allowed to simply gather at the classroom door; we had to line up before we went inside. Likewise, when the bell rang for recess, we could not just leave; we had to line up first. There was a boys' line and a girls' line, and whichever line was the straightest and quietest got to go outside first. Whenever the class walked anywhere—be it to church on First Fridays or simply to our next class—we had to be in lines. If the lines were not straight, the class was reprimanded; God help the unfortunate child who fell out of formation.

The irony of it all was that the submissive obedience mandated by The Line simply made the children want to rebel, which defeated the Line's very purpose. The control the teachers were trying to achieve via The Line was at cross purposes with the natural energy of children.

A common scenario when dealing with Bean Counters.

**Bean Counter Axiom #49:** *Disorder—marked by the loss of control over one's environment—is not to be tolerated. As the natural tendency of order is toward disorder, it is imperative that unleashed energy be corralled and remolded into an orderly state.*

Bean Counters continued to affect my life throughout junior high as well. In seventh grade, I became extremely bored with school. My teachers had a tendency to reduce complexities into formulas, making the marvelous into the mundane. I wasn't being encouraged to question, to challenge, to *think*. And I was a little suspicious.

So I started reading the encyclopedia.

It began unintentionally. I was thumbing through volume 21 of *World Book* looking for information on West Virginia for a report. Suddenly, I realized there were lots of interesting things that began with W. I read the entire article on Frank Lloyd Wright and immediately harbored an ardent (albeit short-lived) desire to be an architect. I read about whales (and Wales). Warsaw, Poland. Watergate. Andy Warhol. The Whiskey Rebellion of 1794. I even read the inordinately long (twelve pages) article on wheat. About two hours had passed before I finally found West Virginia and wrote my report. Reading the encyclopedia soon became a daily activity. I was learning interesting things they didn't spare time for in school.

> **Bean Counter Postulate #128:** *The shortest distance between the end and beginning of an essay is a straight line, which means you should ignore all the curious little diversions in between (like the difference between a blue and a humpbacked whale).*

More recently, I've had to deal with yet another type of Bean Counter. As a volunteer for the March of Dimes Birth Defects Foundation, I lobby state legislators for passage of March of Dimes-sponsored bills. I am trying to be a voice for people who are less fortunate than I. Yet, the first time I lobbied, I discovered I faced opposition. A legislator told me that what I was trying to achieve was a good idea, but it would cost far too much money and was therefore impractical. This struck me as incredibly illogical. What's more important, money or the life of a child?

Typical Bean Counter reasoning. He was only thinking of the beans.

> **Bean Counter Corollary #63:** *Do you promise to support the bean, the whole bean, and nothing but the bean, and forswear to use the bean for any purpose other than propagation of the bean?*

As I approach college life, I look back to see the pervasiveness of Bean Counters and their philosophies. They permeate politics, seep into social issues, and clutter up the classroom. And I have tired of them. What I desire, where I aim to spend my college years, is that environment that sees beyond the bottom line of the bean, that is not threatened by the curious and the creative, that understands—as with encyclopedias and soups— that the complexity of our existence is rarely reducible to the bean, or the formulations of the Bean Counters.

Because I am not a bean counter. I make soup.

## *Penafiel* by Katie Giebler

The gypsies are out and about, running errands early one Penafiel morning.

A cluster of old women bundled in exotic silks of deep burgundies and violets chatter in Spanish as they crowd into the minuscule bakery store on the corner of the alley. There, the women choose from steaming pastries drizzled with glaze and oozing with fruit jam, and cakes topped with fresh strawberries and kiwi embedded in mounds of creamy, vanilla icing like snowy peaks on mountaintops. Soon after, eight-year-olds on their way to school clamber inside the quiet bakery with a few coins in their hot, tiny hands for a warm, sticky, cinnamon roll speckled with sugary raisins.

Two alleys away, a boisterous roar of laughter echoes from outside the village bar. A handful of roguish Spanish men circle around a table, involved in deep conversation, passionately throwing their arms in the air in exasperation to make a point in their complicated argument. Thin, cotton shirts barely button over their round bellies like sausages ready to burst out of their casings. Broad chests reveal wisps of gray and white hairs that tremble when they chuckle. Across the cobblestone street, an ongoing line is already forming this early in the morning at the famous candy shop.

Sweat glistens on the poor cashier's brow as he struggles to fulfill every child's order from the myriad kinds of candy. Children of all ages elbow their way to the front to get the best candy before it is gone. Endless shelves go on as far as the eye can see, a fascinating array of red, yellow, and green-colored candies. The village favorite is the foot-long, watermelon flavored gummy candies, sparkling with sugar that melts in your mouth the instant your tongue caresses it. Root beer bottle candy is popular, surprisingly as sweet and bubbly as old-fashioned root beer soda.

Enveloping the stores and shops is the residential area, housing the small population of 5000 inhabitants. Penafiel houses tower above the village folk, standing nearly 60 feet tall. Because none of the houses is built horizontally, people strain their necks from their windows to engage in boisterous conversation with neighbors, illustrating a skill unmatched anywhere else. Not one shred of the sun's rays permeates the streets of this village, due to these gargantuan houses. Garments, dresses, and trousers dangling from balconies to dry like puppets dancing in the wind create a soothing and rippling contrast to the rigid buildings. Servants dressed in starched, striped uniforms step outside their front doors to beat rugs free of their dust, as the particles diffuse and glimmer in the sunlight.

It is an hour after sunset when lights shine in an ancient, lonely castle sitting atop its knoll, ruling over the landscape as a symbol of the military construction that kept watch over the movement of the Moors. This stoic, grave edifice stands in contrast to the warmth and liveliness of the inhabitants of the village. Lights in the castle create a magical glow over the whole village similar to a distant star.

Penafiel never sleeps; the celebrating and feasting last into the warm nights. Persistent babble emanates from restaurants, wineglasses still clink, and the rhythm of the pulsing music in the discotheques palpitates throughout the village.

There are no horizons on the dry moorland on the village of Penafiel. Summer sends its winds, which wave under a sky of cinnabar. This magical place with its mystical, gypsy inhabitants makes one spellbound; wishing that one could escape to Spain and be a Latin gypsy for the night.

## *Memories from the Mosque* by Huma Attari

A man calls out, "Allah-o-akbar, Allah-o-akbar," signifying the start of prayer.

Fancy terminology would define the guy as a muezzin, someone who calls the prayer, but I like to refer to him as one of my dad's friends. And in an even more typical assumption, my dad's friend would be in a minaret, saying *adhan*, the call to prayer, generally disturbing the neighbors with the deep, solemn words. It does not look like the typical mosques that can be seen on "20/20" specials reporting about the elusive, exotic Middle East. Instead, the mosque, or SABA Center, affectionately dubbed the Center, is a regular building. Its light coral, stone-studded walls with splashes of white paint covering recent graffiti blend indiscriminately with Walgreens to the right and the Christian Child Care Center to the left.

People are streaming into the building: men go to one side and women to the other. As a common cultural practice, men and women are segregated; and if it complete segregation is some sort of religious practice, I wonder what Quran they're reading. As people scurry inside they grab one of the multitudes of prayer rugs that are shaded in various bright reds, greens, yellows, and oranges from a black metal cabinet near the door. They are rolled down against the gray carpet. The original color had been a light gray, but repeated spillage of tea, Coke, and food has made parts of the carpet permanently dark gray. Or maybe it was a light gray—you can never tell.

The prayer has started. Everyone goes through the same motions in unison: bowing, kneeling, standing, and genuflecting. A few people who have been running late quickly bow and kneel, trying to catch up with the rest. From an outside perspective, all the kneeling and bowing seems to be some sort of distorted exercise, a mix of Pilates and stretches. And in a sense, it's true. The prayer is an exercise, with infinite and deep meaning behind the Arabic words. The same Arabic words that people have recited for thousands of years. Once it has ended, everyone joins hands and recites a *dua*, a small prayer, which asks for unity and peace. Only half the people that usually come are here: two weeks ago, a majority of the people voted that the resident *alim*, or priest, be kicked out for general incompetence and a misunderstanding of a $25,000 donation (the *alim* thought it was his to distribute). After much ranting and raving the resident *alim* left, taking half the Center population with him. It looks like we won't be needing to build a bigger Center after all.

*Dua* ended, people start to fold their prayer rugs, some precisely and others with little care. Then they are all shoved back into the black cabinet and stacked haphazardly: the next person who takes something out will have an avalanche of prayer rugs fall on them. My prayer rug dutifully shoved in, I turn and greet my friends and sit down with them, far away from the front, where no aunties (the title of respect given to anyone older than 29) can yell at us to be quiet, but not so far back that we're near the bathroom, where the sickly sweet smell of floral air freshener wafts through occasionally. As I make myself comfortable I am asked if I'm coming tomorrow. "If my parents make me," I quip. We all roll our eyes in agreement and share the common suffering of being dragged to the mosque, especially when there's a new episode of "Roswell" or "Dawson's Creek" on TV. I slightly zone out as my friends argue who's better: 'N SYNC, Backstreet Boys, or Tupac. 'N SYNC seems to be winning. Around me, little children are running around in circles, banging anything that causes loud noises, while their mothers comment to anyone who will listen about how much their child has grown and has become a nuisance. It is a common topic between mothers to complain about their children one minute, and in the same breath brag about them.

A little kid, I don't know how old (all I can tell is that he is young), runs up to my circle of friends and stands there on wobbly knees, hands stretched out for balance, with a bewildered, confused expression on his face, as if to ask, "What are you doing here?" We all smile indulgently at him and tickle his stomach, and the conversation regarding whether-or-not-Justin-Timberlake-can-be-called-cute-with-that-afro     continues. My friend, Farha, gently turns the little kid around, and as he hesitantly leaves, she turns and declares that Justin is one of the ugliest guys she has ever seen, worse than the guys at the Center. The Justin Supporters quickly and loudly protest; to be called uglier than the guys at the Center is one of the worst things that one can say. But fact is fact: most guys at the Center are pathetic losers. If one declared, as one Center boy did, his life intention to work at 7-11 for the free slurpies and marry a well-endowed Mexican woman and still expect everyone to like and be proud of him, one can only conclude that he is a pathetic loser.

Despite potential embarrassment, the boys seem to do exactly what their mommies don't want them to do. All the girls joke about poor, unfortunate Reza, who went to the Winter Ball, only to have his mother come in and drag him off by the ear when she saw that he was dancing (with a girl, no less!). As if their inability to say a sentence without swearing and the fact that their pseudo-ghettoish clothes (the kind you see in rap videos) are supposed to impress everybody isn't enough, their lack of intelligence is beyond comparison. One Center guy said, and I quote, "I'd rather fail algebra than do geometry because I've heard it's hard." A common debate between friends, we can't decide what's worse: their lack of appearance, personality, or intelligence. As Farha so nicely put it, "It's guys like that who make women lesbians."

Though not factually true, looking at the guys at my mosque makes one really wonder about the validity of the statement. The Justin Supporters are still talking about how he is not like the guys at the Center, when an auntie turns around, glares, tells us to be quiet and pay attention. In unison, we roll our eyes, mutter a few choice words, and turn to face the front and listen to what the speaker is saying (something about how the Taliban in Afghanistan is a distortion of true Islam). Dutifully listening I notice the auntie herself is talking. Nudging my friend, I jerk my head toward the auntie who is gossiping to her friend about how so-and-so auntie did this and that and ohmygod, can you believe she did that too? My friends and I give each other disgust-filled looks, mouthing, "Damn the hypocritical aunties." Maybe we should tell them to be quiet, but no, you can never tell someone older than you what to do. Resigned, we start whispering, only to have the gossiping auntie and her friend turn around, and glare at us to be quiet. Zahra waves as they stare. They cluck their tongues and turn back around, commenting to each other about how they were once good, obedient children, and never talked during a sermon. "My teenage son is so obedient and good, thank God, and what are these girls doing these days?" Another woman joins in, talking about how these girls always talk, and where are their mothers who should be controlling them? I then see her child running round in circles, hitting people, slapping the television screen (the speaker is on the men's side, and there is a television hook-up so the women can see and hear the speaker), and shouting baby words at the top of his voice.

The speaker's voice is grave as he announces a current event: Fifteen people in Pakistan, while in a mosque, were killed by hand grenades thrown into the building. Heavy, shocked silence fills the room. The only sound is the little children running around; they soon quiet down as they sense something is wrong. Everyone looks around in disbelief, and all experience the pain of knowing that people were murdered, quite possibly for their beliefs, the same belief we have.

Despite the hypocritical aunties and pathetic boys, we are all a close-knit community. Together, we all pray for the ones murdered.


### *It's All Relative* by **Audrey Erpelding**

> *"It's too scary for me."*

> *"I think it's hardest on my mom; she cries every night."*

*"I've just avoided as much news as possible. "*

*"If you support the war or not, what about the troops?"*

*"It's hard not knowing."*

Our parents had Vietnam.

Our grandparents, World War II. So, is it a shock that our generation must deal with war?

Maybe it's just a shock for me.

He is twenty-four years old, tall, dark, and handsome, a second lieutenant in the Air Force. He's my brother.

I've always been supportive of Dave's dream to become an Air Force pilot. When he enrolled at the Academy, I was more than supportive and happy to meet his fellow, clean-shaven cadets in blue. My priorities have since changed. With the constant news developments in the War on Iraq, I can't help wonder what the repercussions will be for Dave.

**Newsflash:** AT LEAST 148 COALITION DEATHS CONFIRMED IN THE WAR

> *I see the other families that have had sons or daughters die, and it's hard to think that I could get a call from my aunt saying that my cousin has died.*
> —*senior Sara Frausto on cousin Robert*

It doesn't really hit you until it affects someone you love. Death is incomprehensible. I've been raised to believe that you live your life, and hopefully, at a ripe old age, you pass on to the next. I can't understand why men and women my age would want to jeopardize their lives. It's difficult to understand why Dave is so passionate about the military. He and his friends think they are invincible. They're not. But I guess if you're to survive in the armed forces, you need that frame of mind.

Every day, I see soldiers on the news who aren't much older or younger than myself. I think of people like Pfc. Jessica Lynch. She's nineteen-years old. I grab my *Newsweek* magazine and think, "She looks like someone I would have been friends with." Except that she's experienced more in our one-year age difference than I will probably experience in ten, twenty years. I don't think I would have lasted in her situation. I'm amazed at the courage and the strength of Jessica and all our soldiers, but at the same time it feels unfair that we must test their limits.

**Newsflash:** 250,000 AMERICAN AND BRITISH TROOPS HAVE BEEN DEPLOYED

> *To me, the biggest frustration is that [my brother is] National Guard. He's supposed to be holding guns at airports. They're not supposed to be sent overseas for undisclosed amounts of time.*
> —*science teacher Suzanne Lyons on brother Nathan*

Dave graduates from pilot school this May. If he gets his requested "training pilot" position, he'll stay in a quiet, safe little border town— Del Rio, Texas—for at least another year. If not....I hate the unknown. It's somewhat comforting to know that right now he's flying planes over flat lands in the states rather than overseas. I know that he's excited about the war, and that's probably where he wants to be right now. Dave would be flying for military missions and not studying for check flights.

**Newsflash:** MORE TROOPS EXPECTED TO BE SENT OVERSEAS

> *[Michael] has two guys who have volunteered to take his place if he does get called out, and with the camaraderie of the military men, for him, he's tremendously humbled, but also feeling, "That's not right." So, he's now torn, thinking, "If I do get called it is my turn to serve. I signed on the dotted line to do that."*
> *—religious studies teacher Sharon Bouska on future son-in-law Michael*

In times of conflict, heroes appear in the most unexpected places. There are many men and women like those who offered to take Michael's place.

It's comforting to walk around campus and see the yellow ribbons adorning trees. I remember seeing them for the first time. My dad was pulling into the parking lot one morning. He smiled and simply said, "That's nice. I'm glad you guys are doing that." Those ribbons are a constant reminder that although there is so much conflict in the world, there is hope for peace.

**Newsflash:** CARE PACKAGES BOUND FOR THE TROOPS

> *It was cool because there were a variety of views on the war, but it didn't matter. We were there for one cause: supporting the troops.*
> *—sophomore Dina Yacoub*

Lotion, lip balm, socks, and lollipops. That's what I'm in charge of. Finally, there is something I can do here and feel like I've made a difference. Social Studies teacher Amy Fields decided to start a school-wide effort to gather goods and forgotten necessities and combine them to create care packages for our troops in Iraq. "It was the students [who inspired me to start this program]," she said.

Isn't that all that matters? Signs hang in the halls with messages of peace and hope for a swift homecoming. Moments of silence between classes and after school. Yellow ribboned pins passed around in homeroom. Whether or not students are in support of the war, they support the troops.

## Lesson Ideas

- **Toys**: Scatter a number of games and toys on the classroom floor (checkers, jacks, pick-up sticks, cards, marbles, dice, etc.) and have students determine different ways they can categorize them.

- **Spices**: Pour a variety of spices into small cups and place on a table in front of the class. Ask students to smell, look at, and, if possible, taste each spice. Then they should generate a list of characteristics for each one, sharing their lists with the class.

- **Music**: Explaining that most pop music involves some combination of verses and choruses, play any current or past popular song, students following along with a lyric sheet (online sites such as www.lyrics.com provide downloadable lyrics; additionally, most performers have websites with lyrics). Have students indicate on the lyric sheet when verses shift into choruses or other musical passages. Playing two or three selections, direct students to explain how songs differ in their structures.

- **Magazines**: For homework, tell students to pick up copies of two magazines. Then, scanning the table of contents of one, they should provide a written explanation for how the magazine is organized. After doing the same with the second magazine, they explain in writing how the structures of the two publications are similar and different.

- **Architecture**: Using slides, posters, or calendar shots, pin up pictures of buildings whose construction differs. Engage students in a discussion on how the buildings differ in design and how each design carries out its building's function.

- **Structuring Movies**: I use the following worksheet to prepare students for structuring critical essays. Drawing off their knowledge of popular films, the exercise (which can be worked on in groups or solo) provides an easy entrance to structuring by pulling from areas students feel more comfortable with.

Effective writing requires specificity in phrasing: word choice, syntax, and tonal variation. Chapter 6 explains how style is the conscious choice of specific language and expression.

This exercise will acquaint you with several approaches to structuring your material for a critical essay. Working in a small group, discuss any movies you have seen and group your ideas about them in the structures below. For each movie you select, determine a focal idea and sections. For instance, for "Classification," your focus might be the kinds of heroes in *The Lord of the Rings*, each section listing a different kind of hero.

**Classification**: Places information in categories.

*Focus*: Kinds/types of _____

    1.

    2.

    3.

**Chronologic**: Places sections in a sequence of time.

    *Focus*: The stages/development of _____

    1.

    2.

    3.

**Dialectic**: Places sections in a sequence of time, but the third item is a compromise of, or balance between, the first two.

*Focus*: Kinds/types of _____

    1.

    2.

    3.

**Cause-Effect**: Places information in an "if...then" sequence, emphasizing how one condition produces a final result. Your focus should be a particular condition or idea that follows from another action or condition.

*Focus*: How _____ is developed/created.

   1.

   2.

   3.


**Comparison**: A single idea is discussed as it appears in two, similar contexts. The intent is to show how that idea takes on perspective when we see it from two angles.

   *Focus*: How we understand or define _____

   1.

   2.

   3.


**Continuum:** Discuss a single idea as it is represented by a range of events or characters. An extension of a comparison approach, a continuum helps us understand an idea or concept after having studied several examples of it.

   *Focus*: How we understand or define _____

   1.

   2.

   3.

# Chapter 6

# Developing Voice:
# Rhetoric and Poetics

---

**Focus**: Style is the crafting of phrases, pinning down of specifics, and selection of elements that maximize a passage's meaning and aesthetic potential.

---

**Sections:**
- Diction
   - Denotation and Connotation
   - Wordplay
- Syntax
   - Literary Faux Pas
   - Sentence Patterns
   - Punctuation
   - Reading for Punctuation
   - Editing and Revision
- Tone: Detection and Employment
   - Humor and Tone
   - Humor Types
- Writing Assignments
- Imagery, Tightening and Editing: A Sample
- Student Samples
- Resources
- Lesson Ideas

*In fact, the special qualities of writing are best understood when seen as changes in phrasing, sentence structure, and organization made, precisely, in order to adjust to the loss of vocal and facial expression, gesticulation, feedback, collaboration, and the other characteristics of conversation.*

—James Moffett, *Teaching the Universe of Discourse*

*Experiment. Be dangerous. Play with words, mixing the curt
with the lofty. Play with chains of words. Play with phrases
and clauses and dashes and full stops. Mix short and long, neat
and nasty.*

—Constance Hale, *Sin and Syntax*

When Andy Warhol's "Campbell Soup Can" drew critical applause, a California grocer cheekily stacked a pyramid of cans outside his store next to a sign reading, "Buy the real thing." The intended slap at pop art pleased Warhol, whose purpose wasn't solely to create art. He'd wanted to create a dialogue: about what art is and isn't, about commercialization, aesthetics, values, shifting focus away from elitism and onto the world of the mundane.

Pop art targeted the complacency of "looking," the way habit deadens our senses so that we fail to see the world afresh. If Roy Lichtenstein's giant clothespin, standing nakedly in a downtown Philadelphia square, arrested our attention and provoked comment, well, that was the point. And like Clause Oldenberg's toilet or Wayne Thiebaud's mechanical replications of plates of pie, pop art reproduced the common so that we saw it differently or, perhaps, saw it as if for the first time: its form, color, design, and function.

In this manner, pop art parallels the strategies of rhetoric and poetics, which instruct us in writing not the merely serviceable, but the provocative and emotive. For the prosaic writer, words are no more than functional; for the stylist, they are kinetic. Put another way, the former values the denotative; the latter, the connotative. At its most powerful, language is transcendent, suggestive. It is oriented not toward the thing itself, but toward what the thing hauls with it into the mind's eye. Warhol was not

concerned with the soup can; he was concerned with what the soup can made his audience think.

The Greeks defined rhetoric as the act of making speech persuasive, and poetics as the art of making language beautiful. These are conscious manipulations of the written material, the treating of words to produce effects beyond their one dimensionality. Language resonates as we utilize rhetorical devices to produce intended effects. Rhetoric and poetics, then, are the art of achieving predetermined effects through conscious manipulation of language.

Dividing this chapter into the categories of diction, syntax, and tone,

I range wide across the field here, covering punctuation, phrasing, sentence patterns, style, and voice, in order to argue that these areas are united by their common emphasis on the elevation of language from the functional to the effective. I also focus less on a sequential approach to their instruction than on weaving them into the curriculum. And they are taught best, I believe, when integrated directly into student composition rather than via drills unconnected to simultaneous writing.

# *Diction*

*A simple list of words makes up a vocabulary; the accurate, careful **use** of these words in discourse makes good **diction**.*
—C. Hugh Holman, *A Handbook to Literature*

*Words, words, words.*
—William Shakespeare, *Hamlet* (II.ii.192)

*In the beginning was the word.*
—John 1:1

A love of writing begins with a love for words. Dictionaries, repositories of culture and heritage, explain how thought evolves. And the thesaurus illustrates how English hybridized and bastardized other languages until it contained myriad shades of meaning, allowing nuance and subtlety of expression.

Words operate in dialogue with thought: what we conceive of only exists when we have words to express it. Similarly, a fine knowledge of words enables clarity. The point of vocabulary is not to pass the SAT; the point is to sharpen thinking.

Here's a tale: Centuries ago, excavators unearthed caverns under the city of Rome. Beneath the Roman streets they found art, rural and primitive, detritus of a folk culture. The small caves, called grottoes, were filled with the stuff, but it was art that offended the sensibilities of contemporary critics, who, seeking to designate the sublevel quality of the work, called it "grottoesque." Time shortened the word to "grotesque," a description we have applied to ogres, war, fascism, torture, violent film imagery, and social beliefs. This is how we dialogue with words.

In 1986, Rich Hall released the first of two compilations of fabricated words called *Sniglets*. A few of the excerpts:

> *Aquadextrous*: adj. Possessing the ability to turn the bathtub faucet on and off with your toes. (10)

*Expressholes*: n. People who try to sneak more than the "eight items or less" into the express checkout line. (31)

*Kedophobia*: n. The fear of having one's sneakers eaten by the teeth on the escalator. (46)

This is how we play with words, altering, bending, and redefining them to suit our thinking. They are bred of sounds and fury, dead languages, and street culture. Prescriptive grammarians tell us which words to use and when to use them—France has its Academy, which legislates language. Fine and well. But language evolves: it lives and words are birthed, have their moment, and die. Courtiers once plucked raisins from a bowl of ignited brandy, a game called "flap dragon"; "bellytimber" once referred to food; a person as rotund as a pig was branded a "porknell"; and heretics burned at the stake were "firefanged," a phrase derived from overcooking barley or cheese. Such words sound alive despite their passing.

Words are exactors, measurers of meaning. Perhaps a rose is a rose is a rose, but a dock is not a wharf is not a pier—the first is the body of water next to the wharf or pier, the second is the wooden structure that hugs the shore and boats tie up to, where they "dock," and the third is a wharf that extends into the water, perpendicular to the shore. When we demand specifics using concrete language, we are insisting on exactness—the term or phrase that is most fitting, the most apt. The more precise, the more we bring the light of thought into befuddling darkness.

So words are not the purview of vocab worksheets, language exams, spelling quizzes, or drills. They are the verbalization of thought, the breath of insight. Revel in them.

## Denotation and Connotation

The effective use of diction lies in distinguishing between a word's denotative and connotative meanings.

The stripped down poetry of the early twentieth century Imagist movement illustrates this sensitivity to the suggestibility of language. In the writing of William Carlos Williams, Hilda Doolittle, Ezra Pound, W. H. Auden, and others, we feel the impact of phrasing that relies on connotation. Note the way Gary Young uses images to create theme and mood in "In August":

> The tangled chimes made little music as the wind picked up;
> It was warm and the small, hard persimmons were still
> green in the swaying branches of the tree.
> Nothing moved in the windows. Yellow poppies
> closed as the light was dimming, and somewhere jasmine was
>     in bloom.
> The breeze reached the rabbits in their pens and settled them.

> The sky was empty of any bird. All things needing rest rested,
> and there were nine of us sitting silently at the table
> sharing the same air that washed over and passed on.

Young combines a tone of calm ("The tangled chimes made little music"; "Nothing moved in the windows"; "The sky was empty of any bird"; "The breeze reached the rabbits…and settled them"; "nine of us were sitting silently") with that of anticipation: "the wind picked up"; persimmons are gestating ("still green"), and "jasmine was in bloom." August comes at the height of summer but anticipates fall, and the poem reinforces this theme of transition in the image of poppies that close "as the light was dimming" and in the picture of the "same air" that washes over the diners and passes on. "In Autumn" is a compressed narrative, depicting the impact of nature's shift on the land and the family sheltered inside—"at the table"—as "all things needing rest rested." This is show-not-tell language, Young employing images to convey his mood and theme.

Like late nineteenth-century European painting, modernist poetry was influenced by Japanese landscapes as depicted in the nation's art and writing. The centuries-old tradition of haiku—three-line arrangements of fixed syllable counts—relied on the connotative, image-based depiction of the natural world, as in the work of the seventeenth century writer, Basho:

> From all directions
> Winds bring petals of cherry
> Into the grebe lake.

> Sleep on horseback,
> The far moon in a continuing dream,
> Steam of roasting tea.

> The sea darkens;
> the voices of the wild ducks
> are faintly white.

> Ill on a journey;
> my dreams wander
> over a withered moor.

Haiku works on the development, modulation, or juxtaposition of images. This stripping down of expression to the elemental image parallels trends in modernist painting, as in the work of Pablo Picasso, whose minimally sketched *Don Quixote* captured the frail yet proud stance of Cervantes's hero. The artwork recalls the artistic proclamation of Stephen Daedalus from James Joyce's *A Portrait of the Artist as a Young Man*, who declares, "the artist, like the God of the creation, remains within or behind or beyond or above his handiwork, invisible, refined out of existence, indifferent, paring his fingernails" (183). Like the poets, painters, and sculptors reacting to the emotional excesses of Victorian romanticism, Joyce/Daedalus argues for reduction, insisting that the artist make his mind known not through intervention, but through suggestion. His materials, declares Daedalus (soon to be an architect), must speak on their own without the explicit, noisome voice of the creator. This we can do if we select our materials carefully; words—like stones, color, or sound—are more powerful for their reverberations than their definitions.

## Wordplay

Play is experimental, and when we play, we test boundaries. Children who create games craft rules that establish what is and isn't acceptable, and thus compare their versions of reality with what their parents do. By twisting the known and accepted, we test its strength and validity, questioning if perhaps there isn't a better way to see or understand. Simultaneously, then, play validates and invalidates, challenges and approves, the delight we experience from our freedom. To take risks intoxicates: whether it be testing a scientific hypothesis, juxtaposing odd color pigments, adding a flatted note to a musical chord, or violating grammatical rules for literary effect.

More often than we tell students, writing involves play, and their own work must be allowed to stumble, make mistakes, and get it all wrong. As Mina Shaughnessy has noted in her study of grammar, teachers can instruct students by examining the errors they make and why they make them. Risk taking is an invitation to avoid the clichéd and the formulaic, to understand—when we see that something fails—why another way works. I find this concept most teachable when dealing with the foundations of language in wordplay.

Inviting students to see the color and fun in words heightens their sensitivity to the possibilities of language. Knowing how words work and how they use sound or logic to create meaning makes their careful selection easier. And making students aware of—as Gyles Brandeth describes it—the joy of lex requires no extensive lesson planning or units. I draw from many of the books listed at the end of this chapter three to create five-minute opening or closing remarks, playing games or reading a passage. Bookstores abound with books investigating the history, meanings, aspects, or possibilities of language, but I've found the particular books listed at the chapter's conclusion entertaining and enlightening.

# *Syntax*

*...Every word is at home,*

*Taking its place to support the others,*

*The word neither diffident nor ostentatious,*

*An easy commerce of the old and the new,*

*The common word exact without vulgarity,*

*The formal word precise but not pedantic,*

*The complete consort dancing together.*

—T.S. Eliot, *Little Gidding*

Irked by her husband's penchant for swearing, Olivia Langhorne once tried to up the ante against him by unleashing a verbal stream of invective. Her spouse, satirist Mark Twain, stood calmly in the afterglow of the tirade before responding, "You got the words right, Livy, but you don't know the tune."

Artful syntax is about knowing the tune, mixing sentence elements, as essayist Pico Iyer says, "with all the silent discretion of a hostess arranging guests around her dinner table" (133). Diction is selecting the apt term; syntax is arranging those terms for maximum effect.

The sections that follow explore writing techniques aimed at making students more conscious of how to phrase what they mean. Students' awareness of the variety of sentence patterns, alternative phrasings, oral components of punctuation, and the precision of editing empowers them. These sections can be taught individually or sequentially, strung out over a semester or more, or placed at the center of a writing course.

## Literary faux pas

Literary faux pas are the messes that make bad writing, those sloppy and ineffectual results of inexact expression. I teach these early in any course on writing, and students use the list as a reference for peer editing.

### Killer Bees

Poor writers rely heavily on "be" verbs as their main verbs. For instance, a weak sentence might read, "It is very dark out, and the lights are dim." But revised phrasing and dynamic verbs produce better writing: "Dimmed lights barely penetrated the darkness." "Be" verbs comprise the following: is, am, was, were, are, be, being. Though "be" verbs used sparingly are appropriate, an over reliance on them produces dull writing. When you find "killer bees" dominating your writing, revise your sentences to replace them with more dynamic, action verbs.

### Gummy There's

"There is" and "there are" create weak, ineffectual sentences, as in "There are three reasons why I think Anastasia killed Julia." Revise this sentence to make it stronger: "For three reasons, I believe Anastasia killed Julia," or "Three reasons compel me to accuse Anastasia of Julia's murder."

### Opening Articles

The articles "a," "an," and "the" are integral parts of our language. However, repeatedly opening sentences with articles produces dull writing, and effective writers find ways to eliminate them. For instance, "The storm clouds raced across the sky" can easily become "Storm clouds raced across the sky." If nothing else, begin your sentence with an introductory phrase to give it a different opening: "Massed and tumbling, the storm clouds raced across the sky."

### Pathetic Fallacies

Victorian writers coined this term in reference to personification that is unrealistic. As personification is the giving of human/personal qualities to inanimate objects (as in "The wind howled all night long"), bad personification (pathetic fallacies) is the use of personification in an overly emotional or verbally sloppy manner. This can create language so silly it becomes distracting, as in the following: "The sun shone happily down on us, and the wind played merrily with our hair. Birds sang cheerily as we ran, and even the flowers seemed to dance with us." Writing this sophomoric becomes ineffectual. Because the elements of sun and wind, and natural objects like birds and flowers, don't really have these emotions, this passage ultimately fails to accurately describe the impact of the setting. If the writer wants to communicate an atmosphere of happiness and frivolity, that can be done without dumping all the emotions on objects that don't experience such emotions. *interesting.*

### Hallmark Card

Overly dramatic writing, like pathetic fallacies, distracts the reader and draws our attention more to the phrasing than the content. Writers unable to communicate specifically the emotion or scene they envision rely on "Hallmark card" writing in an attempt to manipulate readers through their emotions. Hallmark card writing is often characterized by a reliance on pathetic fallacies, clichés, lack of specificity, and hyperbole:

> I was furious that she had stolen my boyfriend. It was the worst day of my life. I had never been so angry, so angry I could have killed her. Steam was literally coming out of my ears as I watched her saunter into the cafeteria.

First, steam never comes out of anyone's ears, literally or not. Second, relying on extreme statements is a weak attempt to manipulate the reader into caring for the speaker: it is highly doubtful that this was indeed the "worst" day of her life, and it takes a lot to actually murder another human being. Finally, this passage lacks details, simply informing us that the speaker was "furious" and "angry."

### Show not Tell

Great writing is characterized by specificity that supplies details that communicate clearly to the reader an exact image, emotion, or thought. For instance, as Rebekah Caplan has noted, telling the reader "The pizza was delicious" (36) communicates nothing. With no employment of the senses (i.e., any appeal to taste, sight, touch, smell, sound), this passage fails to create in the reader's mind the pleasure of the pizza. This writer might well find her pepperoni pizza delicious, something that I—who finds pepperoni not all that tasty—would disagree with. Instead, hearing her make this statement, I would envision her eating my favorite—Canadian bacon and olives—and imagine a pizza far different from the one the writer is drooling over. Hence, she fails to establish in my mind the pizza before her. Look for details: the way pepperoni curls into a bowl, rimmed with black, filled with golden oil; the way cheese—usually mozzarella and cheddar—congeals in streaks of dark white and off-yellow, with small eruptions of grease; the way crust rises unevenly about the edges, a visual shading of golden brown to ash black. In short, don't TELL us the pizza was delicious: SHOW us. When you find yourself making summary statements, look for details. If the details aren't truly there to begin with, then you can't make your summary/telling statement anyway.

### Clinky Clichés

You've heard them: "It's not over till the fat lady_____," "I was so hungry I could eat a _____," and "I cried till my eyes turned _____." If you can complete these sentences, you've encountered clichés, phrases used so often they come to us automatically. That's the problem. Clichés aren't found in good writing; they're a substitute for good writing. Writers who rely on clichés tell the reader they can't think of the specific details that would more clearly pin down what they want to say; instead, they opt for a "tried and true" (another cliché) phrase. Clichés bore the reader and communicate your lack of specificity.

### Excessive Verbosity

Too many writers recreate the pauses in their thinking, using unnecessary phrases as if treading water. For instance, a sentence reading, "From what I could tell, his response was really exaggerated and completely unnecessary" swells with pointless adverbs and excess phrasing; this could be more simply stated: "His response was exaggerated and unnecessary." Long sentences have their place (witness the way Hawthorne crowds levels of thought into his extended clauses), but writers often confuse length with depth. If you can say the meaning simply, do so, and leave the longer sentences for your more intricate explorations of meaning.

# *Sentence Patterns*

Teaching sentence patterns does double duty, providing instruction in punctuation as well as syntax. I've produced a changing list of sentence patterns over the years, but Harry R. Noden's *Image Grammar: Using Grammatical Structures to Teach Writing* (from which many of the ideas below are drawn) provides an undergirding philosophy to his collection of patterns. Noden argues that effective phrasing is fundamentally about finding and arranging details. Sentence patterns are not merely about structure; they're about the orchestration of specifics. Encouraging writers to tease out the appropriate image, Noden teaches rhetorical strategies that emphasize detail.

## Basic Grammatical Structures

### Participials

Expanding a sentence through the addition of participles or participial phrases enables a rider to sketch the shadings of a scene, as Ernest Hemingway does in this passage from *The Old Man and the Sea*:

*Shifting the weight of the line to his left shoulder and kneeling carefully*, he washed his hand in the ocean and held it there, *submerged*, for more than a minute, *watching the blood trail away and the steady movement of the water against his hand as the boat moved*. (56–57)

A writer, for example, might say, "The storm clouds drifted across the sky," but note the accretion of specific detail if he writes, "Massed and darkening, storm clouds drifted across the sky."

### Absolutes

Absolutes combine nouns with participles to act as modifiers, as in this passage from Anne Rice's *The Mummy*:

The scream froze in her throat. The thing was coming towards her—towards Henry, who stood with his back to it—moving with a weak, shuffling gait, *arm outstretched* before it, the *dust rising* from the rotting linen that covered it, a *great smell of dust and decay filling the room*. (72)

The truncated concision of absolutes adds punch to a sentence. Rather than write, "The guitarist plucked at the strings," add absolute phrases: "Fingers flying, hair streaming to his shoulders, the guitarist plucked at the strings."

### Appositives

By restating a noun, appositives shade the meaning of an image, giving it depth and contour, as Cornelius Ryan illustrates when he describes ships in this passage from *June 6, 1944, The Longest Day*:

Plowing through the choppy gray waters, a phalanx of ships bore down on Hitler's Europe: *fast new attack transports, slow rust-scarred freighters, small ocean liners, channel streamers, hospital ships, weather-beaten tankers, and swarms of fussing tugs*. (243)

As with absolutes and participials, appositives provide specifics:

A collection of trash—*tiny starfish, moss, sea conchs, crabs, pieces of kelp*—sit atop the lobster's shell.

*Discover the elusive Spanish wolf, the graceful Flamingo, and the majestic Imperial Eagle*, some members of Spain's unique wildlife.

### Adjectives shifted out of order

Students often overload adjectives with upfront details: "The large, red-eyed, angry bull moose charged the intruder." Such constructions force the reader to wade through a river of information before finding what is being described. A better construction might read, "The large bull moose, *red-eyed and angry*, charged the intruder." In addition to making the sentence more manageable and providing rhythm, "red-eyed" and "angry" receive emphasis when shifted behind the noun. Arthur Conan Doyle employs this technique in a scene from *The Hound of the Baskervilles*: "And then, suddenly, in the very dead of the night, there came a sound to my ears, *clear, resonant, and unmistakable*" (72). Again, the final adjectives give attention not to the sound, but to its qualities.

## Sentence Rhythm

The syntactical arrangement of elements within a sentence creates rhythm, indicating where we focus, when we breathe, how the reading should sound. The following constructions illustrate how content can be wed with form to achieve effective writing.

### Repetition

Winston Churchill knew the power that repetition can bring to a single word, as when he argued for war against Germany: "*Victory* at all costs, *victory* in spite of all terror, *victory* however long and hard the road may be; for without *victory* there is no survival." Repetition brings emphasis to an idea or image the writer wants most intensely to convey: "He was a cruel *brute* of a man, *brutal* to his family and even more *brutal* to his friends."

### Coordination

As Ernest Hemingway's writing illustrates, a string of coordinating conjunctions can create a strong, pulsing rhythm:

> In the bed of the river there were pebbles *and* boulders, dry *and* white in the sun, *and* the water was clear *and* swiftly moving *and* blue in the channels. Troops went by the house *and* down the road *and* the dust they raised powdered the leaves of the trees. (*A Farewell to Arms 3*)

### Parallelism

Whether through phrases or clauses, parallelism creates a musical quality in a sentence, as Abraham Lincoln understood when composing the final lines of his Gettysburg address: "That that government *of the people, by the people* and *for the people* shall not perish." The employment of three prepositional phrases creates parallelism in both structure and rhythm. Journalist Hunter S. Thompson makes his case against Richard Nixon by employing a series of relative clauses that pile up accusations:

> And Hoover at least had the excuse that he "inherited his problems" from somebody else—which Nixon can't claim, because he is now in his fifth year as president, and when he goes on TV to explain himself, he is facing an audience of 50 to 60 million *who can't afford steaks or even*

*hamburgers in the supermarkets, who can't buy gasoline for their cars, who are paying 15 and 20% interest rates for bank loans, and who are being told that there may not be enough fuel to heat their homes through the coming winter. (The Great Shark Hunt 156)*

### Periodic sentences

Periodic sentences build tension and anticipation as details define an image before its appearance closes the sentence:

> Sketch a simple picture of azure waters, gentle breezes, and a protected anchorage; add a wash of tropical sunset colors—and you have a portrait of Cruz Bay.

> Across the plains of Salisbury, in a field of waving grass, standing like sentinels, the rocks of Stonehenge rise.

### Run-ons, fragments, and comma splices

Writers know that run-ons, fragments, and comma splices are perfectly legal when they achieve an effect superior to conventional phrasing. Tom Wolfe violates grammar rules repeatedly when he wants to create the sound of the human voice, instill drama, or suggest the circumlocutions of thought itself, as in this passage from "The Girl of the Year":

> That girl on the aisle, Baby Jane, is a fabulous girl. She comprehends what the Rolling Stones mean. Any columnist in New York could tell them who she is...a celebrity of New York's new era of Wog Hip. Baby Jane Holzer. Jane Holzer in *Vogue*, Jane Holzer in *Life*, Jane Holzer in Andy Warhol's underground movies, Jane Holzer in the world of High Camp, Jane Holzer at the rock and roll, Jane Holzer is—well, how can one put it into words? Jane Holzer is This Year's Girl, at least, the New Celebrity, none of your old idea of sexpots, prima donnas, romantic tragediennes, she is the girl who knows...The Stones, East End vitality...

## It's Greek to Me

Making students sensitive to the structures of Greek composition can be both entertaining and enlightening. A list of such sentence patterns would be exhaustive; here are just a few types Greeks employed to create voice and effect.

### Antithesis

As the name suggests, antithesis is the joining of identical structures that contain opposing thoughts. Shakespeare employs antithesis when he has Brutus defend the killing of Caesar: "Not that I loved Caesar less, but that I loved Rome more."

### Anaphora

Churchill, well schooled in the classics, knew the power of anaphora, the repetition of a word or phrase at the beginning of succeeding sentences: "We shall not flag or fail. We shall go on to the end. We shall fight in France, we shall fight on the seas and oceans."

### Chiasmus

Whereas antithesis repeats a structure, chiasmus involves inversion of that structure. For instance, "soon to be delivered" would be followed by "delivered too soon." One of the more famous examples of chiasmus is John Kennedy's, "Ask not what your country can do for you; ask what you can do for your country."

### Hyperbaton

Hyperbaton is any rearrangement of syntactical elements to place emphasis on a particular word, usually located at the end of the sentence.

Down the field and through the tacklers ran the Heisman Trophy winner.

His kind of sarcasm I do not like.

She had a personality indescribable.

### Zeugma

Linking two words to a verb or an adjective which is intended for only one of them is an example of zeugma. The second word creates a shift in tone (often dramatic or humorous) when yoked to the common verb or adjective.

He excelled in sports; I, in loafing.

Al Gore won the popular vote; George Bush, the presidency.

# Punctuation

*Writing must somehow compensate for the loss of voice features such as stress, pitch, and intonation, and for the loss of gesture and facial expression. Correspondence offers an excellent opportunity to teach some of the real functions of punctuation, diction, and stylistic devices. Commas, dashes, and semicolons, ironic word choice, reversal of word order often do what we do other ways in speaking face to face. Writing should be taught as an extension of speech. Nowhere is this more sensible than with punctuation. Generally, much of*

> *writing technique is a matter of simulating or replacing vocal*
> *characteristics.*
>
> —James Moffett, *Teaching the Universe of Discourse*

> *Grammar cannot be taught so as to strengthen writing—or*
> *even to make it correct—unless it is learned in the context of*
> *writing within which we can at appropriate moments show it*
> *to act usefully and beautifully.*
>
> —Marie Ponsot and Rosemary Deen, *Beat Not the Poor Desk*

As Moffett states, punctuation is a guide to speech, a notion traceable to its origins in the transcriptions of orators in classical Greece and Rome. Wanting to reproduce in the reader's mind the sound of the original presentation, writers developed coded marks indicating where to pause, what to emphasize, how to shift tone, and when an idea was complete.

Punctuation guides the reader to hear the author's voice, so writers must first determine how they want their work to sound: how the voice shifts volume, intensity, and pitch. Knowing that, the author then selects the punctuation that directs the reader to produce that vocal pattern. As Moffett notes,

> The author knows he must use typography as a set of signals indicating to a reader where the stresses and pauses are and how the intonation goes. This is what the breaking and punctuating of sentences on the page is all about anyway. The rules are merely an attempt to generalize the relations between sound, syntax, and sense. But no one ever has trouble punctuating orally; the problem is rendering speech on the page. Children who don't learn how to punctuate in twelve years of rules could learn in a few months by having other students misread their own dialogues back to them. (109)

Readers who torture a passage often fail to reproduce the writer's voice because they do not know what each punctuation mark dictates. The classic illustration of this comes from the final act of Shakespeare's *A Midsummer Night's Dream*, when a nervous Prologue reads the prologue for a performance of "Pyramus and Thisbe," placing his periods in the wrong spots:

> If we offend, it is with our good will.
> That you should think, we come not to offend
> But with good will. To show our simple skill,
> That is the true beginning of our end.
> Consider then, we come but in despite.
> We do not come, as minding to content you,

Our true intent is. All for your delight
We are not here. That you should here repent you,
The actors are at hand; and, by their show,
You shall know all, that you are like to know.
(5.1.108–116)

As Theseus notes at the conclusion of this grammatical mess, "This fellow doth not stand upon points." The passage illustrates how punctuation enables a dialogue between writer and reader, the former knowing what marks convey his voice and the latter knowing what those marks direct him to do.

"Reading for Punctuation" is a handout I distribute to clarify how punctuation sounds. After reading the handout with the students, I distribute an essay for a class read-around, each student reading a small section aloud, seeking the tone the punctuation suggests.

## Reading for Punctuation

### PERIODS

A period indicates the end of a complete thought, so the voice should drop to its lowest level in the sentence.

Ex: He was tired after working the entire weekend.

Ex: Doing homework until well after midnight wasn't April's idea of fun.

### SEMICOLONS

A semicolon, like a period, indicates the end of a thought. It divides two thoughts within a sentence. Therefore, like a period, the voice should drop to the lowest point.

Ex: Things had gone too far for Michael; he decided to do something fast.

Ex: The drive to the beach had been long and hot; the return home hadn't been any better.

### COMMAS

A comma indicates a temporary break in the complete thought, so the voice should drop partially, but not as completely as after a period or a semicolon.

Ex: He wasn't terribly upset by his team's defeat, but he wasn't happy about it either.

Ex: After waiting in line for six hours, John and Mary got seats in the back row.

## INTERRUPTIONS

Interruptions, also known as parenthetical thoughts, do as their name suggests: they interrupt the thought being expressed. Interruptions can be signaled by the use of commas, dashes, or parentheses. As if confiding a secret, the voice should drop in pitch for the duration of the interruption.

Ex: The overworked senator, although he wouldn't say so, was irritated by the questions.

Ex: That self-satisfied man—God knows how I hated him—did better than the rest of us.

Ex: The problems that plagued the committee (lack of money and long working hours) prevented it from achieving its goal.

## DASHES

Dashes indicate a complete and abrupt break from the thought. The voice should change pitch, and sometimes volume, completely.

Ex: Panic rising in him, John said to the robber, "I'll cooperate with anything you—don't do that!"

Ex: It's going to be fine, I said to myself, I'll just—who am I kidding?

## ELLIPSES

Ellipses at the end of a thought indicate that it is trailing off, as if unfinished. The voice should drop with uncertainty, not finality as with a period.

Ex: "Maybe if I find another job," mused Caryn, "or I could go to school or get a loan or..."

Ex: We might go to New York or Miami Beach or maybe even Canada...who knows?

## QUESTION MARKS

Question marks come at the end of a thought, but unlike periods, which express certainty or finality, they indicate bafflement or uncertainty. Therefore, the voice goes up or stays at the same pitch.

Ex: I looked at him defensively and asked, "Is that what you really want to do?"

Ex: Isn't it our purpose to help whoever we can?

## COLONS

Colons do not indicate the end of a thought, but they signal a movement toward the thought's completion. Therefore, the voice should drop at the colon and read everything after it in a lowered pitch.

Ex: After twelve hours of work and three days of little rest, he could arrive at only one conclusion: he needed to sleep.

Ex: He would need a number of items to make the camping trip a success: sleeping bags, tent, gas stove, and fishing gear.

## ITALICS

Italics are a writing device to indicate emphasis. Sometimes capital letters are substituted for italics. The voice should increase in volume and pitch.

Ex: I hated him for going through the drawer: those were *my* things.

Ex: He was the man, the *very* man, who had robbed my father.

## Punctuating for Meaning

Each of the sentences below can convey multiple meanings, depending on the way it is punctuated. Ask students to punctuate each sentence and then explain what meaning their punctuation conveys.

Edgar the alligator is hungry

When it comes time to eat my brother we will

The teacher said I was failing

Because I couldn't see the future was bleak

That car with the UCLA decal is the one I want

Since no one volunteered James finish the work

Please bring Mr. Johnsons Romeo and Juoiet to the concert

The men standing by the dock are ready

There is only one thing to do what you want

---

*Essayist Pico Iyer's "In Praise of the Humble Comma" is a wonderful illustration of the philosophy of and sound possibilities in punctuation.*

The gods, they say, give breath, and they take it away. But the same could be said—could it not?—of the humble comma. Add it to the present clause, and, of a sudden, the mind is, quite literally, given pause to think; take it out if you wish or forget it and the mind is deprived of a resting place. Yet still the comma gets no respect.

---

It seems just a slip of a thing, a pedant's tick, a blip on the edge of our consciousness, a kind of printer's smudge almost. Small, we claim, is beautiful (especially in the age of the microchip). Yet what is so often used, and so rarely recalled, as the comma—unless it be breath itself?

Punctuation, one is taught, has a point: to keep up law and order. Punctuation marks are the road signs placed along the highway of our communications—to control speeds, provide directions and prevent head-on collisions. A period has the unblinking finality of a red light; the comma is a flashing yellow light that asks us only to slow down; and the semicolon is a stop sign that tells us to ease gradually to a halt, before gradually starting up again. By establishing the relations between words, punctuation establishes the relations between the people using words.

That may be one reason why schoolteachers exalt it and lovers defy it ("We love each other and belong to each other let's don't ever hurt each other Nicole let's don't ever hurt each other," wrote Gary Gilmore to his girlfriend). A comma, he must have known, "separates inseparables," in the clinching words of H. W. Fowler, King of English Usage.

Punctuation, then, is a civic prop, a pillar that holds society upright. (A run-on sentence, its phrases piling up without division, is as unsightly as a sink piled high with dirty dishes.) Small wonder, then, that punctuation was one of the first proprieties of the Victorian age, the age of the corset, that the modernists threw off: the sexual revolution might be said to have begun when Joyce's Molly Bloom spilled out all her private thoughts in 36 pages of unbridled, almost unperioded and officially censored prose; and another rebellion was surely marked when E. E. Cummings first felt free to commit "God" to the lower case.

Punctuation thus becomes the signature of cultures. The hot-blooded Spaniard seems to be revealed in the passion and urgency of his doubled exclamation points and question marks *('¡Caramba! (¿Quien sabe?),* while the impassive Chinese traditionally added to his so-called inscrutability by omitting directions from his ideograms. The anarchy and commotion of the 60s were given voice in the exploding exclamation marks, riotous capital letters and Day-Glo italics of Tom Wolfe's spray-paint prose; and in Communist societies, where the State is absolute, the dignity—and divinity—of capital letters is reserved for Ministries, Sub-Committees and Secretariats.

Yet punctuation is something more than a culture's birthmark; it scores the music in our minds, gets our thoughts moving to the rhythm of our hearts. Punctuation is the notation in the sheet music of our words, telling us where to rest, or when to raise our voices; it acknowledges that the meaning of our discourse, as of any symphonic composition, lies not in the units but in the pauses, the pacing and the phrasing. Punctuation is the way one bats one's *eyes,* lowers one's voice *or* blushes demurely. Punctuation adjusts the tone and color and volume till the feeling comes into perfect focus, not disgust exactly, but distaste; not lust, *or* like, but love.

Punctuation, in short, gives us the human voice, and all the meanings that lie between the words. "You aren't young, are you?" loses its innocence when it loses the question mark. Every child knows the menace of a dropped apostrophe (the parent's "Don't do that" shifting into the more slowly enunciated "Do not do that"), and every believer, the ignominy of having his faith reduced to "faith." Add an exclamation point to "To be or not to be..." and the gloomy Dane has all the resolve he needs; add a comma, and the noble sobriety of "God save the Queen" becomes a cry of desperation bordering on double sacrilege.

Sometimes, of course, our markings may be simply a matter of aesthetics. Popping in a comma can be like slipping on the necklace that gives an outfit quiet elegance, or like catching the sound of running water that complements, as it completes, the silence of a Japanese landscape. When V. S. Naipaul, in his latest novel, writes, "He was a middle-aged man, with glasses," the first comma can seem a little precious. Yet it gives the description a spin, as well as a subtlety, that it otherwise lacks, and it shows that the glasses are not part of the middle-agedness, but something else.

Thus all these tiny scratches give us breadth and heft and depth. A world that has only periods is a world without inflections. It is a world without shade. It has a music without sharps and flats. It is a martial music. It has a jackboot rhythm. Words cannot bend and curve. A comma, by comparison, catches the gentle drift of the mind in thought, turning in on itself and back on itself reversing, redoubling and returning along the course of its own sweet river music; while the semicolon brings clauses and thoughts together with all the silent discretion of a hostess arranging guests around her dinner table.

Punctuation, then, is a matter of care. Care for words, yes, but also, and more important, for what the words imply. Only a lover notices the small things: the way the afternoon light catches the nape of a neck, or how a strand of hair slips out from behind an ear, or the way a finger curls around a cup. And no one scans a letter as closely as a lover, searching for its small print, straining to hear its nuances, its gasps, its sighs and hesitations, poring over the secret messages that lie in every cadence. The difference between "Jane (whom I adore)" and "Jane, whom I adore," and the difference between them both and "Jane—whom I adore—" marks all the distance between ecstasy and heartache. "No iron can pierce the heart with such force as a period put at just the right place," in Isaac Babel's lovely words: a comma can let us hear a voice break, or a heart. Punctuation, in fact, is a labor of love. Which brings us back, in a way, to gods.

# *Editing and Revision*

Editing and revision are distinctly different activities. Editing focuses on correcting small errors, such as spelling, punctuation, or wording. Revision is more ground-zero based: the phrasing and diction of the sentence, paragraph, or essay itself are altered. Editing deals with mechanics; revision aims to elevate composition from pedestrian prose to arresting writing. However, when students edit and revise (solo, in groups, in front of the class), they benefit from a guideline of what to look for.

Teachers find peer editing hit-and-miss. Clearly, most students lack the revision skills of their teachers. But like Shakespeare's quality of mercy, editing blesseth him that gives and receives. Beyond the potential benefits to the writer, editing enables the editor to recognize weak or ineffectual writing, and because students are armed with the handouts I've provided (Literary Faux Pas, Sentence Patterns, Reading for Punctuation), they can spot problems and suggest revisions.

Depending on the assignment, editing guidelines vary, so I draw from the general list below.

## Revision Checklist

1. **Rewrite your attention getter in the introduction.**

   For fiction:
   - Start with a description of the setting using sensory detail.
   - Start with a character in action.
   - Start with a character's thoughts or a description of the character.
   - Start with a conversation between characters.

   For nonfiction:
   - Start with a story.
   - Start with an example.
   - Start with a question.
   - Start with a definition.

- Start with a startling fact.
- Start with a well-written summary.
- Start with a quotation.

2. **Rewrite your conclusion.**

   For fiction:
   - Conclude with a final description of a setting.
   - Conclude with the character's thoughts.
   - Conclude with the character in action.
   - Conclude with a final conversation between characters.
   - "Frame" your essay: conclude by tying back to your introduction in some way.

   For nonfiction:
   - Conclude with a thought-provoking question.
   - Conclude with a call to action.
   - Conclude with a thoughtful synthesis of what you've written. (Explain what it all means when seen as a whole.)
   - Conclude with an appropriate quote.
   - Conclude with an evaluation (your opinion on the quality of the work).
   - Conclude with a reference to a parallel idea or event.
   - Conclude with a reference to a contemporary discussion.

3. **Add details**. Avoid common names (like red, yellow, and blue for colors), but don't overdo it with your thesaurus (beryl, cyanic, pavonine—which are all blue, by the way). *Example*: "The iron-gray clouds promised to flood us with rain by mid-afternoon."

4. **Use specific nouns.** Not car, but Porsche; not store, but K-mart; not dog, but St. Bernard; not street, but Woodruff Avenue; not girl, but Susan. *Example*: "Rainey chased her mother's Honda Accord all the way down First Street."

5. **Use specific action verbs.** Not walk, but saunter; not run, but sprint; not talk, but chatter; not see, but glimpse. *Example*: "John shuddered and cringed in the heat."

6. **Add "sound" details**, but avoid using the words hear or sound. *Example*: "The Christmas paper crackled and crinkled beneath the toddler's excited feet."

7. **Add "smell" details,** but avoid using the word smell. *Example*: "The scent of cinnamon and oranges floated from the kitchen into our warm dining room."

8. **Add "touch" details**, but avoid using the words feel or touch. *Example*: "The burlap bag rubbed against my bare leg like sandpaper as we waited to start the three-legged race."

9.  **Add unique and creative figurative language.**

    *Simile*: "Butterflies stream toward flowers like dead leaves in the wind."

    *Metaphors*: "Her voice was a soft song lulling me to sleep."

    *Personification*: "The wind roared as it hurtled down the avenue."

10. **Vary sentence patterns.** Begin with a subordinating conjunction, slip in a participial phrase, construct a periodic sentence, use parallelism, or repetition.

11. **Vary sentence length.** Include short sentences (1–5 words), average sentences (6–15 words), and long sentences (16+ words). *Example*: "I was terrified. Dusty cobwebs floated across my skin as I hurried to leave the old house. The tiny sliver of light slanted from where the front door opened into warm sunlight miles away."

12. **Vary sentence beginnings.** Don't start two sentences in a paragraph with the same word or letter unless you are purposely using repetition. (Challenge: Start every sentence in your piece with a different word.)

13. **Avoid killer bees.** You will usually have to reword or rearrange the sentence in order to use an action verb.

14. **Show, Don't Tell.** *Dull example*: She was angry. *Exciting example*: She threw her books across the room and slammed the door as she stormed out.

15. **Make sure you have a clear organization:** attention getter (introduction); several paragraphs of development, elaboration, and detail; and a clincher (conclusion). Consider different ways to structure your paper:
    - Classification
    - Associational
    - Spatial
    - Illustrative
    - Comparison
    - Continuum
    - Interwoven
    - Episodic/fragmented
    - Chronologic
    - Dialectic
    - Cause-effect

16. **Use transition words** to guide your reader through your essay. *Example*: "First, I did my homework. Then, I washed the dishes. Finally, I brushed my teeth and headed for bed."

17. **Avoid all the earmarks of Hallmark writing:** pathetic fallacies,

clichés, overly dramatic language, hyperbole (unless for comic effect).

18. **Examine the effect of your punctuation.** Does it clarify or confuse? Does it replicate a voice? Does it add verve or punch to the writing?

19. **Spell correctly.**

## *Tone: Detection and Composition*

*Dying is easy. Comedy is hard*

—Edmund Keane

The recognition of tone is the mark of sophisticated readers and writers, an observation reinforced by the number of tone questions on AP exams. But I also teach tone to make students sensitive to diction and syntax, as both its detection and employment require an awareness of the connotative qualities of language.

As tone is the implied attitude toward the subject, it requires an understanding of the word choice and phrasing that create that tone. Therefore, we can teach students to detect tone by examining a writer's selection of diction and syntax. In humor, no less than other literary realms, the selection of specific words and phrases—right down to the sounds some words generate—determine the success of the endeavor.

The trick of humor is identifying the denotative and connotative aspects of what we write. What the words say is only a literal meaning; what they mean casts the passage as ironic, sarcastic, understated, hyperbolic, absurd, or farcical. When our audience tells us they "don't get it," what they don't get is the connotation. We've all experienced the disappointment of telling a joke to a literalist, someone who hears only the denotative level, followed by the laborious process of explaining how the joke works. I once had a friend who never laughed at sitcoms, who'd sit deadpan in front of the television screen and occasionally declare, "That's funny," without cracking a smile. Apparently, her comedy elevator never reached the connotative level.

Be forewarned: comedy is probably as hard to write as it is to detect, and teenage humor runs the gamut from gut buster to pathetic, but the learning is in the doing, and students able to identify and then utilize comedic techniques become sensitized to the specifics and aptness of word, phrase, and image choice.

Finally, comedy writing is an excellent way to develop writing skills, its emphasis on tone requiring sensitivity to phrasing. As George Hillocks, Jr., argues in *Teaching Writing as a Reflective Practice*, the art of writing satire, for example,

offers resources that encourage, perhaps demand, seeing in different ways, resources that are tapped in no other writing done in school: all the tools of the satirist—diatribe, exaggeration, understatement, symbolism, irony, travesty, and parody. (131)

## Humor & Tone

More complicated comic writing is situational or character based, what critic Northrop Frye called high comedy, but to make comedy accessible to students, I begin with phrasing. Short and direct, comic phrases are building blocks for more extended passages and works. Students can compose phrases as they learn the following humor types:

### Understatement

Understatement occurs when a statement denies its opposite as when *The Catcher in the Rye*'s Holden Caulfield declares, "It isn't very serious. I have this tiny little tumor on the brain." (43)

### Hyperbole

An exaggeration or extravagant statement used as a figure of speech. Carl Sandburg uses hyperbole in "The People, Yes," when he writes, "It's a slow burg—I spent a couple of weeks there one day."

### Absurdity

Absurd humor is based on extreme juxtapositions in tone, subject matter, or imagery. Popular after WW II, it's rife in the work of Monty Python, Woody Allen, Joseph Heller, early *Saturday Night Live*, or *National Lampoon*. *The Onion*, a parodic periodical, employs absurd juxtapositions, as in its headline about a WW II story on the bombing of Dresden: "Dresden fire-bombed; Thousands of enemy Tea Sets, Clocks, Ornamental Statues Destroyed" (65). Nonsequiturs (literally, "it does not follow") involve a serious statement followed by an absurdly silly one, as when Woody Allen declares, "Of all the wonders of nature, a tree in summer is perhaps the most remarkable; with the possible exception of a moose singing 'Embraceable You' in spats."

### Irony

Irony is the difference between how something appears and what it actually is, so that we say one thing while meaning another. Irony can be situational, as when Don Quixote believes he is a knight-errant fighting giants as he attacks a windmill. Greek literature abounds with irony, from the picture of the blind seer Teiresias (who "sees" in ways Oedipus cannot) to Midas, who—granted the gift of a golden touch—finds his life made miserable by the consequences.

### Sarcasm

Sarcasm is a vitriolic kind of irony, the underlying meaning meant as an attack. Oscar Wilde sarcastically derided the lowbrow tastes of Victorians when he declared, "The public is wonderfully tolerant. It forgives everything except genius."

## Humor Types

The field of humor has far more types than the three I list here, but these are the most accessible for students and are staples of humorous literature.

### Parody

Parody is imitation done for humorous effect. Requiring knowledge of the original, a parody engages us by its recall of the original's diction and syntax, but the tone of the original is likely out of sync with the newer subject matter as illustrated in Andrew Barlow's send-up of Robert Fulghum's "All I Need to Know I Learned in Kindergarten." Capturing the simple, pedantic voice of Fulghum's work, Barlow's employment of a similar tone in the context of a horrific event creates a deliciously ironic twist.

*All I Need to Know I Learned by Having My Arms Ripped off by a Polar Bear*

For me, wisdom came not at the top of the graduate-school mountain nor buried in the Sunday-school sand pile. For me, wisdom arrived during a visit to the home of our trusted friend the polar bear. Actually, I suppose "trusted friend" is something of a misnomer, because last year I had my arms brutally ripped from my torso by a fifteen-hundred-pound Norwegian polar bear. How and why this happened is an interesting story. For now, though, let's take a look at some fun lessons about our good friend Ursus maritimus, the polar bear. Here's what I learned:

-Share everything. You might be thinking, "Really? Even with polar bears?" Yes, share especially with polar bears. Actually, the word "share" does not exist in a polar bear's vocabulary, which consists of only about three hundred words. Give everything you have to a polar bear and do not expect him to share it. It did not occur to the polar bear who took my arms from me to share them in anyway afterward.

-Polar bears are meticulous about personal cleanliness. A typical polar bear will feast for about twenty to thirty minutes, then leave to wash off in the ocean or an available pool of water. The polar bear who feasted on my arms did exactly this, leaving to scrub up in a nearby lake. Good hygiene is fundamental.

-In nearly all instances where a human has been attacked by a polar bear, the animal has been undernourished or was provoked. In my case, the bear was plump but deranged. Consequently, my attacker bear was spared the execution that typically follows an assault. My proposal—that my polar bear have his arms ripped off by a larger polar bear—was rejected by the authorities. No lesson here, I guess.

-The town of Churchill, Manitoba, is known as the "Polar Bear Capital of the World." According to legend, when a bear ambled into the Royal Canadian Legion hall in Churchill, in 1894, the club steward shouted, "You're not a member! Get out!" and the bear did. This story is almost certainly fictitious. During the first ten minutes that a polar bear was removing my arms from my body, I repeatedly shouted, "Stop!" "Get away from me!," and "Please—oh, my God, this polar bear is going to rip my arms off!," but the animal was unfazed. The lesson in this is that you can't believe everything you hear.

-Beware of blame-shifting. The authorities speculated that the nasty scene may have begun when I grabbed onto the polar bear's fur. At first, I thought, Gee, maybe that's right—I must have done something to get him so sore. But now I reject this suggestion. Why would I grab his fur?

-Things change. As a child, I used to delight in early-morning "polar-bear swims" at my summer camp. Now I don't even feel like swimming anymore, because I have no arms.

-Summing up: l. Do not run from a polar bear. 2. Do not fight back. 3. Don't just stand there. Whatever you do, it will teach you a lesson.

-Never judge a book by its cover. Polar bears hate this.

-When a male polar bear and a human are face to face, there occurs a brief kind of magic: an intense, visceral connection between man and beast whose poignancy and import cannot be expressed in mere words. Then he rips your arms off.

### Wordplay
Wordplay is the heart of short phrasing, from puns to turn-of-phrase to farcical constructions. Poet Ogden Nash was a master of all varieties of wordplay, as these samples illustrate:

- A husband is a guy who tells you when you've got on too much lipstick and helps you with your girdle when your hips stick.
- I sit in an office at 244 Madison Avenue, and say to myself, you have a responsible job, havenue?
- The Bronx? No thonx.

A subtle play on the meaning or sound of a word is a turn of phrase, as when fifties rock legend Little Richard abandoned his music career to become a preacher, declaring, "I gave up rock 'n' roll for the Rock of Ages."

"All in the Family" character Archie Bunker was famous for his malaprops, as when he decried the notion of cremation, declaring that he didn't want his ashes "kept in a urine on the shelf." Malaprops are verbal misphrasings, intentional when the artist is in control, and entertaining when the speaker isn't, as in these samples from student history compositions:

- Adam and Eve were created from an apple tree. Jacob, son of Isaac, stole his brother's birthmark. One of Jacob's sons, Joseph, gave refuse to the Israelites.

- The inhabitants of Egypt were called mummies. They traveled by Camelot. Moses led the Hebrew slaves to the Red Sea, where they made unleavened bread, which is bread made without any ingredients. David was a Hebrew king who fought the Philatelists. Solomon, one of David's sons, had 500 wives and 500 porcupines.

- The Greeks invented three kinds of columns—Corinthian, Doric and Ironic. The mother of Achilles dipped him in the River Styx until he became intolerable. In the Olympic Games, Greeks ran races, jumped, hurled the biscuits and threw the java. The reward to the victor was a coral wreath. Socrates was a famous Greek teacher who died from an overdose of wedlock.

- In the Middle Ages, King Harlod mustarded his troops before the Battle of Hastings. Joan of Arc was canonized by George Bernard Shaw. The Magna Carta provided that no free man should be hanged twice for the same offense. William Tell shot an arrow through an apple while standing on his son's head.

Farfetched plot twists and incongruities are staples of farce, a verbal wordplay often employing absurdity. A staple of vaudeville, Depression-era radio programs, and current sitcoms, farce is foundational in the musings of columnists like Dave Barry:

> *What is and Ain't Grammatical*
>
> I cannot overemphasize the importance of good grammar.
>
> What a crock. I could easily overemphasize the importance of good grammar. For example, I could say: "Bad grammar is the leading cause of slow, painful death in North America," or "Without good grammar, the United States would have lost World War II."
>
> The truth is that grammar is not the most important thing in the world. The Super Bowl is the most important thing in the world. But grammar is still important. For example, suppose you are being interviewed for a job as an airplane pilot and your prospective employer asks you if you

have any experience, and you answer: "Well, I ain't never actually flied no actual airplanes or nothing, but I got several pilot-style hats and several friends who I like to talk about airplanes with."

If you answer this way, the prospective employer will immediately realize that you have ended your sentence with a preposition. (What you should have said, of course, is "several friends with who I like to talk about airplanes.") So you will not get the job, because airline pilots have to use good grammar when they get on the intercom and explain to the passengers that, because of high winds, the plane is going to take off several hours late and land in Pierre, South Dakota, instead of Los Angeles.

We did not always have grammar. In medieval England, people said whatever they wanted, without regard to rules, and as a result they sounded like morons. Take the poet Geoffrey Chaucer, who couldn't even spell his first name right. He wrote a large poem called *Canterbury Tales,* in which people from various professions—knight, monk, miller, reever, riveter, eeler, diver, stevedore, spinnaker, etc. —drone on and on like this:

> In a somer sesun whon softe was the sunne
>
> I kylled a younge birde ande I ate it on a bunne.

When Chaucer's poem was published, everybody read it and said: "My God, we need some grammar around here." So they formed a Grammar Commission, which developed the parts of speech, the main ones being nouns, verbs, predicants, conjectures, particles, proverbs, adjoiners, coordinates, and rebuttals. Then the commission made up hundreds and hundreds of grammar rules, all of which were strictly enforced.

When the colonists came to America, they rebelled against British grammar. They openly used words like "ain't" and "finalize," and when they wrote the Declaration of Independence they deliberately misspelled many words. Thanks to their courage, today we Americans have only two rules of grammar:

> Rule 1. The word "me" is always incorrect.

Most of us learn this rule as children, from our mothers. We say things like: "Mom, can Bobby and me roll the camping trailer over Mrs. Johnson's cat?" And our mothers say: "Remember your grammar, dear. You mean: `Can Bobby and I roll the camping trailer over Mrs. Johnson's cat?' Of course you can, but be home by dinnertime."

The only exception to this rule is in formal business writing, where instead of "I" you must use "the undersigned." For example, this business letter is incorrect:

"Dear Hunky-Dory Canned Fruit Company: A couple days ago my wife bought a can of your cling peaches and served them to my mother who has a weak heart and she damn near died when she bit into a live grub. If I ever find out where you live, I am gonna whomp you on the head with a ax handle."

This should be corrected as follows:

". . . If the undersigned ever finds out where you live, the undersigned is gonna whomp you on the head with a ax handle."

Rule 2. You're not allowed to split infinitives.

An infinitive is the word "to" and whatever comes right behind it, such as "to a tee," "to the best of my ability," "tomato," etc. Splitting an infinitive is putting something between the "to" and the other words. For example, this is incorrect:

"Hey man, you got any, you know, spare change you could give to, like, me?"

The correct version is:

". . . spare change you could, like, give to me?"

The advantage of American English is that, because there are so few rules, practically anybody can learn to speak it in just a few minutes. The disadvantage is that Americans generally sound like jerks, whereas the British sound really smart, especially to Americans. That's why Americans are so fond of those British dramas they're always showing on public television, the ones introduced by Alistair Cooke. Americans love people who talk like Alistair Cooke. He could introduce old episodes of "Hawaii Five-0" and Americans would think they were extremely enlightening.

So the trick is to use American grammar, which is simple, but talk with a British accent, which is impressive. This technique is taught at all your really snotty private schools, where the kids learn to sound like Elliot Richardson. Remember Elliot? He sounded extremely British, and as a result he got to be Attorney General, Secretary of State, Chief Justice of the Supreme Court and Vice President at the same time.

You can do it, too. Practice in your home, then approach someone on the street and say: "Tally-ho, old chap. I would consider it a great honour if you would favour me with some spare change." You're bound to get quick results. (147-149)

## Satire

Satire aims to correct, exposing foibles and ills so that, brought to communal awareness, the problem will be addressed. Aristophanes employed satire when lampooning the failures of Athenian politics, and Romans Horace and Juvenal jabbed at the social follies of the Empire. The intent to attack social constructs appealed to Age of Enlightenment commentators from France's Moliere to England's Addison and Steele, John Gay, and Jonathan Swift, whose "A Modest Proposal" is an extended satirical attack on politics. And as America followed the same path of urbanization, social satirists from Mark Twain to Joseph Heller to Comedy Central's Jon Stewart have targeted their culture's hubris and hypocrisy.

## Writing Assignments

Imitation was more than the sincerest form of flattery for Renaissance writers. Scholars believed replicating the style of Classical writers was a prelude to developing a writer's voice.

The lessons I've developed to teach rhetoric and poetics adhere to this belief. Once aware of the range of stylistic devices, students imitate syntactical structures—paying attention to word choice—to produce a specific tone. As they move into more developed pieces, they direct their attention to diction, syntax, and tone, experimenting with combinations of techniques.

Writing exercises can be as simple as word games, sentence imitation, or tonal reproduction, but I also use them as preludes to, or in context of, more extensive writing assignments. Thus, a teaching unit on style consists of a writing assignment preceded by exercises whose techniques will best aid the student in composing the larger piece. In developing each unit, I keep the following goals in mind:

- Students need to isolate the characteristics of a particular stylistic device to understand how it achieves its effect.

- Having isolated those techniques, students then practice recreating them in stylistic imitations.

- Given subject matter to write on, students create a voice stylistically appropriate for the topic.

- At all times, students need to focus not on the functional, but on the effective, selecting words and phrasing that is most apt.

## Imagery, Tightening, and Editing: A Sample

Alexa Shoemaker, a senior at Georgiana Bruce Kirby Preparatory School, approached me for help on her college essay. Over the course of four weeks, we consulted as she continued to revise her work. What follows are the versions as she composed them. The shift to her final paper illustrates the power of revision, the importance of specifics, and the possibilities for improvement when teacher and student dialogue.

### Version number 1

I used to think that death existed. It never had personally, but people died on film and television and in books, so it was obviously real. The only family member of mine to have died was my grandfather. My only memory of him I take from a photograph of us sprawled out on our carpeted floor. I could say I remember he ate bittersweet chocolate and marmalade, and he always wore a felt man's hat. I could say he was a good man—he helped construct the atom bomb in World War II but petitioned against its use. But I simply don't remember him. And I don't remember his death either. I only remember that it was the first time I saw my mother cry.

I used to think that death existed. That is, until last May I did. It was Mother's Day, a sunny, warm spring day, a day only poets write about. My red-headed friend in the passenger's seat laughed out the window, and I turned left on a green arrow. I only got halfway through the intersection. A woman barreling down Mission Street obviously didn't see her red light, or she chose to ignore it.

Looking back, the accident could not have caused significant harm to my friend, the car, or me. But what surprised me, and surprises me still, is what went through my head at the moment the two vehicles crashed into each other. I didn't think about who had annoyed me the day before, or what homework I had to finish. I thought about the things the poet Nazim Hikmet says, "I didn't know I loved." I thought about people and flowers, printer's ink and shooting stars. I thought about Greece, my favorite place on Earth, and Santa Cruz, my other favorite place. I thought about the thick build-up of paint on Van Gogh's Wheat Field with Cypresses, and how my sister's hand shares the same wrinkles and muscles as mine. I thought about how I wanted to tell people how much I loved them, and I hoped I would still get the chance.

Death does exist, but not in the way most believe. Someone's heart may stop beating, or someone's brain stop working. But then, there are cases in which someone stops being curious, or excited, or silly. There are cases in which someone stops loving the world and cherishing the smallest details. That is death in the truest sense of the word. But when memories don't fade, and the mind and heart stay true to the soul, no one can really die. My heart beats a regular rhythm, my bones are sturdy and my lungs fill with air every few seconds, but I am more alive today than I ever have been.

*My first response to Alexa's essay was that it lacked specifics, relying overmuch on abstractions. I also wanted to play down the tone, believing more images and anecdotes would convey her intent better than some of her language, so we discussed areas where she could provide more details. I also advised her to modulate the tone, supplying some lighthearted moments as well. She returned a few days later with a second version.*

*Version number 2*

Last fall my middle sister brought home her German, unambitious, musician boyfriend. My best friend and confidant for as long as I can remember, she had suddenly become the distant relative at family reunions you give a polite but forced smile. The latest addition to family functions was just the beginning of a year that proved to be more poignant and more enlightening than I could have predicted. I had long been oblivious to the world around me and unacquainted with what my heart needed. Later that year I finally understood how ill my oldest sister really was. She was no longer the energetic, cognizant, strong woman I knew her to be. Instead of traveling to Papua New Guinea and Australia by herself to photograph underwater creatures or single-handedly winning Trivial Pursuit, she only comes home for medical appointments and tests. She has had medical problems since she was nine, but it took me night after night spent holding her hand to fully realize the pain she suffered from her tremors and headaches. Oddly enough, she has become more pleasant company, as she is less apt to tell me what to do.

In May of this year, Mother's Day, I became instantly aware of my own mortality. A woman barreling down Mission Street didn't see her red light or chose to ignore it. The accident could not have caused significant harm whatsoever to my friend in the passenger seat, the car, or me. But what surprised me, and surprises me still, is what went through my head at the moment the two vehicles collided. I didn't think about the girl in my class who didn't care about art, or the carrots and frozen pie crusts I had to buy at the supermarket. I thought about the things—as the poet Nazim Hikmet says— "I didn't know I loved." I thought about the sister I no longer knew, printer's ink and shooting stars. I thought about Greece, my favorite place on Earth, and Santa Cruz, my other favorite place. I thought about the thick build-up of paint on Van Gogh's "Wheat Field with Cypresses," and how the wrinkles and muscles in my sister's hand echoes mine. I thought about how I wanted to tell people how much I loved them, and I hoped I would still get the chance.

Insight into my sister's condition and character as well as a sudden confrontation with myself has changed me over the past year. I can spend an afternoon with my mother or watch the sunset over the cement ship at the beach in Aptos and not worry about what's going to happen the next day. My heart beats a regular rhythm and my bones are sturdy. I love orchids and drinking lemonade and listening to rain, and I am more alive today than I ever have been.

*I liked a lot of the details Alexa brought to this version, particularly the background on her sister in the second paragraph. I encouraged her to find more such specifics as she continued to revise. I also wanted her to play with the structure, feeling the essay was becoming a bit episodic. We discussed her using the accident as a controlling metaphor, the event that culminated in a year's worth of revelations and disturbances. She returned with the following:*

### Version number 3

The eighty-year-old woman barreling down Mission St. failed to notice the bright red light hanging from the steel beam and promptly collided with my white steed of a Volvo station wagon. It was the culmination of a year that proved to be more poignant and more enlightening than I could have predicted.

It began last fall when my middle sister brought home her unambitious German boyfriend. He has had the same apartment for nine years and is too cheap to buy his own drum set. I couldn't see why my best friend and confidant for as long as I can remember had suddenly become the distant relative at family reunions you give a polite but forced smile because of a man too weak to chop wood. I had long been oblivious to the world around me and unacquainted with my heart until the year slowly unfolded.

Later that year, my oldest sister, who loves dachshunds and Coca-Cola, no longer exuded the energy and strength I knew her to possess. Instead of traveling to Papua New Guinea and Australia by herself to photograph underwater shrimp or single handedly winning Trivial Pursuit, she only comes home for medical appointments and tests. She has had medical problems since she was nine, but it took me night after night spent holding her hand to fully realize the pain she suffered from her tremors and headaches. Oddly enough, she has become more pleasant company, as she is less apt to tell me what to do.

In May of this year, Mother's Day, the bittersweet experience of a car accident offered me two gifts: familial love, tenderness, and pampering, as well as instant awareness of my own mortality. The accident could not have caused significant harm whatsoever to my friend in the passenger seat, the car, or me, but I was surprised at what went through my head at the loud, crunching moment. I didn't think about the girl in my class who didn't care about art, or the carrots and frozen pie crusts I had to buy at the supermarket. I thought about the things—as the poet Nazim Hikmet says—"I didn't know I loved." I thought about the sister I no longer knew, printer's ink and shooting stars. I thought about Greece, my favorite place on Earth, and Santa Cruz, my other favorite place. I thought about how the wrinkles and muscles in my sister's hand echoes mine. I thought how I wanted to tell people how much I loved them, and I hoped I would still get the chance.

Insight into my sister's condition and character as well as a sudden confrontation with myself has changed me over the past year. I can spend an afternoon with my mother or watch the sunset over the cement ship at the beach in Aptos and not worry about what's going to happen the next day. I love orchids and drinking lemonade and listening to rain, and I am more alive today than I have ever been.

*Alexa was continuing to dig up details (her sister's love of dachshunds and Coca-Cola) and some nice images in the final paragraph, but I still wanted to tone down some of the language and make the transitions from paragraph to paragraph clearer. I'd felt from the start that the Hikmet quote drew attention to itself and disrupted the flow of its paragraph, so I recommended making it an epigram. Finally, we worked on ways to tighten her language, eliminating wordy passages. Her next version came in the next day.*

### Version number 4

*"I didn't know I loved so many things*

—Nazim Hikmet

The eighty-year-old woman barreling down Mission St. failed to notice the bright red light hanging from the steel beam and promptly collided with my white Volvo station wagon. It was the culmination of a year that proved both poignant and enlightening.

It began last fall when my middle sister brought home her unambitious German boyfriend. He has had the same apartment for nine years and is too cheap to buy his own drum set. I couldn't see why my best friend and confidant thought a man too weak to chop wood was more important than me. Before him, we could make calzones together and watch *When Harry Met Sally*. We could laugh about the time she wrapped an entire bowl of sickeningly sweet French Vanilla ice cream into a paper napkin and hid it in her pocket because she didn't want to offend the restaurateur who had given it to us for free. Those details in my life had gone unnoticed until the year's ensuing experiences heightened my sensitivity.

Later that year, my oldest sister, who loves dachshunds and Coca-Cola, no longer exuded the energy and strength I knew her to possess. Instead of traveling to Papua New Guinea and Australia by herself to photograph underwater shrimp or winning Trivial Pursuit, now she only comes home for medical appointments and tests. She has had medical problems since she was nine, but it took me night after night spent holding her hand to fully realize the pain she suffered from tremors and headaches. Oddly enough, she has become more pleasant company, as she is less apt to tell me what to do.

So on that Mother's Day, a car accident offered me two gifts: familial love, tenderness and pampering, as well as an instant awareness of my own mortality. The accident could not have caused significant harm whatsoever to my friend in the passenger seat, the car, or me, but I was surprised at what went through my head at the loud, crunching moment. I didn't think about the girl in my class who didn't care about art, or the carrots and frozen pie crusts I had to buy at the supermarket. I thought about the sister I no longer knew, printing ink and shooting stars. I thought about Greece, my favorite place on Earth, and Santa Cruz, my other favorite place. I thought about how the wrinkles and muscles in my sister's hand echoes mine.

I recognized at last that life does not go on forever. It is a finite, passing experience that I do not want to miss. I can spend an afternoon talking to my mother or watch the sun set over the cement ship at the beach in Aptos and not worry about what will happen next. I can forgive my sister, enjoy the yellow orchids in the window, drink pink lemonade and listen to the rain splatter on the driveway. I am content knowing that when I come home, the street sign will read the same name, and the five o'clock light will fall at the same angle through the redwoods.

*With this draft, I felt Alexa was replacing more of her abstractions with specifics, making her essay stronger. She'd also brought down the tone, letting her images convey the emotion she wanted. She was tightening her language and shortening sentences, making the essay more reader-friendly. After discussing some additional tightening and rephrasing, she composed her final draft.*

# *Final Draft*

*"I didn't know I loved so many things."*

—Nazim Hikmet

The eighty-year-old woman barreling down Mission St. failed to notice the red light and immediately collided with my white Volvo station wagon. After the previous year spent grappling with doubts about my "identity," the accident reordered my priorities.

My gradual awakening began last fall when my middle sister brought home her unambitious boyfriend. I couldn't see why my best friend and confidant thought a man who has had the same apartment for nine years and is too cheap to buy his own drum set was more important than I was. Before the advent of this party-loving health-nut, we made calzones together and watched *When Harry Met Sally*. One time, she wrapped an entire bowl of sickeningly sweet French Vanilla ice cream into a paper napkin and hid it in her pocket because she didn't want to offend the restaurateur who had given it to us for free. Until the accident, those details in my life had gone unappreciated.

Later that year, my oldest sister, who loves Daschunds and Coca-Cola, no longer exuded the energy and strength I knew her to possess. Instead of traveling to Papua New Guinea and Australia by herself to photograph underwater shrimp, now she only comes home for medical appointments and tests. She has had health issues since she was nine, but it took me night after night spent holding her hand to fully realize the pain she suffered from tremors and headaches. Oddly enough, she has become more pleasant company, as she is less apt to tell me what to do.

And on that Mother's Day, the car accident finally made me comprehend my own mortality. It didn't cause significant harm to my passenger, the car, or me, but I was surprised at what went through my head at the loud, crunching moment. I didn't think about the girl in my class who didn't care about art, or the carrots and frozen pie crusts I had to buy at the supermarket. I thought about the sister I no longer knew, about printing ink and shooting stars. I thought about Greece, my favorite place on Earth, and Santa Cruz, my other favorite place. I thought about how the wrinkles and muscles in my sister's hand echo mine.

Life is finite. Seeing the scattered glass and metal shards reminded me of that. Now, I am content knowing that when I come home, the street sign will read the same name, and the five o'clock light will fall at the same angle through the redwoods. I can forgive my sister's romance and enjoy the yellow orchids in the window. I can also take a trip to the city and immerse myself in Hellenistic statues, Miró paintings, and Mesopotamian cylinder seals. And I can spend hours in a teacher's office discussing *One Hundred Years of Solitude* or stay up all night listening to Eric Clapton and reading Pablo Neruda, just because I want to.

# *Student Samples*

In the student selections that follow, the authors strengthened their writing by employing stylistic devices that made their voices not merely serviceable, but dramatic, whimsical, poignant, amusing, understated, farcical, or angry.

### *Lex Holiday and the Poetic Thing* by Chelsea Grogan

> *Guy on rollerblades*
> *Showing off in Central Park*
> *Oops, I threw a stick.*

I was sitting behind the tiny desk in my tiny office on the first floor of that one floor building in the city, just reading the beautiful poetry of Demetri Martin, when I got a phone call. It was the manager of a bank I knew all too well. I expected a huge bank robbery case but...no. The monotone voice on the other end said that I was late on my payments and that I needed to get caught up soon, or they'd take away my monkey.

I don't own a monkey, but I played along.

The man hung up as quickly as a Jack in the Box burger, and I was just wondering what sad, dateless, monkey-loving soul I'd just saved from a payment, when in he walked. It was my mild-mannered neighbor Jack. He's a surfer from Ohio.

"Lex-dude, have you seen the news?" He always says that, and then I have to respond the same way.

"Nah, dude. I don't have a television or a radio." I didn't have a paper either, but Jack didn't have to know that.

"Then you won't guess what just happened, dude!" I bet I could. Jack always comes to me with some sap story about his dentist suing him or his dog digging a hole under his bathtub. "There's been a guy writing articles in *The New Fruiton Times* about how bad poets are in this city—and I'm his latest victim."

Oh. Good thing I didn't have any money riding on that bet.

"Well, Jack-dude, I don't know what I can do about this. I didn't even know that you were a poet. Why don't you just go over to the Times building and tell the guy to stop?" I said. Sometimes you have to jump-start Jack's brain.

"But, Lex! I came to you because I don't know who the guy is; he's been writing anonymously." Hmmm…probably to avoid house-egg-ings.

"Alright, Jack. Let me get this straight. You…want me…to find the guy and tell him off?"

Jack sighed. "Yes, Lex. You're a detective. You do this kind of thing, right, dude?" I do what I can to pay the bills, win the bread, bring home the bacon, keep the heat on, paint the bathroom, wash the car, cook the celery, play the flute, shine the cat, spike the punch…what was I saying?

"So will you do it?" Oh yeah, that poetic thing.

"Sure; and since you're my friend, I'll solve this case for half the price of a normal case." Jack perked up. Either he liked this idea or his power bar was kicking in. But I didn't have the time to ponder; I had a case to solve.

I bussed it to *The New Fruiton Times* building and arrived at a hair past a freckle. I don't own a watch either.

It was a tall building, as tall as that tall thing I saw that one time, and the elevator was broken. Just my luck. I hadn't had to climb that many stairs since the war; I was a mail boy at the Pentagon. This brought back frightening memories of enemy stamps and renegade letter openers. I shuddered as I finally reached the last step. Good thing that was over.

I found a reporter wandering around and decided to ask him some questions about the editor and who had been here lately and where a guy could get a good poppy seed muffin. Man, those are good.

"I don't know what you're talking about. I haven't seen anyone," he said. But what about the muffin? I was about to ask, when the man continued. "I only come in when I have to. I don't think I want to be a reporter anymore." The man was pacing now and looked like he was about to cry. So, I did what anybody in my position would have done.

I tossed a bowl of soup at him. Good thing there was a lid on it.

"Why don't you tell me your name, kid, and we can have a civilized conversation here." I sat down at his desk and he pulled up a chair, looking as dazed as my Aunt Betsy after a St. Patrick's Day dinner.

"My name's Eddie Paramount, and I don't think we have any poppy seed muffins." What had he been smoking? I brushed off his comment and began interrogating him. I had almost decided that there was nothing suspicious about this Eddie, but he got up to heat the soup and I was able to interrogate his desk.

There was a poem under a stack of papers. It looked like Eddie had written it, but it was called "Damn Poet." Why would Eddie write a poem like this?

> *O you poor hamster*
> *Tragically struck by a spoon*
> *The culprit has run!*

It seemed a hamster had been killed with a spoon. And there was a damn poet involved. Eddie must have been a poet assassin hired to kill hamsters. No, maybe it was Eddie's hamster that was killed by a poet. But I could hear him coming back and covered up the poem.

I decided to discreetly figure out what was going on with this Eddie, if that was his real name. "If you don't want to be a reporter, why don't you do something fun. Like...poetry?"

"WHAT?!" Perhaps he was hard of hearing. But before I could repeat what I said, he piped up again. "I hate poets and their damn poetry." And there was much gnashing of teeth and wringing of hands before he finally admitted that his hamster had been killed by a poet with a spoon.

Eddie was my first suspect and I drew him in my handy-dandy sketchbook as I continued on my way to the editor's office. But, I enjoy creative freedom in my work and gave him a sinister goatee. He looked good. Maybe I should be on one of those reality TV shows; I've always liked the Fab Five. We could be the Fab Six. Too bad I'm not gay. Oh well, I'm not as witty as Carson Kressley anyway.

I eventually made it to the editor's office, but he wouldn't say anything about the mystery critic. Something about editor-writer confidentiality. He did let one name slip, though. Fuse.

I rushed home after that. I had to find Jack.

*********************

His last name is Fuse. But why would Jack send in articles criticizing poets if he is a poet? And why would he criticize his own work? But most importantly, why would he leave his roast in the oven for so long?

By the time I got back to our building, the poor hunk of meat was as black as the bread I eat for breakfast. Man, I need a new toaster.

But there was no time to dwell on such things. I asked Jack about the articles. Was he allied with this Eddie Paramount?

"Dude! Why would I criticize myself?" This kid knew exactly what I was thinking. I hoped he didn't know what I was thinking just then, because it involved a can of pasta sauce and a vat of rising bread dough.

"Lex! Did you hear me? Man, sometimes you remind me so much of Steve Martin in that movie *Dead Men Don't Wear Plaid.*"

"Steve Who?" I hate it when people make obscure references to obscure actors. "Never mind; I said that maybe there's another Fuse in New Fruiton." Jack had to be right. He couldn't be the only one, and it didn't make sense for him to be a suspect. But how could we find out who the other Fuse was?

It was my Harvard-educated cactus Bill who figured it out. He has a PhD in needlepoint, after all, and found the phone book for us.

> *Bill my cactus friend*
> *You are sharp like a Cheese-It*
> *Ouch! Don't touch me dude*

Hey. Maybe I should be a poet.

Jack and I looked up the only other Fuse in town. His name was Pierre and he lived on Tomato Street, a controversial part of New Fruiton. We headed there right away, but Jack seemed distressed. He was as nervous as a jelly doughnut attending an Overeater's Anonymous meeting.

Pierre Fuse was out when we got to his apartment; his shrill old landlady had to point us in the direction of a warehouse he hung out in. What a weird guy. But we legged it over to the next block anyway, and that was where we found him.

"Jack-dude!" Pierre called from a corner as he glanced up from his laptop.

"Hello, Pierre-dude. This is Lex-dude," Jack said as coldly as that cold thing I ate three years ago. He wasn't distressed anymore; now he was angry.

"Dudes." I nodded, wondering what was going on.

"Lex-dude. Pierre is my brother," Jack said to me. "I should have known you would do something like this, Pierre! You were always so jealous of me! But you were the smart one—you went to Harvard, you became successful. Why would you write damaging articles about me?"

"Hold on, Jack....You went to Harvard, Pierre? Did you know Bill? He's about yay high, kind of green, cactusy..."

"Bill....Bill! Yeah! That cactus always had the in with the ladies, dude! We had some totally wild nights back in college! How is old Billy?"

"He's good, he's good. He's actually working at the New Fruiton University...." But I caught the look on Jack's face and decided to change the subject back to the poem thing. "Pierre, how could you do this to Jack? What did he ever do to you?"

"He stole my childhood." Stealing is a criminal offense. "I did everything better than him, but he always got all the attention because he was the youngest! And where was I? In the background with my nose in a book, that's where. Just to get away from everyone and their love of little Jack!" Pierre had walked over to us now and his spit rained on our faces. I felt like singin' but stifled the urge.

"Well, that may be, but you've been getting attention lately with your writing. Maybe you should quit your day job and write full time. I bet you could be pretty good. The both of you could write a book together. Just think: The Brothers Fuse."

"Do you think so, Lex-dude?" they asked. Totally.

They were planning their first creative venture when a certain hamsterless man popped into my mind like a New Year's noisemaker. "Hey, Pierre. Were you working with a man named Eddie Paramount? Did he help you get your articles published?"

"Yeah, dude. Why?"

"I think maybe you should go see him, make him a Fuse brother or something. He didn't like his job, but maybe he'll like writing with you guys."

So they went off and a writing trio was born. They put the past behind them and soon had their first book out: *Flying Dolphins and their Striped Pajamas: A Novel*. All thanks to that poetic thing we did.

***********

Now, here I sit in my tiny office again. Ahh, Demetri Martin. How do you write such beautiful poetry? It's like a piano skiing down Mt. Rushmore with its puppy John the Fetcher.

> *Birthday clown, I think*
> *That you are not that happy*
> *One balloon dog, please*

### A Snapshot of Tragic Youth *by Christine Takaichi*

Like the solitary beacon of a lighthouse, my brother Matthew hunches before his computer, alone in the dark night with nothing but the comfort of the blaring screen. The large window to his side shows his thin, weak-looking silhouette, which inspired his nickname "Quasimodo." His beady black eyes stare unblinkingly forward, most likely at a picture of a Korean pop singer. Most pathetic about this image is that the sickly-looking seventeen-year old boy looks completely oblivious to the tragedy of his life.

Computers seemed a likely outlet for Matthew. Always attracted to the uncool, boring, and nerdy, at the age of five he wanted to be a minister. We still listen to the tapes of him belting out Christian songs for old time's sake. Even though I was two years younger, I could sense that Matthew would always be far from what was considered cool. Soon my uncle introduced Matthew to the sad, sad world of videogames, and Matthew's chance for interaction with other children his age disappeared. Atari. Nintendo. Gameboy. Super Nintendo. Nintendo 64. Play Station. Play Station 2. I watched as Matt channeled his need for friends and a life into the land of Mario and Kirby, spending hours developing bad posture in front of the television screen. Still, I said nothing, ever. Even when Matthew declared that Pokemon was the coolest thing since the Power Rangers and began playing the card game with other misfits at lunch. By then, I was going through a personal crisis of my own. Coming from my socially inept family, I lacked the crucial abilities to relate to children my own age and at one point began a Losers Club. In addition, some sadistic twelve-year-old introduced me to Old Navy and my closet became a nightmare of nerdy clothes.

Eventually Matthew made the transition from videogames to computers, part of the natural evolution geeks undergo. Where else could he find entire web pages dedicated to photographs of dog feces? He was transfixed. Matthew proceeded to spend all of his savings, including his *babysitting money* (that's right, Matthew was the only boy in a Red Cross babysitter's course) on computer parts. By freshman year he was struggling at his new high school, not only because he looked much younger than fifteen thanks to a lack of exercise and sun, but also because he had finally caught up with everyone else and realized that playing card games at lunch was a no-no. Forced to learn the crucial social skills he should have gained while sitting in front of the screen, Matthew lumbered through freshman and sophomore year. It wasn't until junior year that Matt discovered his true identity: student of AP History. No conversation about Matt omits references to his history class. But now he has finally found something else to do with those long hours on the computer besides reading about computer installations: talking to fellow dweebs who eagerly await the SATs.

Now that Matthew has embraced the loser within, I am coming to terms with being dealt a tough hand of cards in life. I had no mentor to teach me fashion sense or boy-trapping skills: I had to rely solely on the publications deemed appropriate by my mother: *Newsweek* and *American Girl* magazine. While I could easily rattle off Fareed Zakaria's article about the war on terrorism and make homemade crafts, associating with other children my age terrified me. In addition to the lack of guidance, I developed a phobia of shaking other people's hands, which created a rather weak first impression when I saw someone's outstretched hand, panicked, and ran away. My sole mentor throughout the terrifying process of growing up without social skills was Matthew. When I was terrified of beginning middle school, who reassured me? (He told me that I'd get stuffed in a trashcan.) Who else taught me how to judge Beanie Babies on their cuteness in our Beanie Baby Club, which he was the president and treasurer of? (I was the vice president and secretary. We were always looking for new recruits but none of them had that "Beanie Baby" star quality. Besides, we didn't know anyone in the neighborhood.) And what would I do without his advice? "[Your current] grade is so easy. Wait `till you get to [my current] grade. You won't have straight A's anymore." (So far, his predictions have been off.)

Matthew will not abandon his post at the computer in our den: rain or shine, he rests like the Sphinx of Egypt overlooking the Sahara desert. In fact, I expect that he will always be here, living at home with our parents. I myself have decided to join a nunnery. To a simple-minded pedestrian strolling down the street, it may appear a pathetic snapshot of tragic youth: but in this comforting sphere of computers, Matthew has discovered true joy.

### Hola, Abuelo *by Heather Frambach*

My mother's cold green eyes follow me across the room as I walk past her, shuffling quickly under the heavy weight of the long box in my arms.

"Are you done with your homework?" she implores.

"Yes," I reply, staring back with my own cool green stare. She sighs and reluctantly sets her gaze back on the TV, a bright, sharp contrast to the rest of the poorly lit room and the dull, faded blue of the couch she is lying on.

I resume my brisk walk down the dark hallway, eager to unload the contents of the box. Suddenly, my eyes fall upon an old picture on the wall of my mother's mother and father on their wedding day—the only picture of my grandfather in the house. Their bright young faces suck what little light the hallway holds into them. I pause for a moment and stare into my grandfather's eyes. Although the picture is black and white, I imagine that his eyes are a brilliant green, tinged with a light, fiery brown on the outside edge.

"Hola, Abuelo."

I blink as I step into the room at the end of the hall, letting my eyes adjust to the single steel lamp in the corner of the room. Deliberately, I set down the box and carefully empty it of its contents: stamps.

My grandfather was a philatelist.

Becoming more excited now, I pull a thick, heavy book from the box, running my fingers anxiously over the faded blue cover and the gold embossed title: THE GREAT AMERICAN STAMP COLLECTION.

Inside the box, which I now eagerly unpack, are dozens of thick envelopes covered and overflowing with so many stamps I have to take a few deep breaths to even comprehend them.

I remember asking my grandmother about the stamps about a week after she had first dropped them off at our house. Not quite sure about how to bring up the subject, or even how to regard my grandfather— "your husband," "Mom's dad," "Grandpa" didn't sound right at all— one day while we were driving, I said bluntly, "I like the stamps."

"Yo se, Changita. Oh how he lo-o-oved those stamps," she reminisced, jumping right into conversation. "Otros hombres? They spent their money at the bar, but Virgil had his stamps. He was a good man," she declared proudly. I realized this was the first time she had ever said his name in front of me, or anyone, for that matter, though I know she thought about him often from the countless self-help books strewn about her house.

I pick up on things quickly, so I figured I would have no problem with this stamp thing; I'd just pick up where my grandfather had left off. Oh-so-carefully, I lifted a batch of the precious squares until they sat right beneath my nose. I inhaled. They smelled like Grandma's house.

Like tortillas and tamales.

Like stories of Tejanas bellas and how the girls in Mexico can *dance*.

Like a home I had never known.

Like Mexican.

Turning a beautiful 1918 Portuguese stamp in my fingers as if it had been of God himself, I reluctantly set it down and picked up a pair of tweezers. I wasn't about to let the cold teriyaki chicken I'd had not too long ago destroy these treasures.

Surrounded by the huge array of stamps, envelopes, and Bud's Sure-Stick Stamp Adhesive, I dug in. I flipped through the huge blue book, ready to sort and stick just as Grandpa would have done. I decided to start at the end—the latest date in the book was 1961, and he didn't seem to have too many of those. Easy. Smiling now, I dug through the piles of stamps and pushed a batch from 1961 to the front.

OK. Now where do I begin? Small, long. April 1961. Damn it. That's OK, I'll come back.

Cuban issue, June 1961. Big. Roosevelt, May 1961, Prague September Independence issue January Empire State Building December.

No. I really can't do this without him. I was frantic now. Where was my grandfather in all these stamps? No, I'm not looking for Hungary or Canada or Belgium at all. I'm looking for *him*.

Where are you, Grandpa? I wondered silently. Were you good with kids? Would you have been here, showing me everything about your stamps?

I imagined his long, calculating fingers—accountant fingers—guiding me through the tedious process of sorting and placing the stamps. I envisioned his brown, wrinkled face...a smile of affection, maybe. I looked down at my own childlike fingers, thick and clumsy from the clash of Mexican and white in me. I clenched them suddenly, hating everything. I heard my father's elitist doctor-voice in the next room, saying, "You know, if your father's accident had happened today, we would have the technology to save him."

My mother is silent.

Sitting quietly in the sea of cluttered stamps and tears and the thick scent of loss, I realize: everything is in its right place.

# *Resources*

The following works contain observations and information that can begin, flesh out, underscore, or close a lesson. Their background, histories, and examples range from the lighthearted to the insightful, but they also illustrate how entertaining and compelling language is.

*A Pleasure in Words* by Eugene T. Maleska. Maleska catalogues his etymological findings by historical, geographical, and linguistic types: "Our Hellenic Heritage," "Imports from Spain and Italy," "Roots, Branches, and Twigs," and "The Wild and the Tame," among others.

*Anguished English* and *The Bride of Anguished English* by Richard Lederer. A historian, grammarian, and word hound, Lederer has composed a slew of books on the foibles and follies of English. The *Anguished Bride* duo is, as one subtitle suggests, "A bonus of bloopers, blunders, botches, and boo-boos." What makes the books amusing and horrifying is that all the errors have been published, including such confusing headlines as "Million Woman March Attracts Thousands," questionable bulletins like "Immaculate Conception Tonight at 7 P.M.," and fearless declarations like Serena Williams's "If I had not lost, I would have won." Lederer's list of lollapaloozas illustrates the results of bad diction and poor phrasing.

*Circumlocutions:* The Internet abounds with websites providing torturous rewritings of maxims, saws, or Christmas carols (as at members. aol.com/Ifenech/indexlc.html). Deciphering these titles and sayings tests students' vocabulary and word root skills. Kids enjoy figuring out that "Antlered Quadruped with the Cerise Proboscis" translates to "Rudolph the Red-Nosed Reindeer" or "From Dark Till Dawn, Soundless and Sanctimonious" is "Silent Night, Holy Night."

"Daily Dose": *The Washington Post* annually publishes alternate definitions for mainstream words, like these recent winners:

*Abdicate:* to give up all hope of ever having a flat abdomen

*Lymph:* to talk with a lisp

*Testicle:* a humorous question on a test

*Balderdash:* a rapidly receding hairline

*Pokemon:* a Jamaican proctologist

*The Deluxe Transitive Vampire: The Ultimate Handbook of Grammar for the Innocent, the Eager and the Doomed* by Karen Elizabeth Gordon. Steeped in the gothic, grammarian Gordon's books *(The New Well-Tempered Sentence, The Disheveled Dictionary,* and others) bring the macabre to the mundane world of grammar. Gordon deals with the basics from parts of speech to phrasing to fragments, but dips them in deep vats of ennui, menace, and atmosphere.

*Dubious Doublets: A Delightful Compendium of Unlikely Word Pairs of Common Origins* by Stewart Edelstein. A collection of "word pairs of common origins," *Dubious Doublets* tracks down the common source of seemingly unrelated words. "Lettuce" and "galaxy," for example, have a common denominator in the Latin *lac,* meaning "milk." Lettuce, from *lactuca,* came to be so named because of "the milky white sap exuding from the stalk when cut." The milky appearance of the distant stars inspired the Greek *galaxias,* which means milk, and *via lactea* is Latin for "milky way."

*Getting Your Word's Worth* by Rod L. Evans and Irwin M. Berent. This word game collection explores aptanagrams, palindromes, captinoyms, semordnilap, phantonyms, and gramograms.

*Horrible Headlines:* Jay Leno has made horrible headlines a late night fare, but they have a function beyond the entertaining. Explaining how misplaced modification, poor word choice, or strained syntax accounts for such gems as "Something Went Wrong in Jet Crash, Expert says," "Police Begin Campaign to Run Down Jaywalkers," "Safety Experts Say School Bus Passengers Should Be Belted" is educational. Try such Internet sites as www.ebaumsworld.com/newspaperhead.html for examples.

*It Was a Dark and Stormy Night* by Scott Rice. Inspired by Bulwer-Lytton's infamous opening line, Scott Rice sponsored contests soliciting the worst opening sentences for novels thankfully never written. Note this submission: "The lovely woman-child Kaa was mercilessly chained to the cruel post of the warrior-chief Beast, with his barbarian tribe now stacking wood at her nubile feet, when the strong clear voice of the poetic and heroic Handsomas roared, 'Flick your Bic, crisp that chick, and you'll feel my steel through your last meal.'" These delightfully horrid excuses for prose teach by negative example: inappropriate diction has its consequences.

*The Joy of Lex* and *More Joy of Lex* by Gyles Brandeth. Brandeth is a word player par excellence, and his two books are collections of word games. The "Lex" books abound with word histories, obscure definitions, palindromes, anagrams, puzzles, visual gags, crosswords, rebuses, malaprops, gobbledygook, regionalisms, hip rap, and tests of skill too odd to delineate in brief.

*Ladyfingers and Nun's Tummies: A Lighthearted Look at How Foods Got their Names* by Martha Barnette. Barnette investigates categories of food names (i.e., "Foods Named by Mistake," "Food Names Associated with Religion," "Foods Named for What they Look Like") and explains how various names came about. "Linguine," she explains, is Italian for "little tongues," an etymology that not only explains the connection between the pasta's name and appearance but also connects linguine with such language-based terms as "linguist," "lingo," and "bilingual." There's even a distant relation to the mouth candy, "lollypop."

*Madlibs.* Price/Stern/Sloan has published a slew of these fellows, collections of prose passages with missing parts of speech that students fill in to produce pieces sounding like twisted versions of "Jabberwocky"

*Morris Dictionary of Word and Phrase Origins* by William Morris. An etymological compilation that explores such phrases as "down the hatch" (a nautical term comparing the mouth to a ship's hole), "rhubarb" (meaning a heated argument, rhubarb comes from the cinematic fold when film crowds were directed to mutter "rhubarb" under their breaths to indicate anger), and "flapper" (the name for girls of the 1920s who defied social convention and refused to tie up their galoshes, the resultant flapping sound echoing as they walked).

*No Uncertain Terms* by Mark Dittrick and Diane Kender Dittrick. There's a difference, the Dittricks declare, between spumoni and tortoni, calculator and computer, or understudy and stand-by. This short book provides clear and colorful delineations.

*The Play of Words: Fun and Games for Language Lovers* by Richard Lederer. Lederer's collection of words games based on puns, anagrams, metaphors, word roots, similes, definitions, homonyms, eponyms, and others.

*Poetry for Cats: The Definitive Anthology of Distinguished Feline Verse:* Henry Beard parodies a range of popular poetry from Chaucer to Blake to T. S. Eliot, organizing his subject matter around kitty concerns.

*Poplollies and Bellibones: A Celebration of Lost Words* by Susan Kelz Sperling. Evolution occurs in words as well as species, and Sperling has collected some whose passing we might legitimately lament. We learn that a "yeresyeve" is a "gift given at the new year or upon taking office," that "flerd" means fraud or deceit, and "mmfles" are a previous name for freckles.

*The Puzzlemaster Presents: 200 Mind-Bending Challenges:* A regular on NPR, puzzlemaster Will Shortz composes word games that are entertaining and educational. These snippets make for fun class closers.

*Sniglets* and *More Sniglets* by Rich Hall. Hall defines "sniglet" as "any word that doesn't appear in the dictionary, but should." His menagerie of terms veers between mangled word roots ("gyroped: A kid who cannot resist spinning around on a diner stool.") and variations on the familiar ("checkuary: The thirteenth month of the year. Begins New Year's Day and ends when a person stops absentmindedly writing the old year on his checks.").

*Verbatim:* This quarterly from Chicago (http://www.verbatimmag.com) offers amusing and informative articles on words. Fare includes the likes of "Seinfeldisms," an examination of words and phrases that emanated from the sitcom and entered the language of the masses, i. e., "double-dip" ("To dip a chip, take a bite, and then dip the chip again."), "regift" ("To give as a gift something one received as a gift."), and "antidentite" ("A person who dislikes or is prejudiced against dentists.").

*When is a Pig a Hog? A Guide to Confoundingly Related English Words* by Bernice Randall. A horse might be a horse, of course, but a pig is a hog only when it goes to market weighing over 120 pounds. Randall's book is an argument for precision, knowing the difference between seemingly similar words, like the historian's use of "period" when designating an interval of time but "epoch" or "era" when singling out a distinct or radical period.

*Word Games* by Gyles Brandeth. Brandeth's contribution to the world of word games includes spoonerisms, malapropisms, goldwynisms, anagrams and antigrams, and such word sport as botticelli, jotto, hangman, kolodny's game, and balderdash.

## Lesson Ideas

- **Dictionary page.** Colleagues at a previous school developed this lesson. Students prepare a dictionary page containing five or more original words, replete with definitions, parts of speech, pronunciations, and sample sentences. The page is laid out in two columns with headers and a pronunciation guide.

- **Name the colors.** My thanks to Lisa Snow of Christian Heritage High School in Salt Lake City for this idea. Anyone whoever looked to paint a room in white knows the difficulty of distinguishing one shade from another. Manufacturers aim to make the choice easier by providing cryptic titles: oyster shell, dove white, albumen, and plaster of Paris. Bring in a range of color paint chips and let students come up with their own names. As an addendum, play Sarah MacLachlan's "Wear Your Love Like Heaven" (or the original by Donovan) for examples of unusual-yet true-colors: havana lake, rose carmethene, alizarin crimson.

- **Victor Borge.** Video tapes of pianist/comedian Victor Borge's routines include his reading of a prose passage, interjecting verbal sounds indicating the work's punctuation. Borge's collections include *The Best of Victor Borge Acts I and II* and *Victor Borge's Funniest Moments*.

- **Punctuated passages**. Make a list of punctuation symbols and challenge students to compose a paragraph incorporating them all.

- **You can grade poetry**. Students aware of rhetorical and poetic devices write better poetry, and poems are short enough for teachers to grade quickly for immediate feedback. Stylistic devices can also be required for poetry, making grading guidelines specific for teachers and clear for students.

- **Parody.** As Jack Beard's *Poetry for Cats* and Andrew Barlow's "All I Need to Know I Learned by Having My Arms Ripped off by a Polar Bear" demonstrate, parodies require an ear for style and a mind for mimicry. Students can imitate poems, prose, advertising, movie scenes, or television. Particularly fertile fields for parody are the strained similes of romance and detective fiction, samples of which are available on such Internet sites as www.joke-archives.com/toplists/badromance. html, www.topfive.comlarcs/t5012700.shtml, and www.faithfulword. org/goodmedicine/trivia_020bads.html. NPR's "Prairie Home Companion" offers a particularly accurate parody of bad detective fiction in its "Guy Noir" serials.

—·—

Our discussion on induction finishes with a look at its use in analysis, but rather than focus solely on textual analysis, Chapter 7 argues that induction can be used in a range of analytic approaches.

# Piece by Piece:
# The Specifics of Analysis

---

**Focus**: *Analysis is a two-fold process: identifying a work's specifics and then, via induction, explaining how those specifics create the work's focus. A comprehensive writing program teaches varied analytic approaches so students can negotiate a text from several angles.*

---

**Sections:**
- Textual Analysis
- Sociological Analysis
- Psychological Analysis
- Mythological Analysis
- Deconstruction
- The Specifics of Analysis
- Student Samples
- Lesson Ideas

Let me begin with a story.

Once upon a time, I was a very poor teacher (this hasn't changed much). Unable to fund repairs for my 1969 Volkswagen Fastback, I attempted them myself with the aid of a more knowledgeable friend. Ken instructed me to pull the car's engine and tear it apart, piece by piece.

I didn't know a thing about engines, but I figured that if I kept unscrewing stuff, anything could be dismantled. Then, an odd thing happened. Handling the engine's parts, I found out that gas and air are mixed in a carburetor, and that the term "manifold" referred to metal pipes through which that air is conducted. This mixture was then channeled to the engine block where pistons smashed gas and air together, the resulting spark driving piston rods up and down. In short, by tearing the engine down, I figured out how its parts worked together to make the whole operate. (That I failed miserably in repairing the car and had it towed to a dealer, who charged me scads of money to fix my Fastback, isn't the point here.)

This is what analysis does: it tears a text down into its parts and explains how those parts work together to produce the ultimate effect of the passage. The opposite of synthesis, "analysis" is a Greek term, loosely translated as "to unloose, to undo." The *Oxford English Dictionary* refers to this root when it defines analysis as "the resolution or breaking up of anything complex into its various simple elements." In chemistry, the term means "the resolution of a chemical compound into its ultimate elements"; in optics the term is defined as "the resolution of light into its prismatic components"; and in literature itself, analysis is defined as "the investigation of any production of the intellect, as a poem, tale, argument, philosophical system, so as to exhibit its component elements in simple form."

Hence, analysis literally means to examine a subject part by part. In communications studies, analysis is the decoding part of the communication process. Language, a system of symbols, involves the coding of ideas into those symbols a sender delivers to a receiver who decodes them. Analysis, then, is the activity we engage in every time we listen, read, or take in sensorial impressions. Once the receiver has obtained the coded message, he engages in the breaking down of the message into component parts (analysis/decoding/deconstruction) and then inductively works from those component parts to assemble meaning. Put more simply, via analysis we deconstruct; through induction, we ascertain meaning.

Thus, the instructional goal of analysis is to demonstrate how to break a text into smaller parts—its specifics—that are examined in light of their interaction, an examination which yields the meaning of the text. The process works as follows:

- Analysis: The reader breaks the text into its specifics.

- Induction: Those specifics are examined to determine their relation, i.e., their patterns.

- Hypothesis: Those patterns are explained via a connecting idea.

So we first use analysis to identify the component parts of a text. Then, working inductively from specifics to generalities, we determine the text's meaning. The act of analysis thus draws from the same elements that comprise the foundation of structuring: analysis/specifics, induction/sections, and hypothesis/focus.

Having first clarified for students how analysis works, we then teach them a variety of analytic approaches. Secondary level instruction primarily focuses on textual analysis, yet mythological, sociological, psychological, and deconstructive approaches are equally helpful. Indeed, a text that is difficult to approach textually often gives over its meaning more readily via other analytic applications. In addition to providing students with more writing tools, instructing them in a range of analytic techniques gives them choice, which enables them to approach a text with their own understanding and insight. The near-exclusive use of textual analysis on the secondary level is, like the death grip of the five-paragraph essay, more default than planning. Its solo position in the curriculum often reflects a lack of awareness of other approaches rather than a thoughtful consideration of effective methodologies. Teachers tend to teach what they were taught, thus perpetuating the shortcomings of instruction from generation to generation. One argument against teaching other analytic approaches is that students are incapable of using more sophisticated methods. This is the same argument used to defend the primacy of the five-paragraph essay: it's the only structure students can understand. In fact, elementary teachers touch on these types when they teach narrative conflict. Inner conflict (individual versus self) is delineated via psychological analysis; when we teach the individual versus society (any conflict between groups), we are using a sociological approach; and when we teach the individual versus god/fate/the universe, we are employing a mythological approach. Finally, deconstruction is often used in media analysis (determining the motive behind the message), but it is equally applicable to unearthing meaning in fiction and nonfiction.

Deborah Appleman addresses this discussion in *Critical Encounters in High School English*, taking issue with the charge that high school students aren't capable of any analytic approach but textual analysis. As Appleman argues, we do our students a disservice in depriving them of additional ways to tackle a text. Moreover, noting that analysis creates thinking skills that transcend the classroom, Appleman insists that teaching a variety of analytic skills prepares students to broaden their critique of a text to see its cultural implications

> so students can see that they, as readers, are socially constructed subjects. The texts are also constructed in particular social contexts—which may be quite different from their own and which they may need to study—and that different ways of telling stories have consequences. (61)

Finally, the student who struggles with textual analysis may find a mythological approach more accessible. Similarly, she may have difficulties performing a textual analysis on *Jane Eyre*, but find compelling the novel's dissection of economic class, religious warfare, or gender inequalities. And rare is the student who can make nothing of Hamlet's inner conflict. Teaching a range of analytic methodologies not only gives our students more techniques to work with, the concept of analysis itself becomes clearer when students can see its varied formats.

# *Textual Analysis*

*The play's the thing.*

—William Shakespeare, *Hamlet*

Textual analysis gained its greatest emphasis in the twentieth century and is primarily associated with the New Criticism movement that grew in England during the 1930s. This approach to literary analysis disregarded biography and history, insisting that the worth of a text was to be found in the text itself without reference to its authorial or cultural background. Thus, New Criticism stated that we must look at the elements of writing as utilized within the piece under analysis, so that we examine its use of rhetorical, sound, and figurative devices. By understanding how these techniques work together, we begin to see how the ultimate effect of tone, theme, or statement is developed. Thus, we can explain how a piece achieves its ultimate goal via the text alone.

In this analytic method, we examine the work's structure, rhetorical techniques (e.g., irony, tone, etc.), figures of speech, sound devices, and other literary stylings. By examining these specifics, we begin to see recurring ideas we can then explore for the development of a central thesis. In examining the poem "Design" by Robert Frost for example, we might first note that, structurally, the work is a sonnet, leading us to look for the characteristics of a sonnet (e.g., logical structure or a turn at the break). We might then note its imagery, as in the way the color white—austere and cold—contrasts with other colors, such as blue, that suggest life. We might also note the rhetorical technique of posing questions in the poem's sestet, as the speaker moves from detached observer to discomfited participant by noting the spider's skill in waylaying the fly; the speaker wonders what kind of universe could kill such innocence. After gathering all our observations, we then formulate a thesis about the poem's effect.

Ultimately, any analysis must ask, "What effect is achieved?" After we identify the components of a work, we need to ascertain why the author utilized the devices he did. If we isolate a particular simile, or an arrangement of images, we must determine "Why?" By making it clear to ourselves what this device does, we begin to pin down the key ideas of the literary composition.

The specifics of a textual analysis are mainly rhetorical devices. I provide the following guideline for my students.

## Specifics of Textual Analysis

*Visual Traits*: Look at the length of the paragraphs and the arrangement of lines and stanzas.

*Syntax*: Grammatical constructions. Consider the use of pronouns, verbs, adjectives, etc. Which is most emphasized? Note the order of the subject, predicate, complements and modifiers: does their arrangement create a specific tone or voice?

*Sentences*: Length and structure. Look at the number of words, kinds of sentences (e.g., simple, compound, complex, compound-complex), and sentence patterns, including irregular uses like fragments or run-ons. In poetry check out the line (meter) and stanza length. Note the rhythm of the sentences as they work together.

*Diction*: Choice of words. Determine whether the words are formal or informal, concrete or abstract, connotative or denotative.

*Sound Devices:* Look for sound devices: assonance, consonance, alliteration, and onomatopoeia.

*Imagery*: Word pictures. Is imagery a primary device or used sparingly? What mood does the imagery evoke? Examine the images for connotative or symbolic overtones.

*Figures of speech:* Literary devices. Contrast the use of figurative and literal language: simile, metaphor, symbol, personification, reification, metonymy, synecdoche.

*Structure*: Arrangement of ideas: Look for chronological presentation, flashback, stream of consciousness, connection by suggestion, contrasts or comparisons. Is the piece primarily narrative, descriptive, or expository. If the piece is a poem, is it arranged in traditional structures, or is it free verse?

*Point of view:* Speaker. Determine how the author chooses to tell the story. Does the point of view shift?

*Tone*: Tone is the attitude the speaker takes toward the subject matter, the emotional coloring of the work. If, for instance, a friend tells you, "I'm going to get married today," the facts of his statement are clear. But the emotional meaning may vary according to the tone of voice with which the statement is made. He may be ecstatic ("I'm getting married today!"); he may be incredulous ("I can't believe it. I'm getting married today."); he may be resigned ("Might as well face it: I'm getting married today."); he may be in despair ("Horrors! I'm getting married today.").

# *Sociological Analysis*

*Happy families are all alike; every unhappy family is unhappy in its own way.*

—Leo Tolstoy, *Anna Karenina*

As its name implies, sociological analysis is concerned with the way social groups operate. If the psychological is an investigation of the individual, the sociological focuses on groups, clarifying how segments and elements struggle against each other for power or validation.

In much of his work, French intellectual Michel Foucault argued that all relationships are power relationships, whether between king and servant, employer and employee, husband and wife, lover and lover, father and daughter, teacher and student, neighbor and neighbor, friend and friend. Relationships are interactive, and the persons involved set up hierarchies depending on how each perceives the other and what that other brings to the relationship. Foucault notes that the power within a relationship is not necessarily exploitative; rather, power is the understanding participants have as they determine—often unconsciously—where areas of strength and weakness lie, and how each participant is to act with the other. The aim of sociological analysis is to explicate the nature of the power inherent in all relationships.

Whereas psychological analysis attempts to understand characters and their behaviors, sociological analysis targets groups of characters, isolating the conflicts and inadequacies in the arrangement and between individuals within and without those groups. In Classical literature, society comprised those at the top of the power ladder, so that writers examined only that segment of culture with the most influence over others. Aristotle in his *Poetics* argued for this orientation when he insisted tragedy focus on persons in high places. Over two millenia later, Arthur Miller shifted the focus down the sociological ladder when he created Willy Loman, the last name indicating Miller's challenge of Aristotle's definition.

In the last century, cultural critics have come to view society not as a single culture, but as an interaction of cultures: society is less a specific group than a dialogue among groups. This dialogue produces culture, so that an analysis of culture requires an understanding of the groups (i.e., the specifics) that make it up. In this way we might examine *Hamlet* not just as a set of intrigues in the court of Elsinore, but also as an example of women's role in a patriarchal culture (Ophelia and Gertrude), the countervailing world of the commoner (the clowns/gravediggers), the dynamics of family relationships (father-son foils), the sexual behaviors between parent and child (Hamlet and Gertrude), or the uses of class as a power ploy (the killing of Rosencrantz and Guildenstern; the crowd's support of Laertes).

By the close of the nineteenth century, sociological analysis found more fodder to feed on. Whereas the satires of eighteenth century England focused on the aristocracy, industrialization encouraged the rise of realistic and naturalistic writing, moving the focus of discussion further down the social scale. In such a world view, the fate of Stephen Crane's *Maggie* is more than a study of a fallen woman; it is an indictment of the social setting that deprives her of choices. When John Dos Passos composed his pastiche pieces, from *Manhattan Transfer* to *The USA Trilogy*, he broadened the discussion of society to include the disenfranchised. Similarly, sociological approaches to subject matter allowed the examination of gradations within the upper class (the writing of Edith Wharton, Henry James, E.M. Forster, and Virginia Woolf) and critiques of social forces that created an underclass (John Steinbeck, Bernard Malamud, Zora Neale Hurston, Richard Wright, John Osborne, and Toni Morrison).

In the twentieth century, new studies in gender and political history encouraged the founding of feminist and Marxist approaches to literature. Where previous sociological analyses of the works of Charles Dickens focused on his satirizing of English manners and customs, more recent studies have examined his predilection for waiflike female characters and their role within patriarchal culture, while other critics have noted Dickens's critique of class in such novels as *Bleak House* and *Hard Times*. A sociological approach isolates the forces that create conditions under which the characters operate, as opposed to focusing on the characters themselves, as well as the power structures that direct and influence individual and group behavior.

Ultimately, increasing globalization encouraged sociological examinations of conflicting national cultures, as in Chinua Achebe's *Things Fall Apart*, Alan Paton's *Cry, The Beloved Country*, and Julia Alvarez's *Yo!*. Traditionally, social groups have been viewed as those in power, so that European, patriarchal societies have dominated cultural discussions. But the urbanization and industrialization of the nineteenth century increased awareness of groups that, though removed from centers of power, nevertheless interacted with and affected other cultures. As twentieth century notions of cultural identity were redefined, culture itself underwent revision. Sociologists began to recognize a variety of sub-cultures based on gender, economics, education, religion, work, geography, ethnicity, nationality, social trends, and customs.

Nor need cultures be defined by size. The friends we associate with, the colleagues we work with, comprise our most intimate cultures; the most influential culture we operate within are our own families. The discussion of family dynamics has also shifted from the aristocracy to the middle and lower classes, from Louisa May Alcott's *Little Women* to Tennessee Williams's *The Glass Menagerie*, Anne Tyler's many writings, and Asian-American Amy Tan's *The Joy Luck Club*. In our roles as father, mother, daughter, son, we operate within social conventions and familial expectations that develop our primary senses of self, as evidenced by Eugene O'Neill's last works, including *Long Day's Journey Into Night* and *Moon for the Misbegotten*.

The dynamics of power are, ultimately, the purview of sociological analysis. The modern and postmodern eras have been dominated by discussions of the interaction of social groups, from the political (e.g., George Orwell's *1984* and *Animal Farm* and E.L. Doctorow's *The Book of Daniel*) to the colonial (e.g., Joyce Cary's *Mister Johnson* and Brian Moore's *Black Robe*) to the gendered (e.g., Maxine Hong Kingston's *Woman Warrior* and Toni Morrison's *Song of Solomon*), the economic (e.g., *The Grapes of Wrath* and Harriett Arnow's *The Dollmaker*), the sexual (e.g., James Baldwin's *In Another Country* and Henry Miller's *Tropic of Cancer*), to the religious (Chaim Potok's *The Chosen* and Nikos Kazantzakis's *The Last Temptation of Christ*).

In the postmodern era, the complexities and tragic/comic interactions of our social organizations have inspired a number of absurdist visions of culture, as in John Irving's *The World According to Garp* and Joseph Heller's *Catch-22*. Heller explores power systems that direct the fates of his novel's characters, depicting their circumstances as so proscribed that all cultures become destructive. Heller begins by calling attention to smaller groups (e.g., friendships, fighting units) that interact, then enlarges his scope to explore larger cultures and their structures, including the fields of law, medicine, psychiatry, and education. Finally, in an overarching comment on the nature of power groups themselves, Heller ups the ante to show how these larger groups are themselves contained in the patriotic abstractions of nationalism and corporate maneuverings, all of these subsumed, as he illustrates, within the cosmic culture of the universe itself—the ultimate catch-22—the symbol of the illogicality of all systems. By exploring cultural levels in this way, Heller comments on the difficulties of finding meaning and individual validation within these structures. Sociological analysis is a powerful tool for students, which provides multiple perspectives from which to view an author's work.

# *Psychological Analysis*

> *Why then will you say that I am mad?*
>
> —Edgar Allan Poe, *The Tell-Tale Heart*

A twentieth-century movement, the psychological approach to literature developed after critics realized that Sigmund Freud's analysis of the personality could be applied to characters and their motivations. In detailing the inner mind, Freud supplied writers and critics with an understanding of the workings of inner conflict. Though Freud's work has been added to and revised, an understanding of his principle ideas is helpful in any character analysis.

The salient aspect of Freud's studies in psychoanalysis was his explanation of the subconscious. Most psychology stems from this belief in an area of the mind below the conscious level from which a rich repository of images, dreams, and impulses emerges into the conscious world. Hence, a psychological analysis aims to unearth a character's hidden impulses (i.e., the specifics of personality). Once we understand these impulses, we can explain how they contradict one another and/or contradict societal rules. Put another way, psychological analysis primarily deals with the conflict between what a character unconsciously desires and a contrary desire on the part of the same character that violates social norms. Though Freud's early model of the subconscious and conscious mind has been revised by many of his followers, his original model makes a good starting point for an understanding of his early thinking. Seeking to explain the way our sense of self develops, Freud delineated three aspects of the human personality: the id, the subconscious part of our perceptual-conscious mind that is marked by impulses toward pleasure, aggression, and instinctual behavior; the superego, that part of the mind shaped by societal rules and which checks the impulses of the id; the ego, the resultant personality that guides us in our social behavior as we attempt to balance our private impulses within our social setting.

Freud's model thus operates like a dialectic in that the human personality results from the conflict between the interior and the exterior environment. Freudian psychology's aim was the unearthing of the subconscious so that the patient could more fully understand why he reacted to his environment as he did. Hence, Freud's work encompassed the study of dreams, hidden/repressed memories, associational thinking, the role of the family in establishing initial patterns of behavior, and the suppression of sexual and aggressive impulses.

### Identity
Freud's contribution to self-understanding was to add the dimension of the subconscious. Previously, our sense of identity was developed from what we consciously knew of ourselves, what we saw in our daily behavior. But by suggesting that a large—perhaps the largest—part of our identity is shaped by a hidden portion of our minds Freud complicated the issue of identity by noting that how we behave is not who we are, but is instead the result of conflicting desires and impulses. Thus, a full understanding of our identity required more knowledge about an interior world we had only modest access to. As psychoanalysts investigated this conflict between our interior and exterior worlds, they saw behavior as a compromise between the two, a compromise that hid the inner battle disguising a range of mental states.

### Clinical Behavior
By seeing the self as a result of conflicting impulses, psychoanalysts

first explained aberrant behavior and then more socially common behavior. At one extreme, they saw the destruction of the self—its failure to reconcile internal and external demands—in sociopathic behavior (individuals unresponsive to social regulations), schizophrenic behavior (individuals unable to create a dominant ego), and neurotic behavior (individuals overly accommodating of social expectations). But as twentieth century studies continued, it became apparent that most individuals partook of some of these clinical conditions, particularly as it is nearly impossible to reconcile the self-serving desires of the id with the communal expectations of the superego. In short, psychoanalysis also documented milder forms of identity complexes such as depression, a mental state wherein the self is unable to accept the resolution of the conflict between id and superego. In such an individual, an ego/personality is still formed but operates in a hindered state, much like a car engine operating on only four of its six cylinders. Such a machine can function, but without full efficiency. Hence, psychoanalysis aimed to clarify for the patient how various impulses conflict; the resulting understanding becomes the first step toward resolution of the inner conflict.

### Repression

The key to psychoanalysis is releasing hidden fears, anxieties, and impulses that operate beneath the conscious level, but, nevertheless, control the patient's behavior. The importance of unearthing these hidden areas was related to another of Freud's theories—the consequences of repression. Despite our use of denial, Freud insisted that emotional impulses—e.g., anger, sorrow, fear, sex—do not disappear. Instead, they are manifest in other, more socially acceptable ways. Thus, a son frustrated by his inability to please a parent may redouble his efforts to appear perfect rather than confront the parent. Similarly, a woman who feels unable to control social expectations regarding her appearance may seek such control by disciplining her own body, resulting in such eating disorders as anorexia and bulimia. What begins as a form of psychological survival—the repression of an emotion one finds unpleasant—in time becomes a clinical behavior that wreaks more havoc than the original impulse would have. Freud's major work in the area of repression dealt with the most socially unacceptable emotions: aggression and sexuality. He suggested that the repression of aggression occasionally results in violent behavior, from the battered child to the aggrieved employee, or was rechanneled into opportunities for social praise, as in the workaholic or fanatic; these conditions are viciously circular and create their own disorders. In discussing the pleasure principle, Freud argued that the repression of sexual desire was at the base of many psychological disorders as patients superimposed social morality on the amoral id. His classic study, based on Sophocles's *Oedipus Rex*, argued that children grow up with natural sexual impulses, first directed toward their parents, which are accompanied by feelings of aggression toward competitors for a parent's affections. Thus, boys feel the desire to "marry" their mothers and perceive their fathers as threats (the Oedipal Complex), while daughters seek to displace their mothers in their fathers' hearts (the Electra Complex).

### Society and the Individual

Ultimately, psychoanalysis requires an understanding of how the individual's interior desires conflict with the world around him. In some cases, this creates an interior conflict as the protagonist seeks to repress impulses he knows to be socially unacceptable (e.g., the characters Holden Caulfield, Gulliver, Huckleberry Finn, Macbeth, Edna Pontellier, Daisy Miller, Willy Loman, Stephen Daedalus, Blanche DuBois), while in other instances the conflict is between the individual's desires and the conformity of his social environment (e.g., Hamlet, Janie Crawford, Jane Eyre, Ralph Ellison's invisible man, Quentin Compson, Elmer Gantry, and the personas in the poetry of Walt Whitman, Emily Dickinson, and The Beats). What undergirds both conflicts is the attempt of the protagonist to create or maintain an identity despite the forces imposed by society or by the self's own superego.

### Existentialism

Many authors—from the writer of *Ecclesiastes* and the playwrights of Greek tragedies to Renaissance essayists, Romantic poets, and modernists—have struggled with their own identity and its place within the larger context of the universe itself. In these works, the superego is that part of the individual created by that individual's perception of what god/providence/the universe is. The spiritual crisis these authors denote is a failure to reconcile the individual's inner desires with the expectations of a higher being. The greater the conflict between his interior world and the world he perceives as dominant and omnipotent, the deeper the crisis. Unable to reconcile the self with god, the writer is often absorbed by guilt and self-recrimination, as characterized in the protagonists of Dostoyevsky, Eugene O'Neill, Jean-Paul Sartre, Albert Camus, Franz Kafka, and Graham Greene.

An interesting aspect of psychological analysis is that, despite its fairly recent arrival, it has been used to interpret literature composed centuries before Freud. Psychological approaches to Shakespeare, for example, have intrigued critics as well as actors, the latter using psychology to provide insights into how to portray dramatic characters. Any work with well-developed characters can be approached psychologically. In *The Scarlet Letter*, for instance, Nathaniel Hawthorne's characters are motivated by guilt, anger, and repression. An understanding of their actions requires insight into their inner conflicts. To comprehend Dimmesdale's silence, it is important to delineate the interior struggle he faces as an adulterer in a community in which he is also the minister. Understanding the nature of this conflict makes his life-destroying confession at the novel's conclusion more compelling.

As Freudian studies moved into the mainstream, they generated more accessible theories, many of which have found their way into high school classrooms. Two of the most popular revolve around the work of Abraham Maslow and Lawrence Kohlberg. Maslow posited a hierarchy of needs, which suggests that man addresses his physical requirements before moving on to self-actualization. Kohlberg hypothesized a continuum of moral development, stages by which humans move from self-centered, punishment-based behavior to more altruistic, enlightened actions.

---

## Kohlberg's Stages of Moral Development

An accessible tool in character analysis, Lawrence Kohlberg's "Stages of Moral Development" is frequently taught in high school classes. It can be replicated in a chronologic or continuum structure, which enables students to detail the progression of a single character or compare a range of characters.

### PRECONVENTIONAL STAGES
**Behavior motivated by anticipation of pleasure or pain.**

*STAGE 1: Punishment and Obedience*

Characters are motivated by fear or punishment. Behavior is deemed good or bad depending on its consequent punishment.

*STAGE 2: Bartering and Exchange*

Characters do right because they are rewarded for such. In this way, morality is not an ethical debate but a bargaining process. Good deeds bring satisfaction, making morality a pragmatic issue.

### CONVENTIONAL MORALITY
**Acceptance of the rules and standards of one's group.**

*STAGE 3: Interpersonal Conformity*

Characters at this level find rewards via approval from others as they conceive behavior in social terms. They do right because others do right and avoid doing wrong because others deem it wrong. They act ethically not as a result of an internal discussion of ethical behavior but because they have learned to socialize their behavior.

## STAGE 4: Law and Order

Society becomes embodied in legal institutions. Characters emphasize the importance of social stability as protected by obedience to laws and a desire for justice. Those doing wrong are to be punished for their debt to society. The individual identifies with social institutions and finds fulfillment in seeing their maintenance. Justice is the reward for upholding the higher order; injustice occurs when that order does not reward right behavior or protect the vulnerable.

## POSTCONVENTIONAL OR PRINCIPLED MORALITY
## Ethical principles.

## STAGE 5: Prior Rights and Social Contract

Stage five characters believe the state exists to guarantee the rights that man is naturally endowed with, as the Founding Fathers argued. One works within the social system because it is likely the best avenue to bring about universal justice. In this stage, one is equally oriented toward the rights and needs of others as well as one's self. The social contract aids the individual, who submits to it to bring about the highest fulfillment; concurrently, the social contract cannot revoke a right the individual is entitled to. For this reason, the individual is actively involved in the construction of his liberties, seeking ethical behavior that follows from reasoned debate and thought.

## STAGE 6: Universal Ethical Principles

Characters in this final stage of development need no social contract or laws to regulate their behavior. Self-motivated and universally directed, they regard themselves and all others as worthy of dignity and respect others inherently, not for reward or sanction. This is most often borne out of a belief that all people are innately good and act accordingly. Goodness is natural and desirable and its own reward.

# *Mythological Analysis*

*"Well, now that we have seen each other," said the Unicorn,*
*"if you'll believe in me, I'll believe in you. Is that a bargain?"*
—Lewis Carroll, *Alice's Adventures in Wonderland*

Despite the connotations of its name, the mythological approach is also a twentieth-century development, since in that century the work of anthropologist James Frazer, psychologist Carl Jung, and mythologist Joseph Campbell overlapped to increase our understanding of folktales and myths. Through such work we have come to realize how these primitive tales contain structures and symbols very much a part of all cultures—including ours—and that these structures and symbols are embedded in all literature, no matter its date of composition.

A list of mythological archetypes and motifs would be overwhelming: a collection of folktale motifs by folklorist Stith Thompson runs to several volumes. Generally, though, an understanding of the structure of the journey—and its attendant characters, particularly the hero—would enable a reader to make sense of the mythological elements of any literary piece. F. Scott Fitzgerald's *The Great Gatsby*, for example, is a tale of lost innocence. As the novel unfolds, we become aware of an initial stage of innocence for all the novel's characters, most particularly Gatsby himself, who was once a youthful, idealistic believer in the American dream. However, as Gatsby sets out on his journey eastward to achieve an aristocratic lifestyle, he is unexpectedly—and reluctantly—waylaid by Daisy, whose promise of eternal youth compels Gatsby to strive, like Icarus, for a lifestyle that can only harm him. By the novel's end, narrator Nick Caraway can only lament and praise the hero's beautiful dream to maintain an innocence that is inevitably corrupted.

Understanding the mythological underpinnings of a work aids our comprehension of the author's intent. In Shakespeare's *Hamlet*, it is helpful to know that tragedy has its roots in Dionysian fertility rites because fertility imagery abounds in the play. The vegetative images repeatedly refer to the Garden of Eden, a myth embodying the loss of innocence and the first intimations of mortality, all of which parallel Hamlet's movement from a loss of innocence to his death. Similarly, awareness of the hero's journey enables us to see Hamlet's development from an innocent to a world-weary adult who passes through various initiations in his quest for revenge.

The core mythological archetypes are the hero and the journey. In various guises—the innocent, trickster, warrior, martyr, sage, and scapegoat—the hero journeys from a stage of innocence through a debilitating initiatory experience to struggle with questions of identity and physical challenge until he resolves his inner and/or exterior conflict. Carl Jung—once Freud's heir apparent—shifted his psychological studies to explore why myths resonate within us. In contrast to Freud's individual subconscious, Jung posited the existence of a universal subconscious, a realm rich in images and symbols that all humans draw from. Universal images and figures—archetypes—suggest that our brains are hardwired to recognize particular images, though cultures create variations of these, a concept mythologist Joseph Campbell explored in his study, *The Hero with a Thousand Faces*. Though Jung's heirs have explored a variety of heroic archetypes, the most common include the following.

## The Innocent

The innocent possesses an innate understanding that has little basis in wisdom or knowledge. Such characters were once called simpletons or silly people, words that have different connotations in our time. In the medieval world, both words connoted divine guidance, silly meaning "blessed." As opposed to the traveler who comes to understanding as a result of experience, suffering, and, hence, knowledge, the innocent understands intuitively. Thus, he is often a child or childlike, whether that be a figure like Pollyanna or a simpleton like Walt Disney's Goofy, who seems to do right despite his ignorance. In the folktale he is typified by Jack, who stupidly exchanges a cow for a few beans. But Jack's trade produces a beanstalk, which connects heaven and earth, and at the top he finds treasure. A typical tale of an innocent is "Our Lady's Tumbler," a twelfth century French legend. This story tells of a tumbler who dedicates his life to the Virgin Mary. Though he is efficient as a tumbler, he is deficient in all the skills of the monastery and unable to worship the Virgin as his brothers do. Thus, while the other monks worship according to monastic precepts, the tumbler can only perform tumbling tricks before a statue of the Virgin. And when his comrades hear of his performances, they angrily hurry to catch him in the act. But as they come upon him, ready to seize him, the statue comes to life, and the Virgin gently reaches down and tenderly wipes the face of the tumbler. Thus, are we all instructed.

## The Trickster

The trickster succeeds through deception, tomfoolery, and playfulness. Because of his irreverence and often disrespectful attitude, he is associated with the young teen, the character who challenges the status quo indirectly and subversively. Indeed, the trickster abounds in teen flicks (numerous John Hughes films contain trickster characters, from *Pretty in Pink* to *The Breakfast Club*) as well as sitcoms wherein teenage children continually outwit their parents (e.g., "Who's the Boss," "Malcolm in the Middle," "The Simpsons," etc.). But the true trickster shows by his antics a deeper truth. Professor Harold Hill of *The Music Man* gives the citizens of River City, Iowa, a self-respect they had not known. Ferris Bueller—another Hughes creation—would teach us that life is to be lived (carpe diem); Pee Wee Herman teaches that the common and the mundane hold surprises if we apply our imagination to them; Bugs Bunny shows that the race does not go to the strongest or the meanest, but to the cleverest. The trickster dominated Max Sennett comedies in the characters of Charlie Chaplin and Buster Keaton (though Harold Lloyd would qualify as an innocent), or the antics of the Marx Brothers. And on television, the trickster shows up as Lucy, Sgt. Bilko, and Hawkeye Pierce. In classical literature, he is found in Odysseus's deception of Polyphemus, Chaucer's "The Miller's Tale," and Shakespeare's fools. Each of these characters charms us, but also teaches us.

## The Warrior

This classic archetype is the character who does not subvert the system, but faces it straight on. While the trickster would ignore the rules, or turn them wittingly against those who make them, the warrior acknowledges them and matches his strength against the established boundaries, which shows us that it is possible to be good, wise, pure, and decent, and still win. Socially, this is recognized as an advance over adolescence as the character works within established limits but overcomes them on their own terms rather than through subversion. As Joseph Campbell has shown, each society needs warriors to show it how to challenge its limitations and defeat them, and our line of warriors stretches from Achilles and Odysseus through Beowulf, King Arthur and Sir Lancelot, until we approach the modern warrior, who is more burdened by restrictions but nevertheless heroically fights them. This type is signaled at the birth of the modern age in Hamlet and echoed today in R. P. McMurphy in *One Flew Over the Cuckoo's Nest*. (Interestingly, because of the nature of his creation, McMurphy also works as a trickster.) The twentieth century's sense of despair and hopelessness has expressed itself through warriors more supernatural than their predecessors; hence, the development of fantastic types like Captain Midnight, Superman, Batman, the Lone Ranger, and other superheroes.

## The Teacher/Prophet

Teachers are often heroes who have returned from their adventures to instruct initiates. Now fully integrated into society, they represent the matured hero who becomes other-directed, consciously going beyond example-setting to instruction, using experience and wisdom to guide others. Such a type is represented in George Lucas's *Star Wars* films in the figures of Obi Wan Kenobe and Yoda, and as Mr. Miyagi in the 1980s *Karate Kid* films. In folk literature we see this type in the wise old man who guides the younger child through dangerous straits. In medieval literature, Merlin fulfills this role. Interestingly, it is not unusual for this type to use elements of the trickster to teach indirectly, at which time he bears a similarity to the shaman of primitive cultures. For instance, in the Sufi religion, the character of Mullah Nassr Eddin teaches his disciples through antics meant to shock them out of their complacency and un-questioning attitude. This is a favored device of Zen Buddhism as well. In a representative Nasr Eddin episode, the famed teacher addresses a group of listeners, asking them, "Do you know what I have to tell you?" When they answer no, he responds that because they are ignorant of such an important truth, he'd best hold his tongue. When he returns the next week and asks the same question, this time they answer yes. He responds with pleasure, telling them that there is no point in wasting their time then, and he leaves. When he returns a third time and asks the same question, half the crowd answers yes while the other half answers no, to which Nasr Eddin responds, "Well, then, those who know can tell those who do not know" and leaves the mosque. Such an exchange would fit neatly into any Marx Brothers movie.

## Wise Fool/Saint

At the end of the spectrum is the character who has returned to a state of innocence, but his condition is the result of a lifetime of experience that has taught him a simplicity that compels childlike behavior. In modern literature, Herman Hesse wrote of such a character in his short story, "The Poet," wherein the protagonist is attracted to a teacher who leads a simple, austere life. Taking instruction from the teacher, the poet eventually moves away from his complex world until, at story's end, he has taken the place of the teacher. The motif parallels Herman Hesse's *Siddhartha*, based on the life of Gautama Buddha. The wise fool is apparent in Jimmy Stewart's portrayal of Elwood P. Dowd in *Harvey*, where the protagonist, after years of clawing his way through the business world, becomes so simplistic as to become a teacher to his family and would-be psychiatrist. The archetype is also the basis for Martin Vanderhoff in Kauffman and Hart's *You Can't Take It with You*. In this play, Grandpa heads a family of eccentrics and social dropouts whose combination of innocence and wise foolishness complement each other and wean Tony Kirby and his stuffy father away from the destruction of their souls by Wall Street.

Each of these types is distinct from protagonists who only entertain, terrify, or amuse us. The point of the innocent, trickster, warrior, prophet, and wise fool is to guide us to an understanding of a truth that eludes us and make us aware of our entrapment in an existence that, for all its realistic appearance, is not reality. By making us aware of, or showing us the way to, a higher reality these archetypes appeal to our need to find means by which we might recapture some sense of paradise that we can no longer apprehend in our state of ignorance or prepare us for a future paradise.

| | **The Stages of the Journey** |
|---|---|
| *Innocence* | In the stage of innocence the world and we are one. We feel no division or separation from others and believe we are, literally, the center of the universe. Suffering is minimal and short lived, and death is a foreign concept. For the most part, our lives are happy and pleasant. |
| *Initiation* | Three kinds of events can occasion our fall from innocence: death, an awareness of evil, and/or sexual awakening. All of these events go counter to the feelings we experience as innocents. Death tells us, first, that someone we love dearly can be irrevocably separated from us; second, it tells us that no one, including ourselves, is immune. Thus, our awareness of death is awareness of our own mortality. Similarly, the success of evil violates our belief in the fairness and justice of the world, contravenes all the lessons our elders taught us about rewarding good and punishing evil. If suffering can exist without compensation and bad deeds go unpunished, then our moral compass has failed us and we are left wondering what is the good of good behavior. Finally, sexuality creates intense desire within us, a desire that can either be initially frustrated or, in the event of a failed relationship, fulfilled and then retracted. The rejection of the emotional intimacy we bring to a relationship makes us wary of loving again, and such a rejection by the person we most trusted damages our confidence in our ability to act wisely. Thus, initiation experiences tempt us to short circuit our emotional/spiritual growth, for the future now looks dangerous and illogical. |
| *Chaos* | The state of chaos is where all art is created. It is the struggle of our existence to reconcile the information revealed to us through the initiatory experience and move on despite our belief that the future holds only more pain and unrelieved suffering. For many, the desire is to move backwards, to return to a state |

| | |
|---|---|
| | of innocence, and employ denial against what we do not want to acknowledge. But true heroes are not defeated by this knowledge, and instead transform it into wisdom. Distilling experience, they reconcile the seeming paradox of good and evil and are strengthened by it. |
| ***Resolution*** | It is important to remember that the hero who advances to the fourth stage does so with open eyes. The hero is not that person who has learned how to evade the knowledge of the fall, but has integrated it into a wider, fuller, and truer vision of the world. It is not sufficient to live *in spite of* the threat of death, but *because* of it. More specifically, the hero realizes that death makes life fragile and temporary; therefore, he lives each moment as if it is his last. In this way, death creates appreciation for life. Mythologically, most heroes advance to the fourth stage, but the intriguing aspect of the modern and postmodern eras in literature is the litany of heroes who fail to achieve the resolution of the final stage: Huck Finn, Edna Pontellier, Jay Gatsby, Willy Loman, Willy Stark, Holden Caulfield. By contrast the heroes and, mostly, heroines of feminist and ethnic literature tend to find a way through the darkness to a kind of peace, usually finding aid through community (in contrast to the male protagonist's desire for isolation) as in the writings of Toni Morrison, Zora Neale Hurston, Anne Tyler, Alice Walker, Denise Chavez, and Julia Alvarez. |

# *Textual Deconstruction*

*Pay no attention to that man behind the curtain.*

—*The Wizard of Oz*

If analysis is the revelation of meaning, deconstruction is the revelation of the meaning behind the meaning. Deborah Appleman writes that "deconstruction is a particular kind of unbuilding, one that takes into account the very nature, weight, and composition of the bricks or constructs it dismantles" (*Critical Encounters 102*). If analysis dismantles the text into its component parts, deconstruction examines the parts themselves: not what they mean, but why they were selected.

This is a powerful tool because it ups the ante on analysis and asks students to understand not what the text means, but why the text exists at all and what the motive was behind its creation.

> For many deconstructionists, the traditional conception of literature is merely an elitist "construct." All "texts" or "discourse" (novels, scientific papers, a Kewpie doll on the mantle, watching TV, suing in court, walking the dog, and all other signs that humans make) are of a piece; all are unstable systems of "signifying," all are fictions, all are "literature." (Appleman 104)

Playwright Bertolt Brecht had something of the sort in mind when he composed his theory of epic theater in the 1930s. Intending that his plays not entertain but instruct, Brecht staged minimalist productions, working with the barest of props, costume and scenery so the audience did not become distracted by the illusion of theater and overlook the text's message. But ironically, even Brecht's plays are text, and the deconstructionist would examine not the meanings Brecht wanted the audience to hear, but why the playwright chose minimalist theater itself, whether in creating his theory of epic theater—an attempt to undermine the illusion of drama—Brecht was merely creating an alternate illusion.

For this reason, deconstruction is the staple of media studies: an examination not of the letter the messenger rides in with, but of the horse he rides atop. If analysis asks, "What does it mean?" deconstruction inquires, "What is its intent?" Consider a truck commercial Nissan released in the late summer of 2001. Set in an iron foundry, the ad's soundtrack is the Chicago blues stylings of Muddy Waters singing "I'm a Man." Into a vat of volcanic hot iron rolls a variety of male icons: raw steak, a Viking helmet, a biker's jacket, and two balls stamped "100% brass." The molten mass is then poured into a mold and stamped, the sides falling away to reveal the truck that rolls off the assembly line. Clearly, the commercial is aimed at a male audience, tongue somewhat in cheek, and entertaining as it solicits us. But the deconstructionist would look beneath the humor and ask why such images convey machismo in the first place. What cultural assumptions turn a piece of cow cadaver into a sign of fertility and what kind of culture finds the evocation of such images so commonplace as to be amusing? And why did Nissan both parody, and yet depend on, such stereotypes to sell what is nothing more than a piece of metal that transports humans?

Applied to literature, deconstruction is immensely provocative as evidenced by the collegiate canon wars. As gender and minority studies have increased, so have attacks on the assumptions of college reading lists. Literary canons are assumed to be the repository of cultural values. If so, then the predominance of Western, Caucasian, male writing in education has raised the curtain on the Wizard of Oz: who, exactly, has chosen our texts, and why should we assume they reflect no bias? In such a debate, Joseph Conrad's *Heart of Darkness* is examined not for its vision of man's innate evil, but for its sanguine presentation of imperialist colonizing. Shakespeare's *The Merchant of Venice* is inspected for traces of anti-Semitism, James Fenimore Cooper's work for sentimentalized depictions of Native Americans, and the canon of American literature for a female who is neither childlike, angelic, nor seductive. When Zora Neale Hurston released *Their Eyes Were Watching God*, many critics praised its evocation of a rural black culture, rich in heritage. But as a black author, Richard Wright blasted its depiction of a black social class he insisted played on white stereotypes of blacks as indolent, simple, and irresponsible. Wright was later derided by feminists—black and white—for attacking a woman's depiction of a male dominated culture. And so it goes.

If utilizing deconstructive approaches to literature sounds like opening Pandora's box, well, that's part of the point. Many educators rely on the (mistaken) assumption that literature yields narrow, conventional meanings. Deconstruction opens up a black hole of possibilities, freeing the student from the grasp of the teacher, encouraging individual exploration of the text. Appleman explains that "instruction becomes less a matter of transmittal of an objective and culturally sanctioned body of knowledge, and more a matter of helping individual learners learn to construct and interpret for themselves" (21). Which seems like the point of education anyway.

# Specifics of Analysis

We teach textual analysis by identifying the use of literary techniques, such as figures of speech, sound devices, structure, and meter. By teaching these terms to students, we give them specifics to unearth and examine in the work under analysis. Mythological, sociological, and psychological analyses can be similarly taught, showing students the underlying specifics that make up the work they are studying. Though all three fields have myriad components, the most common and accessible are listed below.

- Mythological analysis *(individual versus fate/god)*
  - *Stages of the Journey:* innocence, initiation, chaos, resolution
  - *Heroes*: innocent, trickster, warrior, sage, magician, earth mother, scapegoat
  - *Images*: the elements (earth, water, fire, sky); numbers; colors
- Sociological analysis *(individual versus society)*
  - *Groups classifiable in any of the following ways*: class, gender, age, religion, politics, employment, nationality, ethnicity, family, ability, interests, species

- Psychological analysis *(individual versus self)*
  - *Models:* Freudian (id, ego, superego*)*; Maslow (Hierarchy of Needs); Kohlberg (Stages of Development)
  - *Clinical conditions:* neurosis, psychopathia, schizophrenia, manic depression
  - *Drives:* sexual, aggressive
  - *Emotional behavior:* sorrow, anger, joy, depression, etc.

# Student Samples

### *Fiction vs. Reality* by Katie Van Domelen

Where were you when you first found out?

I was 11, when it suddenly came to me that they weren't real. None of them were. Not the Tooth Fairy, not the Easter Bunny, not even Santa Claus survived. At first I completely rejected them; they weren't real and they had no place in my life. But now I'm realizing that it's the cultural heritage these fantasies represent that's important, not their actual existence.

Most children seem to go through this cycle of whole-hearted belief in fantasy to total denial and eventually to an understanding of how the two stages should mix. In Kaye Gibbons's book, *Ellen Foster,* Ellen also goes through these stages. However, contrary to other children her age, she must view the world through extreme realism before, not after, experiencing a beautiful fantasy world of make-believe. Only then can she finally find the balance that allows her to grow and yet still enjoy the dreams and fantasies of childhood.

In the first stages of Ellen's life, she is blunt, realistic and biased towards the world around her. She never sugarcoats anything and she seldom looks beyond the present, real moment. She shows this when talking about the undertaker for her mother's funeral and his pretense of caring: "I would like him better if he said it is my job to care, make more money than you will ever see just to care. That would not offend me" (Gibbons 15). This shows Ellen's impatience with superficial shows of politeness and respect; she only wants and knows what's real. She also feels as if it's her job to take care of those around her and has no illusions of safety or security. When her mother comes home from the hospital, Ellen takes it upon herself to see to her mother's health and well-being. "We peel her dress off over the head and slip on something loose to sleep in. I help her get herself laid in the bed and then I slide in beside her" (5). We can see that Ellen's subconscious longs to be taken care of as she slides into bed beside her mother, the very person who should be caring for her, knowing that in reality she must take care of not only herself but her mother as well.

In the beginning, Ellen wears no rose-colored glasses. She sees the world as it is, no less and no more. She believes there is a God only because at this point she doesn't have the philosophical nature to question what she's been told. But she does not believe in answered prayers. She has no vision of fluffy white clouds and pretty angels or a roving protective grandfather figure as a God. Her visions are of abandonment. In her words, "Everything was so wrong like somebody had knocked something loose....Some wild ride broke and the one in charge strode off and let us spin and shake and fly off the rail" (2). Ellen's reality is cold and harsh. Her imagination doesn't play with toys and furry animals. It dwells in wild amusement parks where she has to save herself from broken rides gone haywire and no one is there to help her.

After Ellen moves out of her home to live with Julia and Roy, she can let her imagination grow, and she begins to believe in being silly and having fun just for the sake of having fun and because someone else can take care of her now. We can see the transformation in the way Ellen describes how she spends her free time with Roy and Julia.

> Every Sunday we would all three lay on the floor drawing each other with blue hair or two noses or something silly. You name it. Or we would all take a part reading Prince Valiant and stand up and strike a pose when it is your turn to read. That was the best. (47)

It is amazing how something so fundamental, that almost everybody has done before, is such a stretch for her. It's something new that she never thought of doing before because it wasn't real. Before, she knew that people didn't have two noses, or blue hair, and didn't draw them that way. Now she is learning that fantasy is much preferable to reality, and she lets it take over. Ellen is exposed to the typical American family through TV and her own devious spy methods. She can see what it is to have a mother and father who provide for the children and who have all the clothes they want, and enough food. But seeing isn't enough; she longs to experience it. In her own personal free time she plays "catalog":

> I picked out the little family first and then the house things and the clothes. Sleepwear, evening jackets for the man, pantsuits. I outfitted everybody. The mom, the dad, the cute children. Next they got some camping equipment, a waffle iron, bedroom suits, and some toys. When they were set for the winter I shopped ahead for the spring...the man worked in the factory and she was a receptionist. They liked to dress up after work. (26)

Ellen's fantasies, while truly out of reach to her, are quite simplistic to most American children. She lets herself dream away about a family that is typical yet special because they love each other. She has lost her death grip on reality and has immersed herself in fantasy. Ellen didn't believe in Santa Claus because Santa Claus had never come to her house. Christmas was only slightly different from every other day because all the Christmas specials were on TV.

But this time she is spending Christmas with Nadine and Dora, and she lets her hopes rise. "All I asked for was the pack of paper but she looked at me like she was thinking of some surprises or just some small treats to go along with it….I bet she is racking her brain to come up with something else for me" (107–108). Again this seems like a small thing to dream about. But to Ellen, who never had a proper Christmas nor dared to dream that she should get gifts at all, it was a big step in imagination. She even went as far as to wait up for Santa Claus: "I stayed all night not able to sleep with…the loudness of my wanting to hear some something landing on the roof" (145). For Ellen, a girl who has had such a rough life, this is the stuff of her wildest dreams. To think that she should get gifts from someone else, not just from herself, is a dream, and it doesn't come true.

Eventually Ellen learns what each and every one of us finally comes to understand: that fantasy and fiction are necessary to complement and enhance the real world, that neither extreme should be exaggerated. When she is finally living with her new mama, she knows how to pretend, but she also knows what is real, as when she is talking about riding the pony:

> The other children know the pony is not specifically mine but they let me play like he is mine….I keep calling things mine but nothing actually belongs to me….But while you use or play with the things here it's Ok to call it yours. When you get through with something clean it up and put it back so the next one can call it his. (15)

Ellen knows the pony isn't hers, but she plays in a fantasy world in which she owns a pony and goes on long rides and adventures. It's the harmless type of pretend that at the end of the day is just pretend. She has other ways of playing. She sometimes daydreams of being a ballerina. "I myself am dying to put on the froufrou skirt and slick top Jo Jo dances around in. Not for somebody to see me but to stand in front of the hall mirror and observe myself private and practice my style of posing" (59).

By the end of the novel, Ellen is content and acts like any other child her age. She knows what's real, but she can read her books and paint her fantasies without getting so caught up in them that she can't get out. Sometimes, when I watch my brother and my sister staring eagerly out the car window searching for the Easter bunny, or running upstairs to safely tuck a tooth under the pillow, or sitting up late trying to hear hoof steps on the roof, I wish I could be like them. Earnestly believing and living in the fantasy. But then I think that if I were young like that again, my eyes would be closed to the real world, and I wouldn't be able to grow and think like I do now. Besides, it's important to have people around who know the secret.

If there weren't, who would hide the eggs?

## The 'Eyes' Have It: Sight, Blindness, and Spirituality in *Jane Eyre* by Katie Turley-Molony

*Amazing Grace! How sweet the sound*
*That saved a Wretch like me.*
*I once was lost, but now I'm found,*
*Was blind, but now I see.*

*Jane Eyre*, by Charlotte Brontë, is a deeply spiritual book in which religion is found at the intersection of sight and blindness. Like the repentant slave trader who wrote "Amazing Grace," Brontë finds salvation in sight and light. That is, her characters show that the route to God is, in varying contexts, smoothed by sight, and that spiritual insight conquers blindness. Brontë reflects the attitudes of her times. While the Victorians often connected physical defects and illness with ungodliness and mental depravity (Douglas 1), their views of blindness were not nearly so negative (Sharman 1). Indeed, Brontë's protagonists (Jane and Rochester) both are, in a sense, blinded—one by love and the other by physical destruction of the eyes—but in neither case is this blindness invincible or permanent. Charlotte Brontë is clearly preoccupied with sight and eyes, as seen in her detailed Study of Eyes (drawn in 1831; Shuttleworth, frontispiece). Both the abstraction of sight and the concrete nature of eyes themselves have spiritual meaning for Brontë.

Brontë fills *Jane Eyre* with physical descriptions of eyes and characters' uses of those eyes. Her portrayal of the eyes of Rochester, Jane, Helen, Mason, Bertha, and St. John as well as those of nameless "orientalized" people indicates her belief that eyes have qualities that can be defined in spiritual terms (Said 5). Jane's love for Helen and for Rochester at different points in the book takes on religious qualities, and nowhere is this more evident than in her remarks about their eyes. In both cases, she has a spiritual epiphany when she is inspired by their eyes. When Jane is unfairly punished by the religiously hypocritical Brocklehurst and becomes, in essence, a religious martyr herself, she finds a kind of salvation in the uplifting eyes of a fellow martyr. Religious imagery defines Jane's view of Helen: "[S]he lifted her eyes. What a strange light inspired through them!...How the new feeling bore me up! It was as if a martyr, a hero, had passed a slave or victim, and imparted strength in the transit" (Brontë 67). When Jane meets Rochester, her view of his eyes is also spiritual, although it is a more Romantic than Calvinist type of spirituality (Landow 1). Jane is spiritually moved by Rochester's eyes: "[T]he light of the fire... in his great, dark eyes; for he had great dark eyes, and very fine eyes, too—not without a certain change in their depth sometimes, which, if it was not softness, reminded you, at least, of that feeling" (Brontë 133).

Through Rochester, Brontë juxtaposes the image of Jane's clear, pure eyes with those of the demonic Bertha (Rich 149–150). In so doing, she represents Jane as Heaven to Bertha's Hell. Rochester quotes directly from the Bible in his optical metaphor:

> [T]his young girl, who stands so grave and quiet at the mouth of hell, looking collectedly at the gambols of a demon....Compare these clear eyes with the red balls yonder—this face with that mask...; then judge me....and remember, with what judgment ye judge ye shall be judged. (Brontë 299)

As in the case of Bertha, eyes can have a negative spiritual meaning as well. Jane finds herself ensnared by St. John's constant stare, making her sense a negative spirituality or superstition. "I found myself under the influence of his ever-watchful blue eye. How long it had been searching me through and through, and over and over, I cannot tell: so keen was it, and yet so cold, I felt for the moment superstitious" (Brontë 404). Eyes can lack spirit as well. Even attractive eyes can be empty. As Jane notes of Mason, "You detected something in his face that displeased.... his eye was large and well cut, but the life looking out of it was a tame, vacant life" (Brontë 193). Brontë connects eyes with the darkness and evil of slavery. Jane Eyre is embedded in the cruel history of trans-Atlantic slavery devoid of amazing grace, and numerous nameless others in the East are depicted as exotic, enslaved, and orientalized through descriptions of their eyes. Rochester and Jane joke of his having a harem: "And what will you do, Janet, while I am bargaining for so many tons of flesh and such an assortment of black eyes?" (Brontë 273).

Going beyond the physical description of eyes, Brontë examines sight itself in religious terms. She views clear sight as a route to God or spiritual enlightenment and darkness or blindness as a sign of spiritual ignorance. Early in the novel, Helen attains salvation through sight. On her deathbed, the devout girl connects eternal life to an ability to perceive God with her own eyes. At the moment in which she sees God, and not before, she believes she will be restored to God (Schwingen 1). She converses with Jane:

> "By dying young, I shall escape great sufferings"...."But where are you going to, Helen? Can you see? Do you know?"
>
> "I believe; I have faith: I am going to God....I count the hours till that eventful one arrives which shall restore me to him, reveal him to me." (Brontë 82)

While revelation is mandatory for Helen, for Jane, salvation through sight does not necessarily require a connection to a traditional image of a Christian God. Jane's spirituality is generally Christian throughout the book, but it also is eclectic, encompassing a maternal spirit. Jane views the matriarchal spirit in the sky as her salvation from the potential sin of adultery proposed by Rochester (Rich 152).

She [the spirit] broke forth as never moon yet burst from cloud:...a white

> human form shone in the azure, inclining a glorious brow earthward.
> It gazed and gazed on me. It spoke to my spirit...."My daughter, flee
> temptation!" "Mother, I will." (Brontë 324-5)

Jane's reply shows her profound spirituality, one formed in the mutual
gaze of Jane and the maternal spirit on one another.

Darkness, on the other hand, represents spiritual ignorance. Lowood
is shrouded in dark, and that darkness breeds disease. Jane notes that
"That forest-dell, where Lowood lay, was the cradle of fog and fog-bred
pestilence" (Brontë 77). What appears to be spiritual insight as produced
by light, however, may ironically impede one's attainment of God temporarily. Traveling through the dark, Jane reaches the seeming paradise
of Thornfield, the Rochester mansion. As she comes upon the house, she
is, in fact, initially blinded by the dazzling light there.

> [The] double illumination of fire and candle at first dazzled me, con-
> trasting as it did with the darkness to which my eyes had been for two
> hours inured; when I could see, however, a cozy and agreeable picture
> presented itself to my view. (Brontë 97)

This foreshadows Jane's blinded relationship with Rochester—ironically blinded by his bright fire, the metaphor Brontë uses to represent
him. Falling in love with Rochester, Jane remarks, "My eyes were drawn
involuntarily to his face: I could not keep their lids under control" (Brontë
177). Jane's eyes, the instruments of her spirituality, are pulled toward
Rochester and away from a previous connection to God. That is, Jane
makes Rochester a false idol and therefore cannot see God.

Jane, a deeply spiritual woman, is concerned. "I could not, in those
days, see God for his creature of whom I had made an idol," she declares
(Brontë 279). When Jane finally understands Rochester for what he is, a
married man, she calls out to God: "'God help me!' burst involuntarily
from my lips" (Brontë 309). Overcoming blindness to see the light once
again may, in fact, be a more effective route to God than never losing
one's sight in the first place. This is made clear with Jane's pleas for God's
mercy and help. Whereas earlier, Jane is unable to control her eyes when
gazing on Rochester, she becomes incapable now of controlling her lips
when crying out for God's help.

Rochester similarly finds salvation following blindness. He has, in
fact, already been moving toward God while recovering from the blindness caused by the fire. "You think me," he tells Jane, "I daresay, an irre-
ligious dog, but my heart swells with gratitude to the beneficent God of
this earth just now" (Brontë 454). This is his first step toward regaining
spirituality. Jane mediates his return to God through her own spirituality and her own clearer sight and insight. Regaining partial sight, Rochester is able to reach closer yet to God by being able to see the child he
shares with Jane, to whom he is now married. Indeed, "he could see that

the boy had inherited his own eyes, as they once were—large, brilliant, and black. On that occasion, he again, with a full heart, acknowledged that God had tempered judgment with mercy" (Brontë 460). Amazing Grace.

The illustration of saving grace through sight permeates Brontë's book. Rochester, wretch that he is, and Jane eventually comprehend Christian spirituality with their own clarity. They see each other, not as idols (for idols cannot bestow human love), but as soulmates:

> I hold myself supremely blest....No woman was ever nearer to her mate than I am....I know no weariness of my Edward's society: he knows none of mine, any more than we do of the pulsation of the heart that beats in our bosoms; consequently, we are ever together (Brontë 460).

# *Bibliography*

Brontë, Charlotte. *Jane Eyre*. New York: Penguin Books, 1997.

Douglas, Laurelyn. "Victorian Attitudes toward Health." *The Victorian Web*. Brown University. URL: http://landow.stg.brown.edu/victorian/health/health11.html (10 Apr. 2001).

Landow, George P. "The Doctrines of Evangelical Protestantism." *The Victorian Web*. Brown University. URL:http://landow.stg.brown.edu/victorian/religion/evangel2.html (10 Apr. 2001)

Said, Edward. *Orientalism*. New York: Vintage Books, 1978.

Rich, Adrienne. "Jane Eyre: The Temptations of a Motherless Woman." *Critical Essays on Charlotte Brontë*. Ed. Barbara Timm Gates. Boston: G.K. Hall and Co., 1990. 142-155.

Schwingen, Mary. "Religious Belief in Jane Eyre." *The Victorian Web*. Brown University. URL: ttp://landow.stg.brown.edu/victorian/bronte/cbronte/jane10.html (10 Apr. 2001)

Sharman, Caroline. "Nineteenth-Century Views of Blindness and Deafness and Jane Eyre." URL: ttp://landow.stg.brown.edu/victorian/bronte/cbronte/sharman10.html (10 Apr. 2001).

Shuttleworth, Sally. *Charlotte Brontë and Victorian Psychology*. Cambridge: Cambridge University Press, 1996.

# *Lesson Ideas*

- **The Hero and You**. In *The Hero Within: Six Archetypes We Live By*, Carol Pearson defines a variety of heroic archetypes and explains how they provide models for contemporary society. But the book also contains an examination students can take to determine which of several archetypes describe them. This two-page quiz is fun for students and piques their interest to learn more about archetypes.

- **Myth and Movies**. I dislike taking class time to show entire movies, so I often provide guide questions students can use as they watch films at home. Film scripts play repeatedly on journey and heroic archetypes, and guide questions enable students to isolate mythological motifs. The accompanying CD-ROM contains guide questions for *Dead Poet's Society, City Slickers,* and *Groundhog Day.* Also, *The Lord of the Rings* and the *Harry Potter* series draw heavily on mythological archetypes.

- **Varied Approaches**. Select a poem, short story, or song and analyze it textually, psychologically, mythologically, sociologically, and deconstructively. I've tried this with such poems as Margaret Atwood's "Siren Song" and W.H. Auden's "The Old Masters"; songs such as Suzanne Vega's "Calypso" and The Eagles's "Hotel California"; and short stories such as Hemingway's "Soldier's Home" and Anne Tyler's "Teenage Wasteland."

- **Deconstructing Media**. Our culture abounds with subliminal messages, and students enjoy taking apart advertisements, music videos, and television sitcoms. Asking why the media uses the images, structures, and voices it does both sharpens students' analytical skills and makes them more culturally savvy.

- **Pop cult Analysis**. Pop culture analysis has invaded the world of movies, sitcoms, and television dramas, churning out a number of books that make serious attempts to explain how our pop icons reflect transcendent beliefs. You can explore some of these arguments in such texts as *The Gospel According to The Simpsons: The Spiritual Life of the World's Most Animated Family; The Simpsons and Philosophy: The D'oh! of Homer; The Matrix and Philosophy: Welcome to the Desert of the Real (Popular Culture and Philosophy, V. 3); Seinfeld and Philosophy: A Book about Everything and Nothing; The Sopranos and Philosophy: I Kill Therefore I Am (Popular Culture and Philosophy).*

—·—

Without a scope and sequence writing program, our lesson plans become little more than isolated achievements. Students need to see how writing techniques can develop and build a coherent experience. *Writing is Dialogue: The Next Step* closes with a discussion on how to bring all the lessons together.

# Unit III:
# A Writing Program

*"The second, and more grave, reason for [English teachers'] failure is that they appear to place the emphasis on 'writing,' rather than on writing-about-something-for-someone. You cannot write writing."*

—S. I. Hayakawa, "The Use and Misuse of Language"

# Chapter 8

# Stew Versus Souffle:
# Scope and Sequence

---

**Focus**: A sequenced program, in the classroom and within the department, makes clear to students, and teachers, how skills are introduced and developed. By pooling its talent and resources, a department can develop a focused writing program that introduces and reinforces—not merely repeats—key skills.

---

**Sections:**
- A Voice in the Wilderness: The Goals of the Teacher
- The Process
- Sample Unit
- Project-Based Learning
- The Gang's All Here: The Goals of the Department
- Philosophy
- Sequential Planning: Stages
- Goals
- What Goes into a Sequenced Program?
- Addressing the Problems
- Program Overview
- Nuts and Bolts

When I first began teaching—young, immature, and very poor—I was in survival mode. My lessons were cannibalizations of the books each department chair handed me, memories of high school coursework, a fistful of ideas from college methods courses, nifty notions lifted from Saturday seminars, and anything creative I could scrape up late Sunday night. My teaching units were ideological collages, assembled with the overriding goal of getting to June. If nobody died along the way, I had a good chance of being rehired.

Planning a year's worth of lessons was like parachuting into the woods: I couldn't see the forest for the trees. I lacked focus, perspective, and therefore couldn't assemble the disparate parts into a cohesive whole. What we had here was a lack of induction.

It was in the third year of my fourth school that the lack of structure got to me, the irritating sense that as strong as I wanted each unit to be, it bore only a tangential relation to the units before and after. I thought I'd invented sliced spam when I began planning units that segued from one to the next, units that picked up and enhanced techniques and progressed through a continuum of ideas. I began focusing on themes, sequencing skills, and finding threads of thought that evolved over the year. This was induction writ large, working up smaller lesson ideas into larger units: it takes a bunch of trees to build a forest.

By my third year at the school, I was department chair, and my frustration was now aimed at the department curriculum. As good as some of our courses were, they didn't connect one to the other, follow through on skills, or work toward any but the most general of department goals. What I was doing in my courses—and what I knew others were doing—I wanted to do department-wide. On all levels, from the department down to individual lesson plans, I wanted to develop a scope and sequence program.

# *A Voice in the Wilderness:*
# *The Goals of the Teacher*

*For assessment to be reflective, it must grow out of a theory related to the particular teaching problem and students. In that sense, testing programs mandated by states and school districts or college English departments have nothing to do with reflective practice, nor do teacher-made tests that are administered without regard to specific teaching or learning problems.*

—George Hillocks, Jr., *Teaching Writing as a Reflective Practice*

*The aim of assessment is primarily to educate and improve student performance not merely to audit it.*

—Grant Wiggens, *Educative Assessment*

If you're a normal teacher, you probably have a number of good lessons plans, a number that you know you haven't got quite right, and a few you are directed to do. Some of the units work together better than others; some address department goals; some you developed because you love a particular book or writing assignment. And if you're a normal teacher, you've been doing this for some time, and you have somewhere between 150–200 students. When the papers come in, your family and friends don't see you for a long stretch. So, when someone suggests you need to overhaul each course, integrating every assignment until an overall goal is clearly attained, it sounds like a great idea that requires a lot of work.

Initially, it does. The payoff's down the road, when your kids begin to anticipate ideas you've laid the foundation for, when skills you've gone over start to sink in because students return to them in progressive assignments, when students refer to and incorporate ideas they learned at the beginning of the course. All scope and sequencing takes time to create, but the improvement in student work is noticeable.

So, to work.

Grant Wiggens bemoans the cart-before-the-horse syndrome in lesson planning, when "teachers choose a favorite activity (such as reading aloud, building a diorama, or conducting a research project) and then look in a very general way for an achievement that might plausibly be related to the task" (122). In other words, most teachers decide how to assess learning *after* they've completed the lesson plan. This is backwards: "Effective learning and school improvement are possible only when we grasp that curricula must be built backward from authentic assessment tasks, the latter providing a rationale and a basis for selecting content, skills, modes of instruction, and sequence" (205). Put another way, we must first decide what students need to learn before choosing the materials, texts, and projects they will encounter. Assessment is not an afterthought; it is determining in advance how students will demonstrate their understanding of the subject material. Having predetermined the goals and assessment activities, we must make those goals apparent to students throughout the unit, and not merely test for them at the conclusion.

For Wiggens, assessment is most effective when it is authentic, "when we anchor testing in the kind of work real people do, rather than merely eliciting easy-to-score responses to simple questions" (21). Assessment, then, is a testing of performance, a performance possible only when students have internalized instruction. As I have argued throughout this book, writing is not about drills, tests, or exams, it is about writing. Assessing writing is not about a student's adherence to formulas, it is about creating authenticity. Wiggens decries the formulaic testing that is the heart of national, state, and local exams, noting that they emphasize the less important aspects of writing: "Many state writing assessments run the risk of undercutting good writing by scoring only for focus, organization, style, and mechanics without once asking judges to consider whether the writing is powerful, memorable, provocative, or moving" (67). Wiggens argues that we most frequently test for "formal" traits—how many paragraphs, avoidance of comma splices, proper placement of a topic sentence—and rarely ask students to communicate persuasively, movingly, empathically, or intellectually. Frequently employing metaphors, Wiggens explains in *Educative Assessment* that drills are a preparation for an athlete, but they are not the athlete's raison d'etre. The quarterback who throws with precision in the pregame drills achieves little if he can't score during the game. The proof's in the putting the ball in the endzone.

Education specialist Howard Gardner writes that assessment tests for the understanding we need to apply our knowledge:

> Understanding is a sufficient grasp of concepts, principles, or skills so that one can bring them to bear on new problems and situations, deciding in which ways one's present competencies can suffice and in which ways one may require new skills or knowledge. (Wiggens 83)

This is not to say that what we ask students to do only in the classroom has no meaning, but if students produce work that matters nowhere but the classroom, we have failed fundamentally as teachers.

## *The Process*

> *What kind of task should we design in light of the evidence we need?*
>
> —Grant Wiggens, *Educative Assessment*

*Determine the Goals*: Ideally, any lesson addresses some larger department goal, but if you're on your own, then determine the goals for your course, the units for that course, and the lessons within each unit. Working inductively, brainstorm all that you find important about the course, all the lessons, ideas, materials, projects, texts, and papers. As you determine which learning experiences are more valid than others, isolate the reasons why, asking yourself what it is you want your students to learn, what values and skills prepare them for post-high school life. What you distill from this exercise will be your goals.

*Determine Assessment Activities*: What evidence will you have that students have met your goals? What activities will enable them to demonstrate their comprehension and understanding? These questions are key, for if we engage students in open-ended discussions, free inquiry, and inductive learning, we will find many traditional assessment tools inadequate. Teachers know the inefficacies of national and state testing, whose questions measure retention more than application. What better ways, then, can we encourage students to demonstrate understanding and not memorization? Consider experiences that require thought and application, from project-based learning to portfolios, visual and oral presentations, and writing experiences aimed at goals beyond writing for the teacher.

*Determine Methodologies*: Having decided what you want to assess, let that goal determine what teaching strategies will enable students to understand the material. Much of *Writing is Dialogue* has aimed to provide methodologies that focus on the conceptual and not the formulaic. A formulaic approach to literary analysis, for instance, provides students with a definition of a thesis and explicit instructions about where it should come in the paper. A conceptual approach, however, clarifies how a thesis works and, therefore, how the student might employ it to achieve his writing goal. A formulaic approach to teaching punctuation will focus on the memorization of grammar rules; a conceptual approach explains how punctuation shapes tone, thereby encouraging the student to replicate the voice in his head by utilizing the nuances of these markings.

*Determine Materials*: Finally, we can ask what texts, visuals, music, readings, film, etc., will best serve our methodologies. What becomes apparent here is that text selection should not guide the curriculum; rather, curricular goals should ultimately determine text selection. As teachers, we all have our favorite song, art slide, movie snippet, or short story, but unless such materials serve the goals of the unit, they are more indulgent than purposeful.

*Prepare the Unit:* It is important that students have some sense of what they will learn and why, and if we have determined our assessment goals, we can state these clearly at the start of the unit. The advantage here is twofold: first, students have a clearer idea how what they have just learned relates to what they are going to learn; second, a stated focus enables students to zero in on ideas and experiences that relate to that focus of the unit and more quickly process instruction. It is then important to reinforce these expectations in the course of the unit, culminating in a final assessment in which all the previous learning finds application. Units should contain some variation of the following:

- **Unit Calendars:** Calendars provide students with an overview of the work ahead, including homework and reading assignments, as well as project due dates.

- **Questions:** Wiggens argues for beginning a unit by asking "essential questions," open-ended debates that students spend the unit researching. I have provided such questions at the beginning of a unit, but perhaps more effectively, I've also guided students in developing their own questions as the unit begins. I once taught *The Scarlet Letter* in a unit on Puritanism, asking students to submit three questions about Puritan culture they wanted answers to. We discussed the formulating of open-ended questions; whereas "How did the Puritans cross the ocean?" is not open-ended, "Why did the Puritans deny religious freedom to others?" is. As students poured through the unit's material, they took notes in preparation for a unit-ending paper that both addressed and evaluated one of their questions. In this way, they demonstrated their understanding of the material and evaluated their own biases and predispositions in a paper that combined analysis with reflection. For a sample response, read Stephanie Brannen's "I'm Just a Big Hyprocrite" on the accompanying CD-ROM.

- **Models:** I use student writing models because as Wiggens asserts,

  > Effective feedback exists only relative to standards, thus to models or model specifications....Even students with talent in a particular area need to discover how much others have done and why study of the great is desirable. (64)

Without models, students are unclear about both the specifics and standards of the assignment. By contrast, a model that is explained and analyzed makes clearer to students what they must aim for as the unit unfolds.

- **Rubrics:** Grading sheets are ineffectual if provided only when work is returned. Creating a rubric forces teachers to be clear about their expectations, and making clear those expectations to students is both fair and instructive. Providing rubrics as the unit opens encourages discussion about why you employ particular criteria. If you value something enough to make it a part of the assessment, discussing that with students in advance focuses them on the task. Creating rubrics is a skill in itself as teachers too often emphasize method over result. Wiggens provides examples and strategies in *Educative Assessment*, and the excellent rubrics College Board creates for its AP testing are available with released exams at www. apcentral.org.

- **Peer Evaluation:** Nancy Atwell has argued that the ability to critique the work of others sharpens our own skills and forces us to clarify not just *what* needs improvement but *why* it needs improvement (we know this as teachers). Peer evaluation frequently fails because students are given minimal direction. However, armed with rubrics, models, and appropriate handouts (e.g., "Literary

Faux Pas," "Basic Grammatical Structures," "Revision Checklist," "Reading for Punctuation"), students are prepared to offer more effective feedback. It is important to encourage both editing (i.e., searching out grammar and phrasing errors) and revision (i.e., re-writing passages to increase their effectiveness). My peer evaluation days take up the entire class (and sometimes an additional day), allowing me time to talk with all students, commenting on their writing and on their critiques. These one-on-one experiences between teacher and student, as well as student and student, are the best ways to offer specific and effective feedback.

• **Final Assessment:** The culminating experience of the unit should give students the opportunity to demonstrate what they have pro-cessed, not merely rehearse information. If we have been clear in our minds what we value most about the unit, how we see it fur-thering the students' individual goals and the department's goals, this activity should demonstrate to them and to us how successful we have been. Wiggens writes that, "Students must be given prob-lems that cause them to use (and want to use) texts and materials to help them conduct inquiry, fashion arguments, and develop quality products" (227). In what ways, we must ask, can students evidence they have internalized the concepts—not merely the information—that has guided the construction of the unit?

The goal of teaching is not coverage, as Wiggens explains, but think-ing. He notes Jean Piaget's hope for learning: "Jean Piaget argued that the student must verify or 'discover' the key truths encountered, not just receive them and play them back unthinkingly as part of a formal frame-work" (229). My goal nearly three decades ago was to get through the material I felt required by contract to cover. I was a novice. Now I believe in the importance of thinking, in the skill involved in parsing an argu-ment until its flaws are revealed like the skin pulled off an onion, in the creation of a voice so strong we are disposed to give it credence, perhaps even belief, and in the deepening of folds within the neural cortex. We do the students no service by meeting our coverage goals. We owe them much more.

# *Sample Unit*

The following unit on the journey is one I have used both with fresh-men and sophomores. Placing it at the beginning of the year, I find it helpful in developing other themes and skills later: mythological analy-sis; the presence of cultural archetypes in literature; and the creation of personal narrative.

**Course: *World Literature***
**Unit: *Mythology***
**Lesson Plan: *The Journey***

*Department Goal:* Enable students to interpret the use of archetypes in contemporary and historical culture.

*Course Goal:* Enable students to identify the use of archetypes in other cultures and analyze their treatment.

*Unit Goal:* Enable students to understand and apply the stages of the journey to their own lives.

***Structure and Methodologies:***

Day One: Introduce the concept of the journey.

a. Assign *Dead Poet's Society* for home viewing and pass out guide questions (copies available on accompanying CD-ROM).

b. Pass out handout of the journey and explain stages (see Chapter 7; journey handout available on accompanying CD-ROM).

*Homework*: Students read "Little Red Riding Hood" and note the stages of the journey.

Day Two: Identify the journey in contemporary culture.

a. Discuss "Little Red Riding Hood" as an example of the journey.

b. Listen to and analyze "I Know Things Now" from *Into the Woods* as an example of the journey.

c. Listen to and analyze "Fields of Gold" by Sting as an example of the journey.

*Homework*: Students read "The Monkey Garden" by Sandra Cisneros from *House on Mango Street.*

Day Three: Continue discussion of the journey in contemporary culture.

a. Discuss the Cisneros story as an example of the journey.

b. Listen to and analyze "The Boys of Summer" by Don Henley.

c. Have students provide examples of movies following the journey structure and document their stages on the board.

*Homework*: Students read excerpt from *The Adventures of Huckleberry Finn* (Chapter 19, dealing with life on the river in an Edenic existence).

Day Four: The journey in history.

  a. Summarize the plot of *The Adventures of Huckleberry Finn*, asking students to note how the journey structure applies to it.

  b. Review excerpt, students identifying words, phrases and images that evidence the journey.

  c. Show excerpt of the river scene from film if time permits.

  *Homework*: Have students read classical work (recommendations: "The Legend of Parsifal," "The Story of Siegfried," or a passage from *The Odyssey* or an Arthurian tale)

Day Five: The journey in history (continued).

  a. Discuss readings as examples of the journey.

  b. Provide other history tales as time allows. This is a great occasion to tell a story, explaining how the journey is the cornerstone of oral storytelling.

  c. Video excerpt from *The Odyssey*, if time permits.

Day Six: *Dead Poet's Society*

  a. Dedicate the class period to reviewing guide questions and discuss how the film touches on various themes of the journey.

**Assessment** (possible activities):

a. Timed writing, a mythological analysis of *Dead Poet's Society*.

b. Provide a story the night before which students will do a timed writing on the next day.

c. Students write about a film or song that reflects their own sense of life as a journey.

d. Students create a storyboard of a well-known tale and document the stages and elements of the journey.

e. Students write their own narrative, explaining how an experience of theirs became an initiation.

# *Project-Based Learning*

A number of schools, private and public, require senior projects, some districts have mandated them, and state frameworks increasingly advocate them. The ultimate goal of a scope and sequence program is to prepare students for a specified objective when they graduate; projects provide evidence whether such goals have been met. Projects require the application of skills students have been learning, so their construction should not be a repetition of previous work. Instead, they should synthesize a variety of skills in the production of a unique product. Projects can involve disciplines and activities outside the school, incorporating community service, political action, surveys, oral interviews, field research, and pretty much whatever interests the student.

In this way, projects also capitalize on the multiple intelligence studies pioneered by Howard Gardner and others, who argue that students learn in different ways. While education is mostly teacher-centered and lecture-based, student learning increases if, first, different methodologies are used and, second, multiple approaches are involved. Some students need to see material, not just hear it, some need to see it represented metaphorically, some need to verbally react to the material, and others need to physically engage the material or respond to it. In short, the wide range of skills required for projects makes possible greater success, reaching students in ways more passive methodologies do not. The September 1999 issue of *English Journal* (accessible at http://www.ncte.org/ej/toc/EJ0891TOC.shtml) contains a number of articles examining the place of research in an English curriculum and how research papers can be modified to become more effective, project-based experiences. In addition, I offer a small list of project-based ideas below. Be creative and come up with a few of your own to flesh out your program.

- *Foxfire*: The Georgia-based Foxfire Fund began in 1966 when Eliot Wigginton instructed students at a semiprivate school to produce the first of several publications which, over the years, would include magazines, texts, specialty books, newsletters, and journals, all based on student interviews with members of the community in an attempt to capture and preserve local history.

- *Websites*: The increasing ease of constructing websites has enabled students to create extensive collections of web pages that combine research, design, photography, and writing, as evidenced by one Cornell University examination of the 1911 Triangle Shirtwaist Factory Fire (http://www.ilr.cornell.edu/trianglefire/default.html).

- *Museum Project:* Searching for a culminating project for a team-taught American literature and U.S. history course, a colleague and I developed a museum project that enabled students to synthesize a range of experiences, observations, and field research. (Find the full project on the accompanying CD-ROM.)

- *60 Minutes:* The CBS news program combines video, interview, and research to produce its segments. I've done similar things with kids that imitate "60 Minutes" or another feature program, the local "Evening Magazine."

- *NPR*: National Public Radio's segments are imaginative, making up for their lack of visuals by taping interviews on location to get audio color, and often incorporating music or voiceovers. These short pieces require students to interview, research, and structure their pieces.

- *Laramie Project:* When Moises Kaufman and his Tectonic Theater Project went to Laramie, Wyoming, after the Matthew Shepard killing, they collected interviews from a wide segment of the community. They turned those interviews into *The Laramie Project*, a compelling depiction of the Laramie community and investigation into the complexity of the murder and its affect on the community. Eve Ensler did much the same thing with her *Vagina Monologues*. These are original approaches to drama, combining interview and reportage with dramatic conventions, and groups of students can create such works themselves. Anna Deveare Smith has produced solo works on the Rodney King beating (*Twilight*) and a racial incident in Crown Heights, New York (*Fires in the Mirror*), in both cases transcribing the interviews and performing all the characters herself. These projects appeal particularly to students with artistic or dramatic interests.

- *Community Outreach:* Schools are increasingly noting the value of community service for students, and projects can address both academic and social needs. Students work with local shelters, groups, or programs, and create written, dramatic, or oral presentations of their experiences. Some schools have gone a step further, encouraging students to get civically involved, approaching city and state governments to enact bills. The March of Dimes has a youth action network that enables students to lobby state legislators and argue for the passage of legislation. Needless to say, such work draws on a variety of skills and behavior that transcend the classroom.

- *Trials*: Literature teachers have occasionally used trials to provoke discussion about the behaviors of fictional characters, and some have widened the field to include historical background. When a social studies colleague and I team-taught an American Culture course, we wanted to introduce the nuclear age in a meaningful way. Anne did so by conducting a trial of Harry Truman, accusing him of murder by dropping the atomic bomb. Students were divided into defense and prosecution teams required to conduct research to back up their presentations. Other students were witnesses or jurors, both roles requiring research and analytic thinking. One school in Washington wanted to put the trek of Lewis and Clark into a similar debate (http://www.longview.k12.wa.us/mont/text/corps/) and required students to perform research to arrive at a response to the project's central question.

- *Artistic Creation:* It's not unusual to require students to create a drawing or sculpture in line with the teaching of a text, but nothing says more long-term projects can't draw from the same skills. Students can write and produce plays, musical revues, or monologues; create photography or drawing portfolios; compose a song cycle; produce a book of poetry; choreograph a dance.

# *The Gang's All Here:*
# *The Goals of the Department*

There is a qualitative difference between a stew and a souffle. The former is a hodgepodge of foods; the latter is a planned dish. Both serve the purpose of feeding us, but souffle beats stew hands down as a dining experience. This isn't an accident. Historically, the stew developed as a combination of whatever vegetables and meats a cook had at hand. Each food item is nutritious and tasty, but a stew is not subtle, which means that though it achieves its purpose, it doesn't make our taste buds dance as does the delicacy of a souffle.

Most department programs are stews: combinations of good books and interesting methodologies, but unless each course works within a coordinated and graduated program of skill development, the overall result is a hodgepodge of learning activities, not an integrated program. By contrast, a scope and sequence program is a souffle; only those activities and materials go into it that will produce the highest quality experience. A cook does not add ketchup to a souffle because he is enamored of ketchup: if the food item disrupts the souffle, he leaves it out.

Let's approach this employing a metaphor more familiar to teachers: there's a difference between a diary and an essay. Though both contain such writing components as anecdotes, quotes, facts, and details, and both employ structure, a diary is a hodgepodge of material, while an essay is that material distilled and organized, advancing an idea stage by stage until it develops an overarching theme. Much as Poe insisted the short story should contain nothing that does not advance the work's dominant effect, the essay (unlike the diary) contains nothing that does not advance its focus. Additionally, we do not allow students to organize sections and specifics randomly. All writing elements must move cohesively from an opening that builds in logic and effect. As the technique of the golden thread evidences, a central idea must run through all the work, so that we know from section to section where we have been and where we are going.

I hope the point is clear. Curricular programs composed of independently valid courses that nevertheless fail to sequentially develop skills similarly fail to move students toward increasingly challenging goals. Like the diary and the stew, they contain all the elements, but they do not organize the elements to produce the most effective results. The predominant weakness of such programs is coursework that repeats rather than enhances. For instance, departments that teach literary analysis each year need to do more than increase the length of the assignments or the difficulty of the texts. Unless students learn and incorporate new analytical skills with each paper, unless they expand their repertoire of structure types, unless they vary their writing styles, unless they employ increasingly different types of research, unless, in short, they simultaneously expand on old skills and incorporate new ones, then they merely repeat from paper to paper what they have learned. Repetition is neither challenging nor effective; rather it suggests that learning does not change with increasing knowledge and maturity.

This is why scope and sequence planning recognizes three stages of skill development and organizes curricula accordingly:

- *Introduce*: In what specific unit, and on what level, will a skill be introduced to the student?

- *Reinforce*: At what level and with what activity will that skill be enhanced, not merely repeated?

- *Master*: At what stage will students be expected to have mastered the skill so as to perform it without additional instruction?

Such a sequentially developed program requires that a department do more than list the occasions on which a skill is taught in its four or six years. Rather, the department must outline how that skill is developed, increasing in depth and complexity, and how it is joined with other skills in activities requiring incrementally sophisticated thinking. Enhancement, not repetition, is the hallmark of an effective scope and sequence program.

If students are to have the highest quality educational experience, writing programs must contain only those activities that together produce the best instruction. Teaching a book, a lesson, a unit simply because we like it is not enough; ultimately, we must ask how each book, lesson, or unit contributes to the whole program. If it doesn't, then it doesn't belong. Planning such a program from middle school to high school graduation—a sequenced program—requires a group of teachers willing to jettison favorite materials and lessons in order to serve not the teacher, but the student. In this, a sequenced program is the ultimate dialogue, the moving between specific lessons and generalized goals; each defines the other, moving in concert toward an overriding vision.

And the first rule for a sequenced program is that there is no perfect sequenced program. Each is as individual as the writing voices we encourage our students to develop. Just as each writing assignment has its unique goals, so does each English department.

# *Philosophy*

A sequenced program develops skills and concepts over several years. Such a program is best created with the cooperation of teachers working to coordinate their instruction. One outcome of a successful program is the development of a sequence of skills from one grade level to the next. Team communication leads to a greater understanding of what has been taught in the preceding years, helping teachers organize strategies and encouraging departments to focus on what students need to learn by the end of the program. This knowledge serves to reduce the amount of time spent on repetition and allows teachers to encourage students to apply past instruction to newer lessons with more challenging concepts.

## Sequential Planning: Stages

- *Goals*: Establish your list of graduation goals, asking what students should have learned by the time they complete your program. For instance, "Students should understand the role of mythology in all cultures."

- *Content and Skills*: Next, establish what specific subject matter and skills students will need to achieve your long-term goals. For instance, "Students should be able to isolate and explain the significance of the journey and the hero in literature."

- *Schema*: Third, determine where your specific content will be introduced, reinforced, and mastered. For instance, "Students will be taught the journey and the hero during first quarter, freshman year; students will discuss additional archetypes in more depth in sophomore year world literature and junior year American literature; students will master the use and application of these archetypes in senior year projects."

- *Evaluation*: Decide what methods of assessment will determine how students are achieving your long-term goals. For instance, "During freshman year, students will isolate examples of the journey and the hero in movies and songs; during the sophomore and junior years, students will apply mythological analysis to produce critical papers; during the senior year, students will demonstrate through projects how these archetypes are a part of our culture."

# *Goals*

The specific goals of a planned program vary from department to department; organizations like College Board offer the following guidelines as a starting point for a discussion. An integrated program should

- introduce all students to higher order thinking, reading, and writing skills at an early stage.

- help teachers develop a continuum of skill building from one grade to the next.

- reduce the amount of time spent on repetition, allowing more time to be spent on new material.

- encourage students to apply and build upon past instruction.

- encourage students to accept responsibility for their own learning.

- open lines of communication between secondary and middle school teachers.

- enhance student performance on standardized tests that require evidence of higher order thinking skills.

# *What Goes Into a Sequenced Program?*

As your department first meets to develop a scope and sequence program, use the following questions to jumpstart your discussion:

- *Goals*: What is it your students should be able to do after graduating from your program? What skills should they have mastered to best prepare them for post-high school life?

- *Content skills:* What skills need to be taught in content areas: reading, writing, grammar, spelling, and oral presentation?

- *Content subject matter:* As you examine your content areas, what specifics will you cover in reading content, e.g., American literature, mythology or Shakespeare; in writing, e.g., analytic essays and poetry; in oral presentation, e.g., dramatic interpretation or recitations.

- *Methodologies*: What approaches to teaching the content are the most effective?

- *Thinking skills:* What thinking skills will your program emphasize, and what learning experiences will you offer to encourage a range of lower to higher order thinking skills.

- *Learning skills:* What aids to learning do your students need, as in close reading, note taking, outlining, test preparation, notebook organization, etc.?

- *Media*: What media will most effectively aid instruction: computers, posters, slides, VCRs, blackboards, and cassette and CD players?

- *Dispositions*: What philosophies will guide the creation of your program? Consider some of the following attitudes toward learning you and your students will internalize:

- Socratic questioning: encouraging open-ended discussions and research.

- Conceptual approaches: teaching both the material and the thinking strategies behind the material.

- Interdisciplinary: demonstrating the connections and parallels between the disciplines of English and other subjects.

- Humanities-based: approach literary concepts from a variety of artistic media.

- Learning styles: Howard Gardner's work in this field demonstrates that the presentation of an idea must take into account the varied ways students learn.

- Thematic structures: organize the materials and units of a course around themes that connect and develop key ideas.

- Student-based learning: look for opportunities to turn students from passive observers to active participants.

- Social issues: address the multicultural, economic, and gender issues of the contemporary world.

# *Addressing the Problems*

The creation of a scope and sequence program can be intimidating. It takes time, commitment, and the buy-in of all members of a department. For those reasons alone, most departments fear to tread where few have gone. But despite these concerns—and others listed below—the benefits of a sequentially developed program are many, and those seeking to convert the hesitant might consider the following arguments:

## Planning requires too much meeting time

No doubt about it, assembling a group of overworked teachers is tough, and teaching commitments often push meeting time into the weekend, summer, or after school. But, like a business investment, time put into a program's creation pays off down the road. When teachers share the creation of exams and units, they relieve themselves of extensive preparation. Similarly, teachers who feel burdened as they cram their courses with all the skills and assignments they feel their students won't get otherwise are freed up when their lessons are dispersed over an entire curriculum. Finally, students coming into a teacher's class with the same preparation relieve the instructor of the need to get everyone on the same page; less time is spent calibrating students as the year opens, allowing a quicker beginning into the meat of the course.

## Teachers are forced to move in lockstep

A writing program can be as regulated or as free as the department desires. Having determined what skills are needed and when they are taught, the department can choose how specific its methodologies and materials need to be. I recommend selecting a core set of assignments around which individual lessons can be planned. For instance, having agreed that short stories will be taught during a particular unit, the department can specify a select group of stories, allowing teachers to add to that group with stories of their own preference. Similarly, after agreeing on what writing assignments a particular level will require, teachers can add to that number with favorite compositions.

## It doesn't happen overnight

True, but nothing this extensive should. Give yourself a good year to flesh out a plan and then another two years before its effects become apparent. Remember also that programs aren't carved in stone. As instructors continue to bring in new ideas and make modifications, the program will evolve. Do not expect to achieve a final product: a scope and sequence program is always a work in progress.

## Nothing needs this much structure

I tell teachers that any lesson within a scope and sequence program should clearly feed into the final goals. This sounds a bit too structured for some. But consider the typical unit. Structurally, a unit is built around a focal idea that is introduced, developed, and then completed, the unit exam determining the student's success in understanding the material. This is a scope and sequence program in miniature. Just as our units are not amorphous collections of unrelated assignments, a department's courses should similarly not be a jumble of disparate learning experiences. Structuring skills so that they develop and increase in sophistication benefits teachers and students alike; the benefits justify the attention to detail.

## Not everyone in the department will buy into it

This is the toughest problem: personalities. Some teachers object to what they perceive as giving up their freedom to become yoked to ideas they might not see the point of. I understand the concerns: I heard them years ago when I was made department chair. We were, as a department, in transition, a little uneasy that no one was stepping up to assume the mantle of leadership when the previous chair stepped down. As we approached and then began the school year, such desperation set in that members even asked if I would do it. Aware of the talented, but maverick, personalities that marked our department, of course I declined. Desperation increased until we reached a compromise: I'd take on the role if in six months the department would consider a scope and sequence proposal. Up against the wall, they conceded, probably figuring that in six months I'd have lost interest. I didn't. I spent the six months meeting with department members individually, asking what they liked about the present program and what, if they had their druthers, they'd revise. And during those dialogues, I stumbled onto a revelation: my colleagues had a lot of ideas, many of which they'd never aired because nobody had asked about them. They were still squeamish about the independence they feared they'd give up, but they all wanted one thing: the best program we could provide for our students. And that's when the focus crystallized for us all: the most important question for our discussions became, "What do our students need to be able to do when they graduate?" Addressing that question forced all of us to consider the importance of what we did. As much as we held to certain books or lesson plans, the graduation goals were paramount: whatever failed to work toward those goals took second to texts and plans that better facilitated our students' education. When January rolled around and I unveiled my proposal, every department member found something of his or hers in the document, ensuring that this was not just the chair's baby. This was a working document even then, and we spent the next weeks modifying the proposal until we had an end result we all felt comfortable with. In retrospect, I know I was lucky to work with the group I had—not all scenarios work out this cleanly—but I also know that we'd all stumbled into the best way to convert the reluctant: mandate nothing; invite input from all; value the insights of your colleagues; and, most important, place all questions about books, methodologies, lessons, and units behind this one: what program would best enable our students to graduate with the skills they need?

# *Program Overview*

Ultimately, the program any department establishes must reflect its own needs and goals, so any model can be little more than a starting point for discussion. What follows, then, is a collection of ideas I've had success with, but this six-year program should be viewed as nothing more than a suggestion. Use it as a guideline, to inspire ideas, or as an example of what you'd prefer to avoid. Like the best writing assignments, you must determine the fit for your own needs.

Following the child development studies of Piaget and others, this program's sequence parallels the student's increasing awareness from self to others to culture. As Moffett noted, this progression involves both perspective (from self to community) and time (from the present to the past):

# Middle School

### *The Personal*

Reflecting the writer's orientation toward the self, writing on these levels encourages the exploration of that self and development of a personal voice. The writer learns how to gather and express his own experiences and views, shaping them into narratives, reflective pieces, and persuasive writing. Middle schools often expose students to the full range of writing experiences their graduates will encounter in high school, and although, to paraphrase Boxer the horse, all learning experiences are equal in importance, some are more equal than others. Developmentally, though students can, and should, engage in selected critical writings, the same skills needed to develop structure, voice, and style can be taught most effectively by focusing on personal essays and reflective writing. Taught in conjunction with such mythological archetypes as the hero and the journey, sequential structures are the most accessible forms of organization for middle schoolers.

# Ninth Grade

### *The Development of Perspective*

Writers begin both to find a commonality of experience with others and track differing results of those experiences. Point of view expands from first-person to include third-person as well, and the writer draws from the observations and experiences of others to bring depth and perspective to his discussion. The emphasis in the ninth grade is twofold: acquainting students with the component elements of writing and teaching additional kinds of research to expand the writing experience to include informative and critical pieces. My recommendation is that literary analysis, as a writing experience, be reserved for the sophomore level, though it should be a part of classroom discussions from the middle grade on. Instead, ninth grade offers a chance to outline the qualities of critical writing in more structurally accessible forms: reports, historical overviews, persuasive essays. All of these can be taught with an eye toward thesis-point-example structuring while the act of textual analysis is wedded with writing on the sophomore level where it is taught as one of several analytic approaches. Finally, style is taught as a specific skill, students made aware of effective uses of diction, punctuation, and sentence structure.

# Tenth Grade

### *The Creation of Context*

By necessity, grades seven through nine explore the experience of the present or the past only as it involves the lifetime of the reader. But by expanding perspective so as to incorporate a past distant in both space and time, the writer incorporates the historical. As in the freshman year, the intent is to enhance depth and perspective, this time placing the writer within a cultural context so as to see what connects him to all cultures and places him within a continuum of time. Most high schools end basic composition and reading courses at the tenth grade in preparation for more specific survey or elective coursework in the upper divisions. To that end, the goal of the sophomore year is to complete writing basics and flesh out the writing continuum. The additional emphasis on analysis complements a more extensive exploration of literature. Many tenth grade reading programs discuss world literature, offering an excellent opportunity to teach varied analytic approaches and cultural perspectives. In such a program, mythological analysis is best taught first, in conjunction with mythological tales. As the reading content approaches the seventeenth century, sociological analysis dovetails nicely with the emerging novel's emphasis on social behaviors. Finally, literature of the twentieth century provides ample opportunities for psychological analysis. Textual analysis can be taught anywhere within the year; programs that structure the year around genres could similarly teach a range of analytic approaches. In conjunction with reading and analytic skills (which go hand in hand), a unit on media analysis offers students subject matter that is accessible, relevant, and appropriate for deconstructive analysis.

## Eleventh Grade

### The Critical (grades 11 and 12)

Students struggle with analysis when they both lack an understanding of the material and have no criteria by which to critique it. But having learned how to mine their own experiences for meaning, and subsequently incorporate the thoughts and experiences of others, writers are better able to develop analytic and evaluative standards. Most English programs spend junior year studying American literature, a course I believe vital to all students. Beyond acquaintance with common cultural themes and texts, a survey of American literature puts students in touch with their culture and, for most students, their heritage. Additionally, the variety of writing in American history provides models for analysis and imitation. Students can produce allegories, memoir, oratory, reportorial pieces, experimental poetry, editorials, and media products that encourage experiments in structure, theme, voice, and style. These approaches to subject matter enable students to see and apply the universals of writing.

## Twelfth Grade

A survey of British literature, offering some of the most challenging reading experiences, similarly provides an opportunity to challenge students in their final year of secondary level composition. In addition to the literary types introduced in American literature, British literature offers the color and experiment of some of the best writing in English. By now, students have been exposed to all the skills the program teaches, and the senior year should be oriented around activities requiring more student choice in their writing experiences. As many schools and districts have begun to recognize, senior year projects are an effective way to achieve many of these goals.

Such a scope and sequence follows a continuum from the personal (suggestive writing) to the contextual (informative writing), which develops the foundations for evaluating experience and insight (the critical). Similarly, analysis develops from that which lends itself to the personal (mythological and psychological) to the contextual (sociological) to the critical (textual and deconstructive).

# *Nuts and Bolts*

What follows is a sample outline of a scope and sequence program. Incorporating many of the elements and assignments discussed in this book, this six-year program illustrates one way to set up a graduated skills sequence. Because this is a guide only, it lacks the specifics a fully developed program would include, wherein all the terms, skills, assignments, and readings would be listed. Instead, this operates as a core curriculum that contains only those areas deemed essential for the program. As such, this guideline leaves room for departments and their members to add those readings, assignments, and skills they feel necessary. Hence, items listed as general descriptions (i.e., "novel," "literary analysis") allow teachers to supply the specific assignment or text they require. Additionally, no specific evaluative tasks are listed, allowing teachers to select the format—objective testing, writings, projects, timed writings—they feel most fitting.

Finally, it is important to see this as a guideline and not a grid. Nothing precludes the teaching of one kind of writing at any grade level if it appropriately challenges the student. This is a philosophical construct, aimed at creating context for a sequentially developed program. As such, it offers stations against which development can be measured, but individual teaching experiences within those stations can vary as much as teachers and students see fit.

This is based on programs I have worked with; thus, the assignments and sequence have been effective for me, but their success for others would of course vary. In that spirit, I offer this as a guide, again insisting that any scope and sequence program a department develops meets its needs in ways too specific for any general guideline to address.

# *Seventh Grade Level*

*Overview*: Approaches to writing. Students will work with voice and varied written formats.

## Unit 1: Descriptive Writing

*Writing*:

- Imagery

- Figures of speech

- Sound Devices

    Assignments: Describe a series of contrasting sites, generating different emotions for each.

*Readings*:

- Short stories

- Poetry

## Unit 2: Persuasion

*Writing*:

- Gathering evidence

    Assignment: Create a product and make an ad campaign to sell it.

*Readings*: Essays and advertising

## Unit 3: Humor

*Writing*:

- Humor techniques

- Sentence types

- Diction

    Assignment: Tell and write a funny personal story.

*Readings*: Humor pieces

## Unit 4: I-Search paper

*Writing*:

- Interviewing

- Gathering evidence

- Making drafts

    Assignment: Write an I-Search paper.

*Readings:* Magazine articles and feature essays

# Eighth Grade Level

*Overview*: Personal experience. Students will encounter elements of mythology (the hero and the journey) and apply them to their reading and writing.

**Unit 1: The Hero**

*Writing*:

- The journey
- Gathering: Brainstorming and observation
- Anecdotes and descriptive detail
- Structures: chronologic

    Assignment: Narrate a personal journey.

*Readings*:

- Short stories
- Poetry
- Myths

**Unit 2: Narrative**

*Writing*:

- Short story elements
- Incorporating dialogue
- Creating character
- Creating setting

    Assignment: Create a short story.

*Readings:* Short stories with varied settings and characters

**Unit 3: Drama**

*Writing*:

- Dramatic conventions

- Stage directions

  Assignment: Groups compose and perform a one-act play.

  *Readings*: Drama selections

### Unit 4: Persuasion

*Writing*:

- Structuring an argument
- Gathering evidence

  Assignment: Compose an editorial or letter to the editor.

  *Readings:* Persuasive essays

# Ninth Grade Level

*Overview*: The first year for most high schools, ninth grade can both reprise elements of middle school instruction and introduce students to the writing fundamentals of the high school program.

### Unit 1: Style Basics

*Writing*:

- Diction: Word choice, word roots, etymologies
- Sentence patterns: "Basic Grammatical Structures" and "Literary Faux Pas"
- Gathering: Brainstorming and observation
- Components: Descriptive detail (images, concrete language, connotative language, appeal to the senses)
- Poetry: Figures of speech, sound devices
- Punctuation: "Reading for Punctuation"

  Assignments:

  - Compose two to three poems, image-based, incorporating

    figures of speech and sound devices.

  - Recitation of original poem.

  *Readings*:  Selected poems

  Autobiographical essays

### Unit 2: Structure Basics

*Writing*:

- Components: Anecdotes, quotes
- Structure
- "Writing's Three Parts"
- Structures: spatial, associational, chronologic, and narrative
- Short story elements: setting, characterization, point of view, tone

  Assignments: Write one essay on a setting and one on a character, both based on personal experiences and acquaintance.

*Readings*:

- Short stories
- Reflective essays

### Unit 3: Style and Tone

*Writing*:

- Gathering: Close reading and note taking
- Tone
- Syntax and phrasing (sentence patterns)
- Humor phrasing

  Assignment: Write a humor piece.

*Readings:* Selected humor works

### Unit 4: Increasing Perspective from First to Third Person

*Writing*:

- Gathering: Interviewing techniques

  Writing assignment: Persuasive essay which includes interview with a friend or family member; final work can be written up or presented orally.

*Reading*: Selected interviews from magazines, radio, other sources

### Unit 5: Critical Writing

*Writing*:

- Analysis of a character
- MLA citations
- Structure: chronologic

Writing assignment: Character analysis

*Reading*: Novel or play

# *Tenth Grade Level*

*Overview*: World literature. Students' first introduction to a survey of literature allows them to sample a range of writing styles and formats. They will also continue their expansion from suggestive to critical writing as they increase their analytic tools.

**Unit 1: *Mythology:*** *The study of mythology as a literary and writing device*

*Writing*:

- Analysis: Mythological
- The Journey; varied heroes

    Writing assignment: Compose a Socratic dialogue, exploring a concept in the style of Socrates; or folk tale, either an original composition or an updating with a stylistic twist.

Readings: Classical works: a play (such as *Oedipus Rex*), folk tales, and myths

**Unit 2: The Renaissance** *Stylistic variations*

*Writing*:

- Sentence patterns: "It's Greek to Me"
- MLA citations
- Structure: Timed writing format, employing preferred structures

    Writing assignments:

    - Reflective essay
    - Timed writing

*Readings*: Essays (Montaigne and Bacon); play (Shakespeare); Machiavelli; Erasmus

**Unit 3: The Age of Enlightenment** *The Art of persuasion*

*Writing*:

- Gathering: Third-person sources
- Components: Facts

- MLA citations

- Analysis: Textual

- Sentence patterns reinforced

   Writing assignment: Timed writing (textual analysis of a poem or writing prompt based on unit reading).

   *Reading*: Poems, essays, plays

**Unit 4: The Industrial Era** *Sociological analysis*

   *Writing*:

- Structure: continuum, cause-effect, dialectic, comparison

   Analysis: Sociological

   Assignment: Research paper

   *Reading*: Novel

**Unit 5: The Modern and Postmodern Eras** *Stylistic experiments*

   *Writing*:

- MLA citations

- Analysis: Psychological

- Structure: Contrast

   Assignment: Experimental poem or prose work and/or timed writing.

   *Readings*: Experimental forms of poetry, plays and/or novel

# *Eleventh Grade Level*

*Overview*: American Literature: The second survey course expands coverage of stylistic offerings. Having learned the fundamentals of the writing program over the first two years, students now begin experimenting more with their own topics, formats, structures, and styles. A list of themes introduced in the first week focuses the year-long discussion (possible themes include the American dream, class structure, religion on the personal and communal level, the effects of geography, the role of the community, economic structures).

**Unit 1: Puritan Culture** *Metaphor and Allegory*

   *Writing*:

- Review figurative language
- Allegory as a stylistic device
- Introduce year-long project (museum project, for instance)
- Mythology: Introduce other incarnations of the hero: innocent, trickster, warrior, and sage

    Writing assignment: Original allegory (could utilize a humorous tone)

*Readings*: Such allegorical works as excerpts from *Pilgrim's Progress*, the captivity narrative of Mary Rowlandson, sermons of Jonathan Edwards, the poetry of Edward Taylor and Anne Bradstreet; *The Scarlet Letter*

### Unit 2: Antebelleum America: *Emergence of the Individual Voice*

*Writing*:

- Suggestive writing: Review reflective essay
- Gathering: Review techniques and components
- Structure: Review structure formats

    Writing assignment: College essay

*Readings*: Critical essays: works by Thomas Paine, Thomas Jefferson, Ralph Waldo Emerson, Henry David Thoreau, Frederick Douglass, Margaret Fuller

### Unit 3: Industrial America: *Detail and Observation*

*Writing*:

- Reportorial writing: composing articles
- Gathering: review interviewing
- Stylistic devices: review techniques

    Writing assignment: Reportorial piece combining first- and third-person perspectives

*Readings*: Journalistic pieces, including work by Theodore Dreiser, Mark Twain, and Stephen Crane; novel with realistic or regional orientation

### Unit 4: Modern Era: *Breaking with Tradition*

*Writing*:

- Structure: Review contrasting structures

- Style: Review sentence patterns

   Writing assignment: Experiment with poetry or prose

*Readings*: Modern poetry; experimental play; novel

**Unit 5: Postmodernism** *Deconstruction*

*Writing*:

   Analysis: Deconstruction

   Writing assignment: Brochure

*Readings*: Contemporary novel, play, and/or poetry

# Twelfth Grade Level

*Overview*: British Literature: Taking "Identity and The Hero" as its thematic center, the senior year surveys British literature and provides more sophisticated writing models and assignments.

**Unit 1: Emergence of the Celtic Hero:** *Literary and Cultural Foundations*

*Writing*:

- Review heroic archetypes
- Review poetry elements

   Writing assignment: Portrayal of a contemporary figure in the style of *The Canterbury Tales*, replete with couplets and sound devices

*Readings*: Excerpts from *Beowulf*, "The Seafarer," and Chaucer

**Unit 2: The Renaissance Hero:** *The scientific method as a means to analysis*

*Writing*:

- Review timed writing
- Review syntax and punctuation

   Writing assignment: Unit-ending timed writing, such as an analysis of a poem from the era studied

*Readings*: Marlowe and/or Shakespeare, the Cavalier Poets, the Metaphysical School of poetry

**Unit 3: Age of Enlightenment:** *Satire as social commentary*

*Writing*:

- Review humor unit for tone and satire
- Review phrasing and sentence patterns

   Writing assignment: Satirical essay

*Readings*: Excerpts from the work of Addison and Steele, Jonathan Swift, John Gay, Alexander Pope, the art of William Hogarth

**Unit 4: Romanticism:** *The Emergence of the personal*

*Writing*:

- Review critical and suggestive writing, particularly their expression in personal and analytic essays

   Writing assignment: Reflective essay

*Readings*: Romantic school of poetry; essays of Charles Lamb, William Hazlitt, Thomas De Quincey

**Unit 5: Victorian Era:** *Social observation and commentary*

*Writing*:

- Review gathering techniques
- Review structure types

   Writing assignment: Analysis of the works of a particular school or author

*Readings*: Novel of social commentary (Dickens, Eliot, Hardy, etc.)

**Unit 6: Modern and Postmodern Era:** *Breakdown of truth and perceptions of reality*

*Writing*:

- Review contrasting structure types
- Review experimental phrasings
- Gathering: review interviewing

Writing assignment: A personal commentary/reflection on a contemporary event or happening, including third-person research and interview. Possible topics might include the place of the mall in modern culture, the effects of advertising on values, the increasing entertainment quality of news or politics, the ramifications of the computerized world.

*Readings*: Experimental selections from all genres

# Bibliography

Allen, Woody. *Without Feathers.* New York: Ballantine Books, 1986.

Appleman, Deborah. *Critical Encounters in High School English: Teaching Literary Theory to Adolescents.* New York: Teachers College Press, 2000.

Atwell, Nancie. *In the Middle: Writing, Reading, and Learning with Adolescents.* Upper Montclair, NJ: Boynton/Cook Publishers, Inc., 1987.

Barlow, Andrew. "Everything I Know I Learned from Having My Arms Ripped off by a Polar Bear." *New Yorker.* May 20, 2002.

Barry, Dave. *Dave Barry's Bad Habits : A 100% Fact-free Book*. New York: Owl Books, 1993.

Basho's Haiku: *Selected Poems of Matsuo Basho.* New York, State University of New York Press, 2004.

Berthoff, Ann E. *Forming Thinking Writing.* Upper Montclair, NJ: Boynton/Cook Publishers, Inc., 1988.

Bloom, Lynn Z. *Fact and Artifact: Writing Nonfiction.* Englewood Cliffs, NJ: Prentice Hall, 1994.

Byron, Ellen. "To Master the Art of Solving Crime, Cops Study Vermeer." *The Wall Street Journal* (May 27, 2005): 1.

Caplan, Rebekah. *Writers in Training*. Dale Seymour Publications, 1984.

Christensen, Linda. *Reading, Writing, and Rising Up: Teaching About Social Justice and the Power of the Written Word.* Milwaukee, WI: A Rethinking Schools Publication, 2000.

Churchill, Winston. *Guardian Century* http://century.guardian.co.uk/1940-1949/Story/0,6051,127386,00.html

Curry, Boykin, Kasbar, Brian. *Essays That Worked: 50 Essays from Successful Applications to the Nation's Top Colleges.* New York: Ballantine Books, 1990.

Dean, Deborah M. "Muddying Boundaries: Mixing Genres with Five Paragraphs." *English Journal* (September 2000): 53–57.

Dickinson, Emily. *The Complete Poems of Emily Dickinson.* Boston: Back Bay Books, 1976.

Dikkers, Scott; Siegel, Robert; Krewson, John; Hanson, Todd; Schneider, Maria, Kolb, Carol, Loew, Mike; Harrod, Tim; Javerbaum, David. *Our Dumb Century.* New York: Three Rivers Press, 1999.

Doyle, Arthur Conan. *The Hound of the Baskervilles.* New York: Signet Classics, 2001.

Eliot, T.S. *Prufrock and Other Observations*. London. Faber and Faber Ltd., 2001.

Ellison, Ralph. *Invisible Man*. New York: Vintage, 1995.

Emig, Janet. *The Web of Meaning: Essays on Writing, Teaching, Learning, and Thinking*. Upper Montclair, NJ: Boynton/Cook Publishers, Inc., 1983.

Forche, Carolyn and Philip Gerard, eds. *Writing Creative Nonfiction*. Cincinnati, OH; Story Press, 2001.

Gordon, Karen Elizabeth. *The New Well-Tempered Sentence: A Punctuation Handbook for the Innocent, the Eager, and the Doomed*. Boston: Houghton Mifflin Company, 1993.

Hale, Constance. *Sin and Syntax: How to Craft Wickedly Effective Prose*. New York: Broadway Books, 1999.

Hall, Rich. *Sniglets*. New York: Collier Books, 1984.

Haswell, Richard H. "The Organization of Impromptu Essays." *College Composition and Communication 37* (1986): 402–14.

Hawthorne, Nathaniel. *The Scarlet Letter*. New York: Bantam Classics, 1981.

Heller, Joseph. *Catch-22*. New York: Scribner, 1985.

Hemingway, Ernest. *A Farewell to Arms*. New York: Scribner, 1995.

Hemingway, Ernest. *The Old Man and the Sea*. New York, Scribner, 1995

Hillocks, George, Jr. *Teaching Writing as a Reflective Practice*. New York: Teachers College Press, 1995.

Iyer, Pico. *Tropical Classical: Essays from Several Directions*. New York, Vintage Departures, 1998.

Joyce, James. *A Portrait of the Artist as a Young Man*. New York: Penguin Classics, 2003.

Moffett, James. *Teaching the Universe of Discourse*. Boston: Houghton Mifflin Co., 1968.

———. *Active Voice: A Writing Program across the Curriculum*. Upper Montclair, NJ: Boynton/Cook Publishers, Inc., 1992.

Morse, Jodie. "Inside College Admissions." *TIME* (October 23, 2000): 74–77.

Nash, Ogden. *Candy Is Dandy: The Best of Ogden Nash*. New York: Carlton Books Limited, 1994.

Noden, Harry R. *Image Grammar: Using Grammatical Structures to Teaching Writing*. Portsmouth, NH: Heinemann, 1999.

Numbers. *TIME*. (March 27, 2000): 27.

Piaget, Jean. *Six Psychological Studies*. New York: Vintage Books, 1968.

Ponsot, Marie and Rosemary Deen. *Beat Not the Poor Desk. Writing: What to Teach, How to Teach it and Why*. Upper Montclair, NJ: Boynton/Cook

Publishers, Inc., 1982.

Potok, Chaim. *The Chosen.* New York: Fawcet Press. 1967.

Reiner, Rob. *The Wit & Wisdom of Archie Bunker.* New York: Popular Library, 1971.

Rice, Anne. *The Mummy or Ramses the Damned.* New York: Ballantine Books, 1991.

Rico. Gabrielle. *Writing the Natural Way: Using Right-Brain Techniques to Release Your Expressive Powers.* New York: Putnam Publishing Group, 2000.

Robinson, William S. "On Teaching Organization: Patterns, Process and the Nature of Writing." NCTE, Volume 21, Number Three, October 1994. (www.ncte.org/tetyc/back/best94.html)

Romano, Tom. *Writing with Passion: Life Stories, Multiple Genres.* Upper Montclair, NJ: Boynton/Cook Publishers, Inc., 1995.

Ryan, Cornelius. *The Longest Day: The Classic Epic of D-Day.* New York: Simon and Schuster, 1994.

Salinger, J.D. *The Catcher in the Rye.* New York: Little, Brown, 1991.

Sandburg, Carl. *The Complete Poems of Carl Sandburg.* Orlando: Harcourt, 2003.

Sayre, Henry M. *Writing About Art.* New Jersey: Prentice Hall, 2002.

Shafer, Gregory. "Composition for the Twenty-First Century." *English Journal* (September 2000): 29–33.

Shakespeare, William. *Hamlet.* New York: Washington Square Press, 2003.

Shakespeare, William. *Twelfth Night.* New York: Washington Square Press, 2004.

Tan, Amy. *The Joy Luck Club.* New York: Ivy Books, 1990.

Thomas, P.L. "The Struggle Itself: Teaching Writing as We Know We Should." *English Journal* (September 2000): 39–44.

Thompson, Hunter S. *The Great Shark Hunt: Strange Tales from a Strange Time.* New York: Simon and Schuster, 2003.

Wesley, Kimberly. "The Ill Effects of the Five Paragraph Theme." *English Journal* (September 2000): 57–60.

Wilde, Oscar. *The Artist as Critic: Critical Writings of Oscar Wilde.* Chicago: University of Chicago Press, 1998.

Wills, Gary. *Lincoln at Gettysburg: The Words that Remade America.* New York: Simon and Schuster, 1993.

Wolfe, Tom. "This Year's Girl," *The Kandy-Kolored Tangerine-Flake Streamline Baby.* New York: Bantam, 1999.

Young, Gary. *Dream of a Moral Life.* Providence: Copper Beech Press, 1990.

Wordsworth, William and Coleridge, Samuel. *Lyrical Ballads: Wordsworth and Coleridge*. New York: Routledge, 1991.

# Recommended Works

Appleman, Deborah. *Critical Encounters in High School English: Teaching Literary Theory to Adolescents*. New York: Teachers College Press, 2000.

> Appleman argues that seemingly sophisticated forms of analysis—deconstructive, feminist, Marxist, and others—are, contrary to popular thought, both accessible and helpful to secondary level students.

Atwell, Nancie. *In the Middle: Writing, Reading, and Learning with Adolescents*. Upper Montclair, NJ: Boynton/Cook Publishers, Inc., 1987.

> Atwell's seminal work explains how to create a student-centered classroom where process is stressed over formula and students compose a range of writing types.

Berthoff, Ann E. *Forming Thinking Writing*. Upper Montclair, NJ: Boynton/Cook Publishers, Inc., 1988.

> Integrating writing theory with explorations of the thinking process, Berthoff's book details how to teach a variety of prewriting strategies from observing to gathering and structuring material.

Bloom, Lynn Z. *Fact and Artifact: Writing Nonfiction*. Englewood Cliffs, NJ: Prentice Hall, 1994.

> In *Fact and Artifact*, Bloom offers ideas on writing about people, places, performances, humor, and controversial topics. This is an immensely helpful exploration of varied writing subjects.

Caplan, Rebekah. *Writers in Training*. Dale Seymour Publications, 1984.

> An early advocate of "show not tell," Caplan's text offers lesson plans on teaching descriptive writing and an extensive section on the I-search paper.

Christensen, Linda. *Reading, Writing, and Rising Up: Teaching About Social Justice and the Power of the Written Word*. Milwaukee, WI: A Rethinking Schools Publication, 2000.

For both its argument about writing as a social act and its defense of personal writing as a necessary part of the curriculum, Christensen's book is superb. The insights, lessons, and student samples are additional gems.

Emig, Janet. *The Web of Meaning: Essays on Writing, Teaching, Learning, and Thinking.* Upper Montclair, NJ: Boynton/Cook Publishers, Inc., 1983.

Citing studies about the way we process information, Emig explains how to teach rhetoric, metaphor, process writing, and multidisciplinary approaches.

Forche, Carolyn and Philip Gerard, eds. *Writing Creative Nonfiction.* Cincinnati, OH; Story Press, 2001.

*Writing Creative Nonfiction* is a collection of essays explaining how to combine observation with narrative and a sampler of effective creative nonfiction.

Gordon, Karen Elizabeth. *The New Well-Tempered Sentence: A Punctuation Handbook for the Innocent, the Eager, and the Doomed.* Boston: Houghton Mifflin Company, 1993.

*The New Well-Tempered Sentence* is one of a slew of Gordon's books (dmfd,d) that bring humor to the study of grammar and punctuation.

Hale, Constance. *Sin and Syntax: How to Craft Wickedly Effective Prose.* New York: Broadway Books, 1999.

As entertaining as it is informative, Constance Hale's book insists that attention to specifics is the hallmark of effective prose. Along the way she puts the instruction of diction and sentence patterns into vibrant prose herself.

Hillocks, George, Jr. *Teaching Writing as a Reflective Practice.* New York: Teachers College Press, 1995.

Hillocks's is a theory-based argument for good writing. The book explains how studies in thinking can aid instructors in teaching composition. The book's final chapters provide a number of student samples and methodologies.

Moffett, James. *Teaching the Universe of Discourse*. Boston: Houghton Mifflin Co., 1968.

————. *Active Voice: A Writing Program across the Curriculum*. Upper Montclair, NJ: Boynton/Cook Publishers, Inc., 1992.

Moffett's work was a paradigm shift in the field of teaching composition. *Teaching the Universe of Discourse* was the clarion call for an expanded writing program molded closer to the human voice. The subsequent *Active Voice* series offered student samples of dozens of different writing formats.

Noden, Harry R. *Image Grammar: Using Grammatical Structures to Teaching Writing*. Portsmouth, NH: Heinemann, 1999.

Wedding grammar and descriptive writing, Noden's book is an alternative approach to teaching punctuation via diction and sentence patterns.

Ponsot, Marie and Rosemary Deen. *Beat Not the Poor Desk. Writing: What to Teach, How to Teach it and Why.* Upper Montclair, NJ: Boynton/Cook Publishers, Inc., 1982.

Ponsot and Deen argue that the nature of inductive experience provides a range of writing ideas to generate more effective composition.

Romano, Tom. *Writing with Passion: Life Stories, Multiple Genres*. Upper Montclair, NJ: Boynton/Cook Publishers, Inc., 1995.

Encouraging students to use their own histories, Romano demonstrates how multi-genre writing can develop and enhance personal voice.

# Index

# About the Author

Jeff House has taught for over twenty-five years in public and private schools. An AP reader and lecturer, he has instructed hundreds of secondary level teachers on writing techniques, providing seminars in the twelve western states for over a decade. In addition to his Saturday and week-long College Board lectures, Jeff has spoken to audiences with AVID, California Association of Teachers of English, National Council of Teachers of English, California Association of Private Schools Organization, and California Association of Independent Schools. He also lectures for and is a consultant to the San Jose Area Writing Project. His published work includes award-winning student publications and articles in a variety of periodicals, including *English Journal*. Newspapers Jeff has advised have received top awards from the Los Angeles Times, the National Scholastic Press Association, and Quill and Scroll. He is currently employed at Georgiana Bruce Kirby Preparatory School in Santa Cruz, California, where he teaches English, journalism, and art history. Jeff lectures on vertical teams, writing, journalism, and AP prep; information on his lectures can be found at www.writedial.com.